The
GREAT WORK
of the
FLESH

"*The Great Work of the Flesh* digs through the world's cultures and long histories to reveal the erotic lore called 'sex magic' that constitutes serious possibilities for us all—far beyond the biologized eroticism of mere sex-drive scientific sexology. In taking these charms, incantations, rituals, herbs, potions, and meditations seriously, we can get glimpses that there are ever more erotic galaxies still out there to be fathomed and shared."

STUART SOVATSKY, PhD, AUTHOR OF
ADVANCED SPIRITUAL INTIMACY AND WORDS FROM THE SOUL

"Alexandrian's study, which is well supported by striking examples, deserves our full attention, for it reveals an aspect of our humanity that is far too often concealed."

CLAUDE LECOUTEUX, PROFESSOR EMERITUS,
PARIS-SORBONNE, AND AUTHOR OF
THE HIGH MAGIC OF TALISMANS AND AMULETS

"In moving away from the typical black magician perspective of eroticism and the occult, Sarane Alexandrian brings much-needed clarity to the depths of sex magic. *The Great Work of the*

Flesh has synthesized the history and methods of this ancient art like no other before it, where we enter a realm of orgasmic wonder. Translator Jon Graham has brilliantly brought Sarane Alexandrian's work to life for the English world."

JASON GREGORY, AUTHOR OF
THE SCIENCE AND PRACTICE OF HUMILITY

"This outstanding work by Sarane Alexandrian, one of the authors best qualified to write it, has now been skillfully and knowledgeably translated into English by Jon Graham, one of those most qualified to translate this work. Don't miss it."

DONALD TRAXLER, TRANSLATOR OF
THE INNER TRADITIONS MARIA DE NAGLOWSKA SERIES

The
GREAT WORK
of the
FLESH

Sexual Magic East and West

SARANE ALEXANDRIAN

Translated by Jon E. Graham

Destiny Books

Rochester, Vermont • Toronto, Canada

Destiny Books
One Park Street
Rochester, Vermont 05767
www.DestinyBooks.com

Text stock is SFI certified

Destiny Books is a division of Inner Traditions International

Originally published in French under the title *La magie sexuelle* by Éditions La
    Musardine, Paris
First U.S. edition published in 2015 by Destiny Books

Library of Congress Cataloging-in-Publication Data
Alexandrian, Sarane.
  [Magie sexuelle. English]
  The great work of the flesh : sexual magic East and West / Sarane Alexandrian ;
  translated by Jon E. Graham. — First U.S. edition.
      pages cm
  Summary: "An inside look at sex magic in Eastern and Western Mystery
  traditions" — Provided by publisher.
  Includes bibliographical references and index.
  ISBN 978-1-62055-378-7 (paperback) — ISBN 978-1-62055-379-4 (e-book)
  1. Magic 2. Sex customs—History. 3. Sex—Religious aspects. 4. Occultism. I.
Title.
  BF1623.S4A44513 2015
  133.4'3—dc23

                                                        2014027365

Printed and bound in the United States by Lake Book Manufacturing, Inc.
The text stock is SFI certified. The Sustainable Forestry Initiative® program
promotes sustainable forest management.

10 9 8 7 6 5 4 3 2 1

Text design by Debbie Glogover and layout by Virginia Scott Bowman
This book was typeset in Garamond Premier Pro and Gill Sans with Helvetica
Neue and Gill Sans used as display typefaces

Contents

Preface

This is not a book of pure fantasy on the subject of sex. Like my *Histoire de la littérature érotique* (History of Erotic Literature) or, more recently, *Le Doctrinal des jouissances amoureuses* (The Doctrinal of Amorous Bliss, my "treatise on the new erotology"), *The Great Work of the Flesh: Sexual Magic East and West* is based on historical references and solid scholarship. Those who have read my *Histoire de philosophie occulte* (History of Occult Philosophy) know it to be a detailed study of gnostic and kabbalistic schools. Furthermore, that latter book represents a profound assessment of "High Magic" based on the many teachers—doctors, professors, or theologians—who practiced it, but gives no credence whatsoever to the nebulous theories of certain "illuminati," or to the harebrained ideas peddled by charlatans. It is a similar spirit that animates *The Great Work of the Flesh* from beginning to end.

Until now the books written on sexual magic have often been content to simply recount stories about witchcraft and embellish them with anecdotes about parapsychological phenomena. One such book, *Magia Sexualis: Mystic Love Books of Black Magic and Sexual Sciences,* by Dr. Émile Laurent and Paul Nagour originally appeared as part of a series on "sexual perversions" in which the same Émile Laurent, a specialist regarding "morbid love," would publish a book on fetishists and erotomaniacs the following year. In direct opposition to Laurent's medical bias, Henri Meslin—an apostate priest who frequented the

Universal Gnostic Church—wrote a 1938 book on the theory and practice of sexual magic, in which he examined the mystical aspects and rituals of occult love, but made no effort to provide any sort of overview. All of these authors, although they remain worth consulting, are now out of date, and it is primarily the subjects they ignored or omitted that I will be analyzing here. New scholarly works and the accounts by initiates of their experience have completely changed the panorama of magical eroticism, and I intend to describe it in its most evolved state.

This subject is one of the most important in the history of amorous traditions and behavior. A great occultist among my friends, Dr. Pierre Mabille, a surgeon and professor at the School of Anthropology, wrote in his book on philosophical anatomy *La Construction d'homme* (The Construction of Man): "Magic, almost as a whole, is connected to sexuality." This is so true that even the operations and symbols of adepts are pansexual expressions. Alchemists name their mixtures the "nuptials" of the King and Queen, or the Brother-Sister "incest"; astrologers refer to the sex of the planets, regarding Venus and the moon as female, Mercury as androgynous, and the other planets as male. Witches and sorcerers, meanwhile, were alleged by the inquisitors to have obtained their powers by copulating with demons during the nocturnal sabbats that they were expected to attend regularly.

Sexual magic can be divided into two types: folk magic and metaphysical magic. The first and most popular type consists of all the unusual and commonly used procedures practiced by people to better their personal lives. There are rites, incantatory spells, and food preparations that make it possible to be loved by someone who does not love you, to cure male impotence or female frigidity, and to determine the sex of the child you wish to conceive.

The second, higher, and even elitist type of magic is handed down by philosophers and is dependent upon the "Royal Art." This consists of taking complete control of one's sexuality and dominating and directing it in a way that brings about the full blossoming of one's personality. In this domain we find the ascetics who use sex to obtain enlightenment and sacred trances, increase their psychic powers, and have an effect on the invisible world.

The sexual magic that underlies both of these forms—the higher and the lower—sometimes belongs to black magic, which calls on demons, and sometimes to white magic (theurgy), which Christian humanists regarded as the only permissible form of magic because it uses only the occult properties of plants, minerals, stars, and universal magnetism. Any activity that claims its success is due to the aid of invisible beings, even angels, smacks of black magic. There is a manuscript in the Arsenal Library, *The Tablet of the 72 Angels,* on which its owner, the Marquis de Paulmy, had written: "This magic is so black and so terrible; it should no longer be allowed to exist."[1] Since the Holy Scriptures nowhere mention these names of the 72 angels who rule the Earth, it is only after death that the faithful will discover whether they exist. Therefore, to summon them for assistance amounts to no less than the invocation of demons.

In sexual magic this distinction between white and black magic became a moot point in the nineteenth century after the deacon Alphonse-Louis Constant—who adopted the pseudonym Eliphas Levi out of his love of the Kabbalah—described "the existence of those fluidic larvæ known in ancient theurgy under the name of elementary spirits."[2] This reduces relations with the invisible beings to a principle of physics: "the evocation of elementary spirits implies power to coagulate fluids by a projection of the Astral Light."[3] He is not giving this name to sunlight or starlight, but the light of the "astral plane" on which move the elementary spirits (souls of the dead) and the elementals (spirits of the elements). Eliphas Levi explains magical phenomena in the following way:

Rendered phosphorescent by the Astral Light, our brains swarm with innumerable reflections and images. . . . Our nervous system— which is a perfect electrical apparatus—concentrates the light in the brain, being the negative pole of that apparatus, or projects it by the extremities, which are points designed for the circulation of our vital fluid.[4]

The invisible beings who assist in magical workings are neither angels nor demons but elementary spirits upon whom names are bestowed out of delusion, for in reality they have none.

Sexual magic's field of action—limited since the Middle Ages to the perspectives provided by the Kabbalah and esoteric Christianity—was expanded over the twentieth century with the contributions from Eastern doctrines, especially those of India and China, which offered, as models, tantric yoga and the Tao. Up until that time in the West, it was believed that magical forces were dark powers governed by demons and that consequently their use depended on diabolical experiments that were harmful to salvation of the soul or health. It was then learned they were luminous forces that determined experiences of the divine and drew the best possible advantage from the "energy centers" of the human body.

The goal of Indian tantric yoga, a later branch of traditional yoga, is *maithuna,* a sexual act performed in a way to make the man and woman counterparts of the god Shiva and the goddess Shakti. At the same time it provides a vital exercise: maithuna gives rhythm to breath and is a method for eliminating thought down to its most innate state. A husband rarely practices this discipline with his wife—although it is done in her presence and she receives consecration from it indirectly—but instead with a courtesan or a girl from a lower caste. The more degenerate the girl is, the greater her aptitude for the rite; tantric authors speak of the *dombi* (washerwoman) as the ideal partner. In other rituals, however, the woman has to be beautiful, young, educated, and initiated by a guru.

Maithuna cannot be performed without advance preparation, during the course of which the neophyte learns to master his senses. According to the technique of the Sahajiya school of Bengal, the man must serve the woman as a servant for four months, sleeping at the foot of her bed. For the next four months, he must sleep on the left side of the bed, then on the right for four more months. After that they will sleep in each other's embrace. Another erotic ceremony, which has eight parts, consists of gradually deifying the woman. During the fourth part, *manana* ("recalling the woman's beauty while she is absent"), the man repeats a mystical phrase three hundred times while internalizing the image of his partner in his mind. She begins to transform into a goddess when, after repeating a spell twenty-five times with his eyes closed, the man then offers her flowers powdered with sandalwood with his eyes open. He then worships the spot where she is sitting, washes her, and bows before her nineteen times while giving her cakes. She places herself on a stool to receive other rites of adoration, then he carries her in his arms to the bed where, with great concentration, they begin the sex act. Coitus must most often be performed without ejaculating; sperm retention is a generative principle for spiritual perfection.

Given the complex nature of its protocol, maithuna cannot be performed every day. For an adept of tantric yoga, doing maithuna once a year is sufficient. Some do it only once in a lifetime. It is therefore not a magic that can be used on a daily basis.

The Tao, which appeared in China about two thousand years ago, sanctified sexuality to such an extent that it was Taoist monks themselves who were the first to teach (and practice) the art of copulating "to restore the essence and repair the brain." For men this means strengthening their vital principle and ensuring a long life and eternal youth, by moving the *jing* (life essence) and increasing *qi* (primordial breath) energy through the movements of coitus. While the greatest importance is attached to positions (or *asanas*) in tantric yoga, in Taoism it is rather by counting the number of penetrations by the penis, and by how shallow or deeply they enter the vagina, that the magical effect is obtained. The sole point of resemblance between Taoist sexuality and tantric yoga is the requisite to not ejaculate. But Taoists allow themselves one ejaculation for every five acts of coitus, and since these do not require the interminable preliminaries of maithuna, they can be repeated frequently. The knowledge of these methods triggered an evolution in Western sex magic. Instead of restricting itself to demonology, it reoriented itself toward physical disciplines capable of increasing an individual's mental energy and influencing events.

Many Americans and Europeans flatter themselves in thinking

they are tantric yoga practitioners, but if they have not first converted to Hinduism, it is an idle boast. As the purpose of maithuna is the identification of the couple with Shiva and Shakti, it is therefore necessary to believe in this god and goddess; otherwise this act is only a parody of what its true disciples are doing. This drawback does not exist in Taoist sexuality because the sexual act is not performed under the invocation of the Chinese deities but in accordance with the Tao, the Great Principle,* which involves the balance of Yin and Yang. A Western Christian can, without feeling he has renounced his faith, indulge in Taoist sexuality as it involves putting cosmic forces into play and not submitting to the gods of a foreign pantheon.

The most advanced tendency, and the one that should now prevail, is the creation of a modern Gnosis of sexuality—in other words, a system that coordinates the similarities and reconciles the opposing aspects of all the erotic-mystical methods that have been put into practice. There are those who call this "composite culture" (the possibility of believing in several religions at the same time) while others connect this tendency to "the oneness of all religions" (the conviction that beneath the variety of all religions everyone believes the same thing), but this runs the risk of ending, on the one hand, in an ideological state of confusion and, on the other, in an excessive simplification. Only Gnosis—used in its etymological sense of "pure knowledge"—functions as a judicious filter for the beliefs in question; only Gnosis allows one to cull the accurate notions from the abundance of ambiguities.

Sexual magic is not a collection of superstitions to be regarded with amused skepticism; it is created out of religious beliefs that have been redirected from their source and concentrated on the physics of love. Furthermore, superstitions are only survivals in the Christian era of the sacred principles that paganism upheld in its pantheistic worship and to

---

*This is how the eminent Sinologist Léon Wieger translated the word "Tao" in *Les Pères du systeme taoiste* (Paris: Cathasia, 1950). Some spell it "Dao" today using the new writing that conforms to pronunciation, but this unfairly depreciates the quotes taken from past experts.

which all citizens were loyal in that earlier period. There is a particular sex magic associated with every religion, and it is the official theologians who disseminate these dogmas. Moreover, it was the very priests of these religions who defined that magic to protect their faithful followers. The people who we find mocking spells and enchantments are typically the nonbelievers, the freethinkers, and the libertines. By contrast it is traditionally the priests, pastors, rabbis, and imams who give such credence to these practices that they persecute anyone suspected of engaging in them.

Can sexual magic be taken seriously by someone who is an agnostic, or a deist like Voltaire (who placed his trust solely in God and rejected all the religions representing him as imposters)? The answer is yes, because there are natural causes that underlie all its effects: the influence of the celestial bodies; the radiant powers of colors, numbers, perfumes, and gestural rhythms; the intensified activity of universal magnetism; and, more specifically, the bioelectricity of the human body. Even belief in elementary spirits, acting in the invisible realm, can be justified.

Consequently, far from concerning myself exclusively with folklore, I am going to specifically emphasize the ethics of the individuals and groups who have operatd according to such beliefs. What I have written here is a breviary of sexual magic, a handbook that conceals nothing. This treatise will be concise, limited to the essential knowledge regarding this topic, and it will be based on the secret teachings of initiatory societies (teachings of the third degree or higher). It deserves the attention of all who seek to expand the reciprocal influence of man and woman, to increase by tenfold the skills relating to their respective sensibilities—which will enable them to embark on transcendent adventures into the deepest zones of reality.

1

The Love Spell
Traditions

The most common magic in antiquity and the Middle Ages was the sort used to help unhappy lovers. Its principal purpose was to manufacture beverages, powders, and mixtures that a man or woman would administer to the individual who they could not otherwise induce to fall in love with them. In Rome a witch was called a *veneficus,* meaning one who prepares a *veneficium,* or love potion. In thirteenth-century France, the bailiff Philippe de Beaumanoir defined sorcery (or witchcraft) in his law-book *Les Coutumes de Beauvaisis:* "Sorcery is when an old peasant woman gives a lackey a medicine for marriage, which will let him take a woman by force of words or herbs or by other doings that are evil."

Love is a form of magic in its own right, and there are many common metaphors attesting to this: to fall under the *spell* of the beloved, to be *bewitched.* Sex magic is nothing more than procuring through artifices the effects of this natural magic that joins lovers together. What makes it a punishable offense is the fact that it is unnatural and not freely consenting. It aims at alienating an individual who is no longer his or her own master, but will succumb without resistance to the desires of the magician. How to make oneself loved? How to retain the love of the beloved individual? How to oust a rival for his or her affections? How to make a child at will? How to abort one easily? How to increase one's sexual prowess? How to make many amorous conquests? How to keep your powers of seduction and sexual enjoyment while growing older? When ordinary solutions are not forthcoming for these and similar questions, then extraordinary measures are called for.

LOVE POTIONS

Potions and philters were beverages intended to transform an individual, primarily by making him fall in love with the person who gave it to him. This is why the Greek word *pharmakeia,* which meant "the use of medicine" (from which the word pharmacy is derived), was also a designation for witchcraft. The witches of Thessaly, the first to enjoy a fearsome reputation, were called *pharmakides.* They used plants from the nightshade family with hallucinatory effects, which they harvested during a religious ceremony in which they left their hair unbound (which attracted elementary spirits). Medea, the most famous magician, stripped naked to cull verbena, a plant sacred to Aphrodite. Belladonna was known as a "witch's plant" because of its frequent use for potions. Its roots and leaves caused dizzy spells or frenetic dancing. Henbane induced temporary madness, and jimson weed caused a stupor that lasted twenty-four hours, accompanied by disturbing visions. The berries of meadow saffron triggered a sense of unreasoning terror, and mandrake root, added as a powder to drinks, caused total delirium. The victims of these potions suffered bouts of mental confusion that left them defenseless against any amorous undertakings.

As magic is based on the law of sympathies and correspondences between beings and things, ingredients that induced lust through analogy were also placed in these brews. Cornelius Agrippa, who in 1533 collected a number of love potions for his *De occulta philosophia* (Three Books of the Occult Philosophy), said they were made from the heart and genitals of animals possessing great amorous ardor, such as doves, swallows, and similar small birds, and the rabbit and the wolf. The flesh of the stellion, a lizard from the iguana family, was often used. Sometimes a vial containing the potion would be placed beneath the straw mattress of a brothel for several days so its potency would be increased by the fornications performed above it. Cornelius Agrippa notes:

> Those who wish to make love spells ordinarily hide or lock away the instruments of their art, their rings, their images, and their mirrors in some evil place, which gives them its virtue by its venereal faculty.[1]

Gerolamo Cardano, speaking in 1550 of the love potions of that era made from cat's brain, menstrual blood, and *hippomane* (a genital secretion from a rutting mare), noted: "These things disturb the mind more than compel the love of the person to whom they are given." In fact these potions were often responsible for fatal frenzies, and their makers were punished as criminals. After drinking a love potion given him by his mistress Lucilia, the epicurean poet Lucretius, the author of *De natura rerum* (On the Nature of Things), committed suicide in the wake of the intense attack of madness it induced. Charles VI died from the love potion given to him by his wife, the Duchess of Cleves. These potions were later replaced by powders to cast on the person who was the target of the seduction, which was much less harmful. The powders contained the same ingredients as the potions, only these were dried and pulverized.

Pierre Le Loyer mentions an affair that was judged by the Parliamentary Court of Paris when he was a young lawyer in 1580. The case was against a young man who had allegedly used powders placed in a scroll of virgin parchment to attract the love of a young girl so that he could take his pleasure of her. He had caught sight of her in the street, and when she passed by him, he had slipped this scroll inside her low-cut dress, between her breasts, so forcefully, that she fell ill from the irritation. The lawyer for the accused said this was excusable, as he had not made the victim take anything in her mouth that would poison her. The young woman's lawyer protested:

> Poison or venom is not only a poisonous potion or herb or drug that is naturally fatal, and when taken by the mouth kills the person.

Poison is also a love potion, an herb, a parchment, a letter, or a magic enchantment that works something against nature.[2]

In his manual the inquisitor Martín Del Rio revealed:

Witches do harm by means of certain very fine powders which they mix in food or drink, or rub on a naked body, or scatter over clothes. The powders which kill are black; those which simply cause illness are ash-coloured (or sometimes reddish-brown), whereas the powder which removes a spell and acts as a medicine is exceptionally white.[3]

Powders were also made to compel a young girl to dance stark naked. The grimoire known as the *Petit Albert* prescribes harvesting marjoram, thyme, myrtle leaves, walnut leaves, and fennel root on Saint John's Eve in June, then drying and powdering the plants before straining them through a sieve:

You must blow this powder into the air of the place where the girl is, or have her take some as tobacco, and the effect will soon follow.[4]

Potions in powdered form were in common use everywhere. In *The Magic Island* (in which voodoo worship is described), William Seabrook recounts how Maman Célie came to the aid of her grandson who had been rejected by the girl he loved. With a dried, powdered hummingbird, a few drops of the young man's blood, flower pollen, and other substances, she made a mixture she put inside a pouch fashioned from the skin of goat testicles. This became a powder that the young man cast in the face of his recalcitrant girlfriend during a dance. She immediately fell in love with him. There is nothing surprising about this: the superstitious individual who found herself the target of a magic spell believed that all resistance was futile; and her seducer, emboldened by this fact, lost all shyness and won her heart.

Sometimes these powdered potions were not thrown surreptitiously on someone, but blended into foods. An eighteenth-century manuscript, *Secrets pour se faire aimer* (Secrets for Making Yourself Loved), recommends "periwinkle ground into a powder with earthworms" and placed in a meat dish. The following instruction is also provided in the manuscript:

> Take three hairs from your balls and three from your left armpit and burn them on a very hot stove shovel, and once they are burned, put them into a piece of bread that you will then place in soup or coffee. . . .The young girl or woman to whom you have given this will be convinced that she will never leave you.[5]

A potion can also take the form of a salve, such as the ointment for the witches' sabbat that allegedly made it possible, when rubbed on the body, to find your way to such a nocturnal gathering. This ointment consisted of mandrake root and the oil in which it had been macerated, skirret, monkshood, cinquefoil, deadly nightshade, and bat's blood. The witch who anointed herself with this from head to toe would fall asleep and have erotic dreams. The sad thing is that under torture she recounted these dreams to the inquisitors who, believing the stories were real and proof that she had fornicated with devils, condemned her to be burnt at the stake. These hallucinations were induced by mandrake, a plant with narcotic and aphrodisiac properties. There are two species of this plant. The male mandrake of spring has white flowers, greenish brown leaves, fruits resembling discolored apples, and a long, thick root that is forked and covered with tiny filaments similar to hairs. This was the mandrake used for love magic and for locating hidden treasures. The female mandrake of autumn has violet flowers, bluish green flowers, and reddish sap-filled fruits. It was medicinal and used by apothecaries. A nuptial wine was made from it and offered on her wedding day to a young girl married against her will. After she drank it, she would not feel any revulsion at allowing her spouse to deflower her.

For René Schwaeblé, an occultist and alchemist belonging to a satanic church, the ointment is the most preferable form of all potions, if it develops, *sui generis,* the odor of the body:

A love potion is a drug whose emanation—more or less pleasant—should first penetrate the skin, then next reemerge; it is a drug that acts specifically on the sixth sense.[6]

For the woman who found herself undesired, Schwaeblé spoke favorably of verbena, though more emphatically recommended the following: "After washing your hands and arms a good long while . . . rub them, always going from top to bottom, with a philter consisting of: essence of cloves, 20 grams; essence of geranium, 10 grams; 95° alcohol, 200 grams." However, he also recognized the efficacy of a potion that was intended to be absorbed—provided that the potion was permeated by the aura of the person who made it: "Place sugar cubes beneath your armpits for twelve hours, and place them in the drink of the gentleman to be enchanted by love. I guarantee you will have results."[7]

It is not commonly known that the seer and doctor Nostradamus, whose prophetic quatrains still inspire sensationalistic commentaries, provided a recipe for an "amorous potion" (*poculum amatorium*), which he claimed was that of a philter invented by Medea and subsequently in common usage throughout Thessaly. Here is a summary of it taken from his *Excellent et moult utile opuscule* (An Excellent and Most Useful Little Work):

Harvest three mandrake apples at sunrise, wrap them in verbena leaves, and leave them out in the open air (or evening dew) until the next morning. Take a magnet stone 6 grains in weight, grind it finely and sprinkle this powder with the juice of the mandrake apples. Add to this the blood of 7 small male birds bled by the left wing, 57 grains of ambergris, 7 grains of musk, 377 grains "of the best cinnamon to be found," 500 grains of sweet flag, 700 grains of *lyris illyrica*, 500 grains of *racina apurusus,* some clove and aloe wood, and finally some suckers detached from the eight tentacles of an octopus preserved in honey.

The next requirement is "Cretan wine double the weight of the whole," an ounce of "the finest sugar" (superfine); crush this mixture in a marble mortar with a wooden pestle. It should then be transferred to a glass vessel with a silver spoon and then boiled over a flame until it takes on the consistency of syrup. This mixture should then be carefully strained through muslin and kept cold in a container.

Nostradamus's potion cannot be used just in any old way. It must be kept on one's person in a small vial. At the appropriate time, a portion "as large as a demi-crown" (around six grams) should be taken in the mouth and then transferred into the mouth of the person to be enchanted. "The way the potion is administered requires a certain prior intimacy between the sorcerer and his subject,"[8] notes René Laroque. This was not necessarily the case in Nostradamus's day, as it was then customary for a woman of high standing, when welcoming a noble guest, to kiss him on the mouth with lips closed. Obviously, however, if the guest would then take advantage of this to regurgitate an "amorous potion," the woman would have raised an uproar. Yet Nostradamus solemnly explains:

> If a man had a little in the mouth while kissing a woman, or a woman him, by casting it with some saliva that would instantly ignite a fire—not a fever-like fire, as it has neither heat nor thirst, but one that burns in her heart to perform the love-act, and with no one but the man who kissed her.[9]

He goes on to say that if some of this potion is swallowed by accident, without any going into the mouth of the lusted-after individual, it is essential to make love with someone else that very same day, "wherever it seems good." Otherwise, the increase of semen it creates will rise into the brain and drive him mad.[10]

A potion transferred from mouth to mouth has incontestable value as a form of sexual magic, and many lovers find pleasure in this procedure for heating up their desire. However, a glass of champagne would probably be more convenient than this concoction containing magnet powder and jellied octopus suckers!

CHARMS

Charm, from the Latin *carmen* (song, verse), is a sacred phrase that creates an enchantment. Littré's *Dictionnaire de la langue française* clearly defines the difference between the two:

> The charm (carmen) is a spell in verse or measured prose to which is attributed the property of disturbing the order of nature. The enchantment (incantamentum) is the action of speaking that spell.

The charm is not always spoken out loud; it can be written down, and some objects are charms because of the secret watchword they contain.

At the request of Catherine de Médici, King Henri III's geographer Antoine de Laval wrote a book in 1584 dealing with "philters, charms, and spells of love." In the book he states that it is Behemoth, the demon of the flesh, who makes them effective. It is difficult to put an end to a charm: "As this illness is above nature, so must its remedy also be supernatural."[11] He recalled that Saint Jerome, in his Life of Saint Hilarion, told of a young man of Gaza who loved a young woman who did not return his love. This young man placed magical characters and images carved in a copper strip beneath her doorsill. She was immediately consumed by an amorous frenzy for him that only Hilarion was able to cure.

Laval spoke at length on magic rings, which were then highly popular, and repeated what Catherine de Médici had told him in this regard. Her husband, Henri II, when he was the Dauphin, received a ring as a gift from a lady of the court. As soon as he put it on his finger, he fell desperately in love with this woman. He no longer wanted to eat unless the food came from her hands. Shortly thereafter the ring was removed while he was suffering through an illness, and at that moment he totally forgot this woman, even her name, although she was at his bedside.

On other occasions a man or woman who wished to attract someone else's lover wore the ring. Here is one way that a charm was hidden inside such a ring: During the thirteenth house of the moon, a topaz and an astral image would be mounted on a gold ring that would be consecrated by being censed in aloe wood smoke. The word *Asmalior* was written on a tiny piece of virgin parchment and placed beneath the bezel with the blood of a sacrificed dove.

Others preferred to use a phrase in gibberish that would subject the individual to be charmed to the mysteries of the logos. In *Secrets for Making Yourself Loved,* the anonymous author offers advice of this nature:

> To command a woman to do whatever you would of her, compel her to look you in the face right between the eyes and when both of you are in that position, recite these words: Kafé, Kasita, non Kaféta, et publica filii omnibus.

Roch Le Baillif, a doctor and member of the Brittany Parliament, claims somewhat naively in his *Demosterion* that certain diseases could be cured in a similar fashion:

> These words: *Irioni, ririori, effera rhuder fere,* written on a piece of bread and given to someone to eat, are a remedy for the bite of a rabid dog.[12]

This derives from the common practice in kabbalistic spells of reciting the beginning of a psalm of David, with each spell having its own particular psalm citation that made it effective. Pierre V. Piobb, a contemporary occult teacher, claimed that the best charm is from the first verse of Psalm 43: *"Deus, auribus nostris audivimus,"* which should be spoken at sunrise on a Friday:

> It will engender love in the heart of the individual you have in mind while saying it (if possible, you should lightly touch this person that same day). The name of the Intelligence that is its ruler is: Se-Feva.[13]

In his book on charms, Leonardo Vairo, prior of Santa Sofia in Benevento, states that they are made, "by sight, touch, and voice, and quite often with observation of the celestial bodies," which is more a definition of bewitchment. Of charmers he says: "They begin their activity under the astral body that rules what they wish to charm." He does, however, recognize the importance of words in tandem with the gesture of touching someone in order to charm him or her: "It is claimed that if some herbs or words are added to the touch, the bewitchment will occur more rapidly." It is similar with regard to the eyes, "whose effect to charm belongs to women, particularly the old dames who also know how to harm with their gaze, especially those with two pupils in each eye or the image of a horse in one of the two." The witches who cast charms with their eyes are a force to be feared: "Their winks cause livestock to abort and become sterile, and spoils their milk." He also explains why so many charms are made with women's hair: "Nature has endowed woman's hair with such power that when burned its odor alone drives snakes away."[14]

This author thoroughly analyzed all the intricacies of such spells. The charm made for adultery differs from the one undertaken for incest or theft. But a charm can have several purposes simultaneously, which complicates its ritual.

> The charm is sometimes called simple, sometimes double, triple, and varied; and this is in accordance with the multiplicity and diversity of its ends and intentions, or the object, or the person, or the quality or nature of the place.[15]

For example,

> if someone uses a charm to win the love of a married woman and if he cuts her throat after taking his pleasure of her, this charm will not have the nature of a single type but of two.[16]

In any event the danger is great. "The person charmed shall soon pass from life into death unless countercharms and remedies are ceaselessly supplied." The Romans ate rose leaves to dispel charms. The

Greeks invoked the goddess Nemesis; while "others believed that the skin of a hyena's forehead [counter-]charmed the charm; others misled the malice of charmers by dragging one leg or the other in front of them." Leonardo Vairo's contemporaries commonly used these counter-charms: "Spitting on your urine right after urinating, or on the shoe for the right foot just before you put it on." Vairo advised reading the Holy Scriptures, giving alms, fasting "to tame and recork the needles of the flesh," taking confession, and prayer, as he sought to establish that the charmer's power was unnatural to man, and was granted by demons in order to sow disorder in the world.

J.-K. Huysmans's friend Jules Bois, who wrote *Le Satanisme et la Magie* to condemn the Satanists of the end of the nineteenth century, believed in the effectiveness of their representation and claimed they equaled those of the Middle Ages.

> I've been looking at a no less effective modern "charm." It is a piece of parchment folded into the shape of a heart; several symbols are inscribed on it; it contains, I'm told, some powdered magnetite, some verbena, and a flower plucked from the tomb of a virgin. It was impossible to carry it on one's person without feeling a bizarre uneasiness. At a certain distance this parchment would influence a compass, and it most certainly disrupted the will.[17]

Jules Bois said that a charm for sexual magic is any note written in ink made from the ashes of a love letter, some magnetite, and woman's milk. He confirms:

> Hair is of great service in love; the person who links his hair with those of his lover, he who, with candle in hand, thrice offers at the altar a little of the sweet cherished mane, so long as he carries it, shall prevail over the hesitant heart.[18]

But the best charm for the adepts of his time, he says, is a secret detail from the architecture of the Alhambra.

This appears to be merely a series of small stones joined together like a necklace in which small rings have been inserted, which on contact produces a kind of psychic electrical current, which is quite alarming.[19]

If a man causes a woman to touch this architectural ornament of the Alhambra, she will fall madly in love with him.

THE MAGIC ART OF ENJOYING ORGASMS AND MAKING CHILDREN

Sexual magic was also called upon for healing the physical failings of a couple. It thereby provided all kinds of remedies for male impotence, whether it was caused by a simple malfunction or due to a spell.

Impotence caused by a spell was the work of a witch, who cast it on a husband on his wedding day because one of his rivals had paid her for this service. She took away his ability to consummate the marriage by casting a curse while tying the laces of a pair of pants into three knots. This was commonly known as "knotting the fly." Saint-André, a doctor for the young Louis XV, recorded this custom from his era:

> The fly is knotted thrice, at three different times, when the priest performing the ceremony says these or those words; the wrongdoer says certain words at the same time from his side . . . as well as the name and surname of the fiancée.[20]

The inquisitors stressed these two points: impotence caused by a spell was inflicted by a witch and not a sorcerer; and it uniquely struck married men, not fornicators. To prevent a witch from causing her husband impotence, a young bride would let her wedding ring fall to the ground at the moment it was being placed on her finger. The Ritual of Évreux in 1606 threatened women performing this gesture in church with excommunication.

Throughout the centuries human sexuality has been contaminated by this cause of impotence, which Saint-André attributed to "the effect of an imagination injured by fear of evil spells," with nothing demonic about it. "A thousand things are blamed on demons every day of which they are innocent." A man convinced that his fly has been knotted could not overcome his impotence by natural means because of his strong mental inhibitions. He would then resort to magical means. The *Petit Albert* instructed him: "The bird known as the green woodpecker is a sovereign remedy against the curse of the knotted fly if it is eaten roasted with blessed salt on an empty stomach."[21] Another prescription seems more effective to me: "If the man and woman are afflicted by this charm, to be cured the man must piss through the wedding ring that his wife will hold while he is pissing."[22] Newlyweds capable of an erotically complicit gesture like this should waste no time in consummating the conjugal act! But the *Petit Albert* notes that the impotence can be caused by knotting a lace of white thread around the penis of a freshly slain wolf, in which case a better cure can be provided by "wearing a ring in which the eye of a weasel has been set."[23]

When the husband's impotence persists interminably, it is necessary to use legal means to hunt down the witch responsible, as she alone is capable of neutralizing the curse.

If the person untying the knots is the one who knotted them, she can simply undo them while taking care to avoid severing or breaking them, as the problem would become (it is said) beyond repair.[24]

Leonardo Vairo has shown that evil spells "can provide hindrance to the coupling of married folk"[25] in ten ways and not only "by repressing or softening the stiffness of the genital member." For example, the husband can introduce his penis into his wife's vagina, but both lose all ability to move and remain paralyzed, one atop the other; or the man cannot ejaculate despite his insistent movements. Or a curse could make them mutually indifferent "by removing and diverting their desire to couple."[26] Finally, the tenth magical cause of impotence, worse than the knotting of the fly, works through fear "by convincing one that the other is misshapen and poorly put together."[27] Leonardo Vairo tells how near Naples he was summoned to help a woman who had never been deflowered by her husband because whenever she drew near the conjugal bed, she would scream with fright and flee. However, she loved him and wanted to enjoy their carnal union. But she had the impression at these times that he transformed into a horrible monster covered with hideous beasts. The priest vainly tried to exorcise her; it was necessary for the witch that was found responsible for this evil spell to nullify it with a ceremony. From that time forward, the couple enjoyed sexual relations and lived happily together.[28]

In cases of purely physiological impotence, the remedies were taken from nature. The authors recommended nettle seed crushed in wine with honey and pepper or summer savory prepared in the same way. The most highly recommended plant was *orchis,* an orchid nicknamed the *satyrion,* but only its root, which gave off the odor of goat. Saint-André explains:

> This plant has two onions at its root that have a fairly close resemblance to testicles. One is firm, smooth, and heavy, the other wrinkled, soft, and light. Botanists give these onions qualities that are quite opposite; they maintain one is good for heating and the other for cooling. The first excites natural heat and the other extinguishes it.[29]

He relates this supporting anecdote:

> Two gentlemen among my friends who heard speak of it decided one day to get two newlyweds to take it, to give the man a fairly large quantity of the one that was good for cooling and putting out natural heat, and to give his wife the one that would excite and enliven it. Consider what happened next and the rumors this incident spread throughout the whole village. The one victim had already accused several ill-intentioned neighbors of knotting the fly . . .[30]

Sex magic also offers all kinds of ways to improve procreation. The primary concern of married couples was creating fine children whose destiny would be crowned by good fortune; hence they sought sure methods for achieving this goal. As a general rule, according to Jean Liébault, doctor and agronomist during the reign of Francis I, the husband and wife should abstain from sexual relations during the new moon, because a child conceived on that night would be born sickly, mentally challenged, deformed, or subject to nervous disorders. He recommended that couples consult an astrologer in order to determine the day and hour when the impregnation would be under "the influence and aspect of some benevolent planet or star" guaranteeing them the best sexual conjunction. This noteworthy doctor from Dijon also spoke out against Aristotle and Galen's claim that women had "a mutilated and imperfect body," by declaring from the outset: "A woman's body is no less whole and perfect than that of a man."

Since at that time it was believed necessary for a woman to have an orgasm in order to procreate, Jean Liébault provided details for a number of extraordinary aphrodisiacs. There are folk recipes that are not to be found anywhere else. Earlier I mentioned the prescription of eating lizard or stallion ("primarily the tip of its prick") in order to achieve an erection. But Liébault alone offers the recipe for "lizard salt" that, if used to season one's food, makes a person tireless in coitus.

> The salt of lizard is wonderful and made this way. Remove the head of any lizard during the summer and take out all its entrails, then fill it with salt. Put it in a dark place until it has dried. Then remove the salt and throw the lizard away.[31]

He has many other unheard-of prescriptions, such as his mixture for "multiplying sperm and making the man potent in the combat with ladies." A bull's penis, dried and ground into a powder, blended with an egg, makes it possible to perform erotic feats, as do "clysters made from the decoction of a goat's head."[32] Liébault created pills he called "hazelnuts that have great virtue in enflaming the amorous matchsticks"— they are made from thirty finely chopped sparrow brains, fricasseed with goat kidneys cooked with clarified honey.

Liébault distinguishes six causes for premature ejaculation, which he treats as follows:

> Take four ounces of lamb's milk, two drams of finely ground, burnt rabbit hair; blend it together and take it every morning and evening before eating. This remedy entirely guarantees all manner of sperm flow.[33]

He was greatly concerned about young couples' "sloppy care of their belly and urine"[34] and instructed them on what the proper state of their intestines should be at the times they are joined carnally. "It would be a good idea before coupling to try to use the toilet."[35] A full bladder is detrimental to love. "You must take a good piss before giving or receiving love's combat, even long before massage the kidneys and the space between the fundament and the shameful parts with a liniment made from quince, blueberry, and mastic,* and a scant portion of vinegar."[36] There is a special diet for impotent old men. "Four ounces of arugula seed and one ounce of ground pepper accompanied and mixed with clarified honey."[37] The couples treated by Jean Liébault's medications ran the risk of becoming rabid with passion and incapable of stopping themselves from making love, but he provides them with a safeguard:

> When you seek some rest and respite from the combat of Venus, you should wash the big toe on your right foot and your carnal desire will suddenly cease.[38]

This intrepid physician did not content himself with having "an infinite number of remedies for increasing sperm, ventosity, and blood, and for making the spermatic spirit fat and thick."[39] He also had remedies for preventing the disunion of couples. For example, in order "to reunite newlyweds who hate and flee each other's company,"[40] he makes liniments for them from a basic mixture of cubeb pepper, musk, and

---

*The mastic of the apothecaries is terebinth resin.

amber. Nothing is more dreadful than conjugal infidelity, but no matter: "several trustworthy authors state that if the husband wishes his wife to know no other but him, he should collect the hairs that fall from her comb, burn them, and grind them into a powder; blend this powder with goat grease and chicken shit, then rub it over himself."[41] Liébault also asserts that if a husband rubs his testicles with the eggs of a crow or swallow, his wife's fidelity will be guaranteed.

It appears impossible to determine in advance the sex of the child one wants to engender, to create a boy or girl according to preference. Human women are not like queen bees, which hatch males or females at will, depending upon the needs of the hive. But as magic is the art of vanquishing the impossible through paramedical procedures, there has been no shortage of authors to teach couples wanting a son the best way to go about it.

Gerolamo Cardano, in his *De subtilitate rerum* (The Subtlety of Things), says that the woman should lie on her right side when coupling with her husband in order to have a son, and on her left in order to have a daughter, inasmuch as Hippocratic doctrine teaches that the male embryo forms on the right side of the womb and the female embryo forms on the left side. Cardano goes on to say that before the sex act, the husband should tie a white band around his right foot if he wants a son and a colored band around the left foot if he wants a daughter. By banding the right or left foot, one compels the corresponding testicle to let its seed spill first.

In his *De occultis naturae miraculis* (The Secret Miracles of Nature), the Dutch doctor Levinus Lemnius recommends the use of the mercury plant or *mercurialis,* a plant from the Euphorbia family whose leaves have laxative and diuretic properties. Lemnius writes that there are two kinds of mercury plant—male and female—and each is quite effective in producing the sex of its gender. If a woman drinks the sap from the male mercury plant for four days, starting on the first day after menstruation, she will give her womb the property to engender a boy; if she drinks the sap of the female mercury plant under these same conditions, it will be a girl.

In his *Trésor des remèdes secrets pour la maladies des femmes* (Treasury of Secret Remedies for Women's Ailments), Jean Liébault states that the woman can become pregnant with a boy from the end of her period to the fifth day of the menstrual cycle; from the fifth to eighth day, a girl, and either on the other days. He also recommends that we take into account the weather, the wind, and the country: "Those who desire a boy should toil rather in the winter and spring than summer; and when the North wind, rather than the South wind, is blowing."[42] Finally, Jean Liébault grants great importance to the time when the conjugal union occurs and says:

> Coitus in the morning engenders males. It has also been seen that the 10th, 16th, and 20th of the month are apt for engendering male children, as the 14th is for females. The 9th works well for either sex.[43]

But the most complete method was described by a doctor of Navarre, Juan Huarte de San Juan, in a treatise published in Bilbao in 1580, *Examen de ingenios para las ciencias* (The Examination of Men's Wits). In it Huarte states:

> In the beginning of the world, and for several years after, woman always gave birth to two children from one pregnancy, of which one was male and the other female. . . . It seems that Nature has reversed this order and children no longer come two by two, and the worst thing is that for every boy that is engendered it is normal for six or seven girls to be born.[44]

During this period the husband will exercise, especially by walking, and remain chaste in order to concentrate his generative strength. He will conjoin with his wife four or five days before her period starts, after which she shall sleep on the right side with her head down and her feet up, for as long as possible. If the couple respects these conditions, Huarte says that a son will inevitably be born to them.

BEWITCHMENT

Bewitchment is when one person performs an amorous action upon another through the intermediary of a magician or else by personally operating as a magician. Enchanters occasionally use potions and charms, but they primarily cast their spells through their eyes, voices, and gestures, like hypnotists. Magic made use of animal magnetism long before Doctor Mesmer established in 1766 that the human body was a natural magnet with a positive and a negative pole, which could attract or repel other bodies. The healing crises that Mesmer triggered in his patients who were suffering from nervous disorders, to whom he transmitted his fluid with the tips of his fingers joined together to form a pyramid, are comparable to those caused by enchanters.

According to Martín Del Rio, bewitchment occurs through physical contagion, which he defines as "any contagion contracted by word, by breath, and by the touching of the limbs."[45] He stresses this power unique to sorcerers: "They bewitch through their breath. This is how they have customarily caused women to give birth prematurely."[46] The most significant case is that of Louis Gaufridi, a priest from Marseilles during the reign of Henri IV, who asked Lucifer, using a conjuration from a grimoire, to satisfy "his immoral affection to take his pleasure of several women." He saw the devil appear to him in a hallucination, as he confessed in April 1611 to the two Capuchin friars interrogating him:

> The Devil told me that by virtue of my breath I would enflame with my love all the girls and women I wanted to have, provided this breath reached their nostrils; and from that time I made it a habit to blow on all those that crossed my path at will.[47]

It must have been an odd sight to see this priest in the streets of Marseille, blowing beneath the noses of any women passing by whom he wished to seduce. "I have breathed upon a thousand girls or women taking extreme pleasure at the sight of them enflamed by my love."[48]

While spending time at the house of a Marseilles gentleman, Monsieur de la Palud, who had three daughters, he fell in love with the youngest, Magdalen, but her mother kept a close watch over her.

> I breathed upon her mother, so that she would take me to her chamber, and take her sport of me when I was in the house, which I could then enter easily so that finding myself oftentimes with the said Magdalen, I kissed her and more.[49]

One detail reveals how Gaufridi acted as a hypnotist: "The first time I wished to take my pleasure of Magdalen, I placed my hand on her forehead and on the place where the Charities claim virginity resides."[50] A libertine would have placed his hand directly on the girl's genitals, whereas Gaufridi, who sought to bewitch her, started with the forehead.

Gaufridi continuously blew on this shy virgin to overcome her modesty:

> The more I blew upon her, the more desperately she wanted her sport of me. I wanted the effect of our lust to come on her initiative: I infected her so thoroughly with my breath that she died of impatience when I was not with her, she came looking for me . . . so I was able to poke her as I wished.[51]

When he grew weary of blowing on Magdalen de la Palud, he gave her a devil named Emodes "to aid, serve, and protect her," and had her write promises to Belzebuth, signed in her own blood. Placed in the Ursuline Convent in Aix, she related her adventures to a companion, who then also believed herself possessed by Gaufridi. Under the control of demons, both of them fought so much that an Inquisition exorcist was called in. This case of bewitchment transformed into a hysterical attack of demonic possession.

Magdalen, complaining of being "perpetually vexed by incubi committing a thousand vile acts," stated that charms had been cast into her mouth. "It is the devil that forces me to open it in order to receive the charms blown upon me through a barrel." She sneezed and coughed as if trying to spit them out; during the exorcisms she rolled around on the ground. During this time Gaufridi had charmed his landlord, Victoire de Corbier, by blowing upon her two times to make her his mistress. Judged by the Provence Parliament, he was condemned to be burned after making amends by walking the streets of Aix with a noose around his neck and a torch in his hand.

Captivation with one's gaze, another glamour of the enchanter, was demonized in the witch trials, but it was merely a hypnotist's prerogative. The famous Belgian journalist Donato, who was initiated into hypnotism by a canon in Brussels, performed wondrous feats at his public exhibitions in Paris. At the Herz Hall in January 1881, where he hypnotized the willing attendees, people saw "around twenty young people dancing, spinning, eating a potato while believing they were tasting a delicious peach, forgetting their name and even their gender."[52] The columnist for *L'Évènement* reported: "The pretty women clapped so hard they ripped their gloves." If a man like this had any inclination to play the Casanova, he would have been able to have all the women he desired. His biographer wrote:

> Donato never used the extremely annoying and ridiculous tricks of his predecessors. He claimed that he did not put people to sleep; he hypnotized them. I would say rather that he *donatized* them.[53]

He stared straight into the eyes of his subject who, under the intensity of his gaze, entered into a state of lucid somnambulism. "Sleep never comes about, unless it is the experimenter's wish," he explained. During a performance at the Fort of Vincennes, he hypnotized two noncommissioned officers who he made mute and immobile and then compelled to jump. To bring an end to this secondary state, Donato would blow on the person's face and the individual would resume normal consciousness. In sex magic the enchanter—even if he shares Gaufridi's religious mania—is merely putting into play the same sort of hypnotic power as was used by Donato.

Breath is still a means for bewitchment even today. Ange Bastiani, in his *Bréviaire de l'amour sorcier* (Breviary of Sorcerous Love) tells how the seer Jessica, in 1969, who worked out of the fourth floor of an apartment house in Montparnasse, told him:

> All a woman who desires someone's love needs to do is blow seventy times over a glass of water that she will then get the man she lusts for to drink. This process needs to be repeated five times.[54]

This may seem ridiculous, but the great hypnotist Joseph Deleuze said: "Magnetized water is one of the most powerful agents you can use. It is given to patients to drink." He went on to explain:

> A glass of water is magnetized by holding it by the bottom in one hand and with the other projecting the fluid across the glass . . . You can direct your breath over the water, you can also sometimes stir it with your finger.[55]

The magnetization is strengthened, in Jessica's method, by multiplying the two most sacred numbers, 7 and 10.

ENCHANTMENTS

Another means for making someone love you is by creating enchantments. In this case the enchantment is achieved by fashioning a wax figurine charged with attractive attributes. In 1329 the inquisitor Henri de Chimay of Carcassonne condemned to perpetual solitude a monk from Mount Carmel who had seduced three matronly women by burying beneath their doorsills a wax effigy of himself in which he had mixed his blood and saliva and the blood of a toad. There are countless examples of this kind of practice.

Enchantments of hate, which seek to slay a rival, and love enchantments have existed since remote antiquity. The heroines of Tibullus and Virgil can be seen making ligatures, or crafting clay or wax dolls, and then throwing them in the fire while invoking Venus in order to make the faithless lover resist temptation as the clay hardened, or bend to the wishes of his enchantress as the wax melted. Enchantment became less amiable at the beginning of the Christian era, however, with the introduction of a character who is entirely absent from the Old Testament and has only just begun to emerge in the New Testament: Satan, a derivative of Seth, the god of evil in Ancient Egypt (where he was revered just like any other god). No Egyptian ever faced legal condemnation for making offerings to Seth, whereas Christians of East and West calling on Satan's aid would have been harshly punished.

The French name for the effigy popularly known as a "voodoo doll" in English is *volt* (from the Dog Latin *voltum,* meaning "effigy"). This consists of a *dagyde* (from the Greek *dagos,* meaning doll, which in this case is a wax doll resembling the man or woman one wishes to enchant and inscribed with magic characters and the individual's name) and a "charge" (vital fluid that animates it). This charge consists of a combination of personal debris (taken from the enchanter or from the victim): fingernail clippings, hair, or pieces of undergarments, together with sacramental phrases that are spoken while carrying the dagyde to a lit stove or fireplace. The wax, by melting, will send the charge to its destination. But if this charge is poorly crafted, it will backfire on the enchanter and destroy him (or her). To avoid this drawback, a "triangular enchantment" is sometimes performed, which means that two people are enchanted simultaneously—one of whom will absorb the backfire instead of the enchanter.

Jules Bois, refusing to give credence to the idea that enchantment was "ritualized hypnotism," reported that his contemporaries used a wax doll on which was drawn a heart that would be pricked with a lemon tree thorn. This dagyde would then be cast into the fire where branches of thyme and sandalwood were burning, while the enchanter spoke phrases intended to similarly enflame the designated individual. But people did not restrict themselves to this activity:

Several demon-worshippers adopted a simpler procedure. They were content with the cursing of an object, most often a food, a drink, or a fruit, and giving it to their intended victim.[56]

The reinette apple,* picked on a Friday before sunrise, is capable of enchanting someone if appropriately prepared, and if, so it is claimed, two needles traverse it in the shape of a cross: "May Asmodeus[†] similarly cross through the heart of the woman I love."[57] Photos were also used by the enchanters of Bois's time, especially for winning back the affection of a woman who had left someone. "Some modern magicians like casting the photo of the one they wish to return into the fire while calling her name."[58]

However, the dagyde was not discarded, but rather it was then customary to make two, one representing the man and the other the woman, and joining them together as if in a passionate embrace. Pierre V. Piobb provided five enchantment recipes using two wax figures—male and female—such as one from the *Picatrix,* a grimoire cited by Rabelais: "Once the image has been made, these words should be said: *Veni de sancta sede Adonay timor qui Omnia ad voluntatem nostrum coarctabit.*" Since nothing malicious is involved in this operation, he concludes:

> [The effect] of a loving charm returning back upon the operator can cause him naught but good, so it seems a waste of time to arm oneself against any backfire in the case of a love enchantment.[59]

Enchantment has been practiced throughout the entire positivist twentieth century with imperturbable solemnity, and it will probably continue to be so through the twenty-first because of the indestructible beliefs of the collective unconscious. In 1928 Doctor Robert Teutsch published *L'Envoûtement* (The Enchantment), a clinical book

---

*[An old-fashioned French apple variety from the eighteenth century. —*Trans.*]

†[A king of demons in Jewish legend. —*Trans.*]

recounting the treatment he gave to numerous patients who had been bewitched. In it he describes the symptoms and remedies for this affliction. He even goes so far as to reveal that he had been enchanted by a female patient whose amorous advances he had rebuffed, and how he cast a counter-enchantment that led to her death. A short time later in 1937, during the Popular Front period when one would have expected Marxist social struggles to exclude such concerns, a Parisian occult scholar using the pseudonym Sabazius brought out a "practical method for work and protection" that dealt with magical attack and defense. It is the most modern manual on this topic and cooly rationalizes its irrational subject matter.

Sabazius begins by describing enchantment through the will:

This enchantment should be made at night, while the bewitched one is sleeping, after the individual has been *touched* during the day and *touched* with the intent that this contact will become an *effective liaison* several hours later.[60]

One must be skilled to do this and capable of "making someone turn around while you are staring fixedly at the center of their throat or the base of their spine, near the sacrum."[61] You should also train every day, practicing exercises at the same hour and place, clad in a garment of white wool, "because white is insulating," concentrating on the spot between both eyebrows, with eyes closed and the body relaxed.

You must visualize more and more the person in whom you are interested. . . . This representation puts the body into a specific vibratory state and permits the emission, toward the targeted spot, of a powerful current directed by thoughts of hatred or love.[62]

However, enchantment by will is an action only exceptional individuals can perform. Ordinary enchanters use procedures that Sabazius analyzes in detail:

The principle consists of *incorporating* the sensibility of the future victim into a material that will condense the neuric force on which you will be able to act at your leisure.[63]

The spell therefore consists of "a condensing material—heightening the sensitivity of this material—the enchantment, strictly speaking, of the sensitized material." Sabazius says that the wax figure is not an essential component of a *volt*. The charge can be relayed by the intermediary of an animal reputed to accumulate fluids (mole, bat, toad, snake, cat).

This author speaks explicitly about sexual enchantments that make use of the magical force a couple gives off during coitus. He states, "This method of enchantment is powerful and very much practiced by modern enchanters."[64] In an enchantment motivated by hatred, which seeks to destroy an adversary, the partner can be a prostitute; but an enchantment to win someone's love requires an unpaid woman. When this involves a woman playing the active role of enchanter, the male partner can take no initiative. In any event "enchantment by sex should be achieved with a passive and willing individual."[65]

Here is the protocol:

The room shall be dimly lit and sandalwood and incense will be burning. The image (photo, statuette portrait, object . . .) representing the person to be enchanted shall be placed close to the operator. During the full duration of the sex act, which is performed in a special way and uses particular positions, *especially at the end,* the operator should keep his or her gaze fixed on the image while formulating in a whisper the wish he or she wishes to realize. The sexual energy that is convulsing through this individual will amplify and prodigiously increase his or her power of psychic projection, and a spell like this, repeated if possible during the weak or malevolent aspects of the enchanted person's planets in accordance with kabbalistic methods, generally succeeds.[66]

Sabazius explains: "The major agent of sex enchantments is the will. Ardent intention suffices for performing all manner of wonders."[67] He offers the enchanter a safety precaution. "The operator should remember that the Name of power is *Shevah*."[68] And he warns against exhaustion: "know that the sex act uses up the vital reserves for ten days."[69] Lastly he tells us that the sex enchantment can also be achieved through zoophilia: "The same rite can be performed by a man or woman alone using an animal of the opposite sex as coadjutor."[70]

If no partner can be found for a sexual enchantment, it is also possible to cast it by masturbating in front of the dagyde. "The love enchanter will perform all the gestures of possession in front of the statuette including the most obscene ones, primarily those of rape, while speaking to it most tenderly."[71] Sabazius adds: "A very common sexual procedure consists of caressing the object to enchant while maintaining an *erection* in hope of heating, impregnating, and giving the symbolic object 'fluidity.'" Furthermore, "another method consists of writing love epistles on paper moistened with blood, which will then be burned in incense burners with the hair and perfume of the beloved woman."[72]

After teaching his readers how to perform enchantments, Sabazius teaches them how to protect themselves. Someone who has been enchanted displays characteristic symptoms, which are more serious in victims enchanted out of hatred rather than love. "It is not suffering that is felt, rather it is a languor, a loss of will, an abandonment of all modesty and resistance toward an individual to whom you had been indifferent."[73] If one has a distinct impression of having been bewitched, a rapid ritual ensues:

The major defense symbol in the West is the sign of the Cross. But a very important observation needs to be interjected here: *it is necessary for this Sign to encompass the entire body.* This sign should therefore start at the forehead and end at least at the level of the genitals, *if not even all the way down to the feet.*[74]

It is a good idea to have a container of water near your bed. "Water, which starts off neutral, will become slowly charged with all the unhealthy effluvia projected at you."[75] Various objects can be used as protectors, like the tooth of a wild animal that has been consecrated as a talisman. "The tooth is the preeminent symbol of a *natural weapon* of defense and counter-attack. . . . You will wear it around your neck or your right wrist night and day."[76] For protection against sexual enchanters, nothing is better than the Ancient Roman *fascinum,* otherwise known as the phallus:

> In the event of danger, a phallus made of coral, wood, or metal would be worn around the neck, on the arm (around the biceps above the elbow), the right wrist (the *positive* side of the human being), or if necessary, over the plexus sacralis.[77]

If one was not available, people would place their hands on an unhewn part of a piece of furniture, "unhewn wood, the act of knocking on unhewn wood, is directly connected to this great phallic tradition."[78]

For his part, Henri Meslin, a defrocked priest who had devoted himself to the worship of Isis, only recommended harmless enchantments by redirecting his readers away from any use of blood. The love enchanter stands before an altar holding an ash box full of salt, a copper candleholder with a green candle, a crystal vase holding a branch of thyme or verbena, and incense burners. "With your arms extended and slightly raised, your hands open and your fingers spread, you shall recite an orison and conjuration to the angels of Venus."[79] He provides the spells taken from the *Keys of Solomon:* "I conjure you Talaroth, Mivig, Crephaniel, Cleuros . . . to repel evil spirits and send them fleeing." The ceremony, following the blessing of the water, salt, and fire, consists of melting wax and embedding in one segment hair, fingernail clippings, the photo of the beloved individual, and a piece of an undergarment she wore. Her name will be carved above this with a copper tip. In another segment of the wax, the operator embeds the same objects coming from him and places his name above them.

Apply the two segments to each other. Bind them together with pink silk thread and seal them in a small, green silk pouch. Then expose the pouch to the smoke of the perfumes while pronouncing the name of the beloved individual three times. . . . Keep the pouch in a secret place.[80]

Henri Meslin was one of three privileged witnesses to a love enchantment in Paris, about which he relates this charming story:

On the magic altar, covered with a sheet of fine white linen, is the portrait of the Beloved surrounded by twelve torches; it is an enormous, almost life-size photograph placed on a bed of roses, violets, and lilies.[81]

Tripods at the four cardinal points held smoking incense burners.

The operator, clad in a loose green tunic, worshipped the image of the Desired One at length. . . . When rising back up, he kissed the portrait on the eyes, the lips, the breasts, the thighs, and the feet.[82]

He evoked the elementary spirits and the spirits of Venus in accordance with the rituals, read the prayer to Ishtar composed by Sar Péladan, drew "a cross surmounted by a circle" in the air with his finger (the sign of Venus), then kissed the sex of the "prestigious portrait, which seemed to stir and come alive through the effect of this erotic liturgy," and ended by lyrically itemizing all the parts of her body:

Your belly, tabernacle of spasms, will only open at my priesthood of love. . . . Your knees will be together and only part when I kneel before them as the hierophant of your charms, and so forth.[83]

According to Meslin this enchantment succeeded beautifully.

After a short while, the society columns in the newspapers

announced the marriage of the amorous magician with the daughter of one of our most distinguished diplomats.[84]

THE LOVE SPELL

Informed authors have drawn a distinction between the love spell and the enchantment, for its primary element is the power of the Logos and not the *volt,* although it sometimes involves the use of a dagyde. For Sabazius this is black magic, a solicitation of the "Spirits of the Abyss" and the greatest precautions are necessary.

> The enchanter should start his spell with the new moon; he should avoid any sexual congress during the first quarter of the cycle (7 days), take only two meals a day, one at noon and the other at midnight, sleep seven hours, and wear a hematite mounted on an iron ring on the index finger of his left hand.[85]

The operator will undertake his own purification in the following manner:

> He shall disrobe completely and pour *holy water* over his forehead, his naked chest, his sexual organs, his hands, and his feet. He shall shave the hair from his arms and legs, as well as that on his face and chest; he shall pluck the hairs from between his two eyebrows. . . . Then, in a large perfume burner, he shall cast seven grains of incense and seven grains of the finest benzoin. Once the smoke begins to rise, he shall pass his face and hands over it, and slowly walk astride it seven times while allowing the ritual smoke to intimately penetrate his sexual parts.[86]

Next, he shall recite the incantation in Latin (for which the author supplies the text) in the light of a black candle, with his eyes fixed on a virgin parchment covered with magic words written with his blood. "The desired result shall not be long in coming," Sabazius promises.[87]

As was the case with Henri Meslin, the love spell has the quality of a sexual extravaganza. "The first things to procure are one or more photos of the beloved individual you wish to be struck by the incantation. If the photograph shows the person nude, that is preferable."[88] Various objects from the individual in the photograph are added such as letters, locks of hair, a handkerchief, and they are all then placed in a green silk bag. Then on Friday evening, the operator will go by himself into a room that will serve as an oratory, in front of a magic altar made from a table of white wood, "but its various pieces must be held together with pegs, meaning assembled without iron or steel nails."[89] The instruments will be copper, the metal of Venus, as are the incense burners for the verbena, sandalwood, and benzoin, and as are the two candlesticks for the green wax candles.

You should be naked beneath a large, green silk robe. If you do not have one, a loose fitting white bathrobe will do, but in this case wrap a green scarf around your neck that should fall over your shoulders like a shawl.[90]

The portrait and the objects of the beloved are removed from the silk bag and the operator will gather his thoughts for seven minutes facing them. Next, he will gaze at the portrait, extend his arms toward it, and solemnly say:

_____ (Here speak the name of the beloved individual) come at my call, guided by the angel Anael who I invoke. Already through the force of my will, your double is permeated by the effluvia of my desire. May this touch your spirit; may your soul join with mine; and may your body consent to the joy. . . . Amen.

He places his open hands over the portrait and objects, mentally asking the beloved for what he desires; then speaks to her out loud as if she were truly present and covers the relics with kisses. "Then slowly bring your hands to your brow, then to your lips, then your heart. Reach out again toward the portrait. Renew your urgent summons and put everything back in place."[91]

It is not absurd to concur with the author that "This operation, done for seven days (seven is the number sacred to Venus), will have an all-powerful effect."[92]

THE OCCULT POWER
OF PHYSIOLOGICAL EXCRETIONS

Excreta have always been regarded as having essential properties, even to the point where doctors have prescribed them in their remedies. Dioscorides treated asthmatics by giving them infant urine to drink, and this medication remained in use into the seventeenth century. When the priest Jean-Baptiste Thiers (during the reign of Louis XIV) mocked "those who wash their hands with urine to deflect evil spells or avoid their effect,"[93] he criticized them mainly for not combating them with prayer. He was well aware that the apothecaries of his day sold urine—exclusively from a boy under the age of seven—to treat asthma. In the chapter on manure in his book of pharmacology, the famous Sienna physician Matthioli said that cow dung is effective against sciatica and goat turds mixed with wine cure jaundice. It was not the naive common folk who overvalued *excreta;* it was the doctors. Pliny the Elder also said of magic: "Nobody will doubt that it first arose from medicine, and that professing to promote health it insidiously advanced under the guise of a higher and holier system."[94]

The difference in evil spells is that the *excreta;* are combined with propitiatory phrases that give them an infernal power. Martín Del Rio indignantly remarks:

> Such sorcerers are even so wicked that they take from women their menstrual fluids to give to men to drink, and take from men their semen for women to eat and swallow; also droppings and other excrements, as several have said in their confessions.[95]

Johann Weyer testified that a witch, accused of having compelled three priests to sleep with her, one after the other, although she was old and ugly, answered publicly when asked what philters she used: "that they had eaten as much of her shit as her arm was fat." Weyer downplayed his scatological admission to spare her from being sent to the stake.

> As for me, I am fully of the opinion that the shit she said she made them eat was nothing more less the filthy pleasures, that these monks like swine wallowing in the mire having often experimented with this old bawd who was practiced in matters of this nature.[96]

However, it is not out of the question that she instructed her partners in the art of coprophagia the better to dominate them.

Women's milk has been a renowned remedy since Ancient Egypt, where doctors recommended it as eyewash for eye ailments. It was subsequently made the treatment of choice for consumptives and those suffering from anemia. We have often heard anecdotes relating how adults of all ages lauded a wet nurse for giving them the teat like a newborn. The use of mother's milk was frequent in magic and was employed, for example, to help resist torture. Servants of the court sold to the accused that had been tortured a flour biscuit kneaded with the blended milk of a mother and her daughter, so they would not feel the pain.[97]

Blood was another magic substance of the highest order: blood from pricking a finger or from a nosebleed, and especially menstrual blood, as it came from the female's sexual orifice in accordance with a cycle indicating it was under the influence of the moon. Doctors like Agrippa and Cardano never tired of praising the occult virtues of menstrual blood: it cured quartan fever when rubbed on the soles of the patient's feet; it nullified all evil spells when put on a doorsill; and so forth. So it should come as no surprise that a girl would believe that she could compel the love of a man with a recipe of this nature: cut open a small loaf of bread still hot from the oven and let nine drops of blood from her period fall into it, followed by nine drops of blood obtained by making her nose bleed;* dry this bread in the oven, then grind it into a powder that the woman will place in the coffee that the man whose love she desires will drink. [98]

In modern-day Paris the fortune-teller Jessica† expressed her outrage at the practice of piercing a pigeon's heart with needles, as some of her customers had done in order to eliminate a rival. She recommended this more natural method: "To bind a man it is common in all lands, and I mean all lands, to put menstrual blood in his food."[99] She specified that a few drops could be poured onto a piece of sugar or in a glass of alcohol or mixed into a cake or sauce. "Note that if menstrual blood is unavailable, it is not inadvisable to use sweat."[100]

The out-and-out libertine, Ange Bastiani (pen name of the writer Victor Marie Lepage, who also wrote detective novels under the name Maurice Raphaël) personally experimented with female sexual secretions when he lived in Toulon with M. J., a pretty Corsican with a fiery temperament.

> The young lady was not averse to using certain oblong-shaped vegetables to obtain some personal orgasms. Frequently we used these vegetables in our meals the next day.[101]

Their aphrodisiac effect was infallible. "I never had cause to regret it."[102] They wanted to verify if this sex magic worked on others and invited two architects and an abstract painter to dinner.

> Some sweet green and red peppers that had played an eminent role in my girlfriend's entertainment that whole afternoon were now on our friends' plates as part of a peperonata.[103]

An hour after dinner, the painter (who had imbibed copiously because of the peppery main course) grabbed a photograph of the host-

---

*Guyon de Nanche indicated several methods for "causing a nosebleed" using mint leaves, celandine leaves, or madder leaves, or by flicking the nose with the finger.
†This fortune-teller was the wife of an expert on esotericism, Louis Charpentier.

ess and tried to hurl himself out a fifth-floor window. A week later the fiancée of one of the architects, a pharmacy student, offered herself to Bastiani at the urgings of her future husband. The third guest was never heard from again.

On another occasion the couple welcomed into their home as guests a naval officer and his mistress, a young widow, to whom they served a salade Niçoise with green peppers, all of which the perverse M. J. had used in her morning masturbation. The widow immediately left her lover and was swept away by a sapphic passion for M. J., who she pursued relentlessly and invited to come spend a week with her in the mountains. After two days M. J. left her, and the jilted lover sent "threatening letters and made lewd phone calls" to Bastiani for six months. The naval officer, now separated from his girlfriend, spied M. J. outside and invited her to his bachelor pad. She accepted his proposition, but he proved to be impotent when she gave in to his demands. These were the disturbing waves created by a magical obscene gesture.

Because of the inner alchemy of the woman, it is logical that the best potions would be those concocted in her private parts. Henri Meslin cited this Arab custom:

A woman who feels her husband's ardor is diminishing, will introduce a date into her vagina every night for seven days. She will leave it there overnight, and in the morning give it to her unwitting husband to eat.[104]

Jessica, who started her career in Morocco, observed there, "the creation of a couscous intended to blind the husband to his wife's bad behavior."[105] A powerful potion was required for this.

For three days in a row she would smear her vagina and ass with honey and then sit naked in the large wooden plate filled with the semolina used to make the couscous. She would then scrape off the grains that remained stuck to her body and set them aside. On the third day, she would wash off her genitals with rainwater that had been exposed overnight to the rays of the full moon.[106]

She would then prepare the couscous with the semolina scraped from her body and this water, by adding oil to it in which a mandrake root had been macerated for seven days. "The woman who serves this to her husband can rest at ease. Even the most jealous husband will be completely fooled and see nothing of her worst transgressions."[107]

The magic of a woman's vulva will magnetize her panties and charge them like a volt influencing whoever—man or woman—touches them. Ange Bastiani even advised an unfaithful husband stricken by his wife's jealousy, to give her the panties, ironed but not washed, that his mistress had worn one day. Not only did her jealously cease, he claims, but the wife became so infatuated with the mistress that he was able to bring them together in the same bed. More seriously, this author has studied the magic effect of a woman who wears no underwear beneath her dress. "The incontestable magnetism inherent to certain mucus membranes, cannot help but be increased by their direct contact with the open air."[108] As an example, he cites

> this strong-minded business woman, considered by everyone to be irreproachable in her behavior, who one day, when she felt herself in a confessional mood, admitted that she never went to any important meeting without slipping away to some discreet spot to take off her panties.[109]

Discussing important matters while her genitals were bare with men who were totally unaware of it, gave her an irresistible self-confidence. Every time she went to these meetings "covered," the discussions turned to her disadvantage. It is easy to see that true sex magic does not consist of demonic ceremonies, but rather actions that draw their effectiveness from the bioelectricity of the genitals.

2
The White Magic of Love

The founder of modern sex magic was an American, Paschal Beverly Randolph, who was born on October 8, 1825, in New York, the illegitimate son of a black woman, Flora Clark, and a Virginia gentleman, William Beverly Randolph, who abandoned him at birth. His mother died of smallpox when he was seven, and his half-sister, Harriet, raised him. Because he was a black man, he had great difficulty in completing school and carving out a place for himself in society. He complains of this endlessly in his writings, calling himself a mixed-blood, but claiming descent through his mother from a queen of Madagascar, and through his father from John Randolph, a member of Congress and Ambassador to Russia. In his youth P. B. Randolph enjoyed the support of a rich philanthropist, Gerrit Smith, an abolitionist and spiritualist. This is how he found himself plunged into the "radical spiritualist" milieu that was extremely active at this time and took the form of revival meetings in which preachers, claiming inspiration from deceased famous individuals in the beyond, gave enthusiastic speeches before frenzied crowds. P. B. Randolph got his start as one of these mediumistic orators: one of his greatest successes was in New York, where he gave a public discourse on "the philosophy of Life," while feeling possessed by the spirit of Benjamin Franklin.

In 1850 P. B. Randolph married an Indian woman who had medicine men in her ancestry. He had three children with her, only one of which survived. During this time he was a barber in Utica, a profession which in those days included the practices of surgeon and healer. In 1853 he gave himself the title of "Dr. P. B. Randolph, clairvoyant physician and psycho-phrenologist." Although he was self-taught in medicine and had no diploma, his abilities as a physician were never questioned. His clientele was satisfied with him. He used Indian remedies passed on by his wife and applied knowledge learned through reading and from his acquaintances. Cuina Vilmara, an Italian scientist traveling through America, revealed medical secrets to him. In 1854 he met two French doctors from the Société Magnétique of Paris in New York, the doctors Bergevin and Toutain, who identified his ability to heal through magnetism. Two journeys to Europe in 1855 and 1857 allowed him to establish contact with the most renowned spiritualist physicians, homeopaths, and hypnotists of London and Paris. Moreover, the Grandmaster of the English Rosicrucians initiated him into this tradition with its long tradition of thaumaturgy. On his return to America, he no longer signed some of his newspaper articles as Dr. P. B. Randolph but as "the Rosicrucian."

The most powerful movement in American spiritualism was that of Free Love, whose adepts did not shy away from engaging in very radical ventures. For example, the Modern Times colony on Long Island, founded by anarchist Josiah Warren in 1853, practiced absolute sexual liberty. Warren's successor, Stephen Pearl Andrews, dubbed himself "the Pantarch." Randolph became involved with the Pantarch and other sexual magi, like the cynic Moses Hall and the mystic libertine, Thomas Lake Harris, but he was critical of their activities and soon sought to oppose them with his own notion of spiritualist sexuality. He published his book *The Grand Secret* in Boston in 1860, the same year he settled in that city. He described this as "the greatest discovery in twenty-five years on a point of physiology," calling it "A New Revelation Concerning Sex." He soon added "The Golden Letter," which was circulated in the form of a manuscript that could be obtained from him for five dollars.

According to Randolph "love is a physical substance." The feeling or passion a person experiences under this name serves to manufacture it and assume its use. This substance is a "neuro-viral" fluid that is made up of three components—electrical, magnetic, and chemical. He calls male sexual fluid *geehr* and that of the female, *keemlin*. When these two separate fluids are mixed during the sex act and manage to merge or combine in the body, they create around the entwined couple an aura, the Ethylle, which has an irresistible power of attraction on entities from the invisible world.

In fact, the universe is bathed in another aerial element that has a different nature from the atmosphere, the Æth, which contains the celestial hierarchies about which the Holy Scriptures speak (the angels, seraphs, arsaphs, and so on) and the Potentialities in their pure state: "Soul seeds (Atomonads) dwelt in the Ether and the Sakwalas or Spiritual Spheres and that in those spheres also existed the germs of all knowledge and power."[1] Men and women have the power to harness them while making love because of the dual nature of their soul.

As he had been teaching since the early 1860s, Randolph believed that the soul was a bipolar "diamondesque," divine white fire (a "condensation and crystallization of God's nervous fluid"), resident in the brain and in the sexual organs.[2]

The negative, electrical, male pole resides in the brain where it holds responsibility for reason, learning, and adapting to facts. The magnetic, positive, female pole was in the male's testicles and the woman's uterus, and it was this magnetic pole that put the individual in contact with the divine, subtle fire of the Æth that feeds the entire universe. The activity of the two poles, especially the magnetic poles, is essential for the creation of perfect things. Without love and the role played by sex, the brain used only half its soul and could produce only botched works.

Randolph was therefore right in claiming to be the practitioner of the "white magic of love." With him there are no demonic evil spells; all the magical powers he attributes to sex come from his concept of the soul, ether, and God. His conceptions were those of a physician, not a dreamer. As he stated in a meeting: "God is Electricity, Movement, and Light." His potions did not derive from grimoires but were medications that he invented such as phloxine, made from hashish, and his two elixirs, phymylle (for nervous exhaustion) and amylle (against imbalances of the passions), which sold for twenty-five dollars a bottle and he claimed were the best two aphrodisiacs in the world. Thanks to these adjuvants and the advice he provided, Randolph's clientele were well equipped to make the best use of their sexuality. If one knows how to perform the sex act as it should be performed, he explained to them, one could attain these results: the restoration of one's health; the creation of a child with exceptional gifts; and the extension of one's life. One could have a decisive influence over another person; improve personal finances or win the top prize in a lottery; or magnetically charge a ring, mirror, or doll, which would then become magic objects.

Randolph stated this fundamental axiom:

> If a man ardently wishes for a force or power, and keeps that wish from the moment he penetrates the women until the moment when he leaves her, his wish is necessarily fulfilled.[3]

Two conditions are required. The first is to formulate clearly in his mind, during their embrace, what he wants to obtain. Next, ensure that their two orgasms are simultaneous, the *expulsive* instant of the man coinciding perfectly with the *exudive* moment of the woman:

> in that moment do these soul-seeds, germs of knowledge, knowledge itself, and magic power descend to, and find lodgment in our souls, the mystic doors of which are then instantly opened and as suddenly closed again.[4]

Therefore a veritable inhalation of the forces of the Æth takes place within the mutual body, and they are what gives the individual the possibility of materializing his will: "The movement of the Will in Love (and not of Will in Intelligence) assures our higher triumphs."

The psyche of the man and woman should be fortified in order to benefit this way from sex. Randolph prescribed daily exercises that he christened with French or Latin-sounding names: volantia, posism, decretism, and tirauclairism. For volantia, which develops one's ability to concentrate and pay attention, a white disk with a black center is fastened to the wall. The individual will stare at the black center of this disk for a full minute, then turn his gaze toward a white surface, on which through an optical illusion, he will see the same disk reversed with a black background and a white center. This exercise should be repeated every day with different colored disks, and after six months "the student will have acquired the capacity to create, while calmly staring at a white surface, a mental form which will attract the corresponding astral body."[5] In Posism, the science of the magic of the gesture, for five minutes every day at the same time, the student will study in front of a mirror the most appropriate poses and expressions for sending or receiving this or that idea.[6] Tirauclarism, "the power of evocation, which permits communication with those who are absent, the dead, and invisible entities" depends on exercises that are performed at night: "Fix in your mind an image or a flash of light, and do not be distracted from it."[7] In this way you will become capable of driving away those thoughts that are foreign to a definite vision. There are no special exercises, however, for learning decretism, which "is the capacity to give inescapable orders"[8] or the "power to create entities capable of living."[9] It is acquired naturally when one's term of initiation has been completed.

Randolph described five positions of the sex act (they are even illustrated by drawings in *Magia Sexualis*), each of which procures a specific magic power. Position 1, in which the man lies atop the woman, face to face, "corrects the senses and the capacities of the operators."[10] In position 2 the man, in doggy style, keeps his chest upright while penetrating the prostrate woman from behind. This position "favors the projection of influence to the exterior (we call that: the exterior circle) upon one or several chosen persons, or upon the higher spheres";[11] and more decisively: "It is propitious for charging a 'volt,' for creating larvae, or for any other aggressive operation against a person."[12] In position 3, which increases and orients the influence to the exterior, the man and woman are seated facing each other, their sex organs slotted together, their upper torsos leaning backward while holding each other up by their hands. Position 4 has the couple seated, facing each other, with the woman's legs crossed around the man's waist and their foreheads touching, for the purpose of realizing a shared wish. Randolph recommends that "if the prayer is only made by one of the spouses, take position number 1. If you will pray together, choose position number 4."[13] In position 5, which is also doggy style, the man lowers himself on his partner's back resting his chin on the nape of her neck. This position "permits the man to influence the woman without her being aware of it."[14] But if the two operators are in accord, "it serves to project a vigorous influence into the exterior circle."[15] These five positions are effective "in conformity to the normal law of opening the aura,"[16] and they can each be performed in turn during a single session.

P. B. Randolph's sex magic falls into a general metaphysics that gives it credibility. He wrote a *Guide to Clairvoyance,* and a treatise, *The Magic Mirror and How to Use It*, in which he put together an overview of the experiments performed by French, English, and American hypnotists for preparing these kinds of mirrors that provoke hallucinatory visions. He used it in his meditations on the invisible world. On several occasions he even practiced "the sleep of Sialam," a near-comatose state during which one receives dreams from the beyond. If he was asked, "How do you know such things exist?" he answered: "Because in the sleep of Sialam I have seen them, and others have seen them like me."* This was how he could write his book *After Death; or Disembodied Man*, which contained two chapters that dealt with sex after death and the marriage of souls in the other world, which are forms of spiritualist erotology in its purest state. Randolph believed

---

*Helena Blavatsky, president of the Theosophical Society in London, while opposing Randolph, borrowed from him this notion of the "sleep of Sialam" for her own writings. It describes a condition when the medium is in a cataleptic state like a fakir and makes his revelations while sleeping.

that souls were born as male and female couples in the Æeth who were combined in a single monad that separated to become a separate man and woman on Earth (each of whom retained a male or female pole, respectively). When a human being died, he would strive to reform the same monad on the astral plane. If the soul of an individual's earthly spouse did not correspond with the celestial partner from whom he or she had been separated, the human soul would wander in search of it. Once it was found, these two halves would regain their former oneness with infinite bliss. They would then enjoy etheric, sexual relations with other units of the same order, for it is the ceaseless amorous conjunctions between the souls of the dead that produce universal magnetism.[17]

In *Pre-Adamite Man* Randolph asserted that humanity did not descend from Adam and Eve but from several Adams and Eves who existed one hundred thousand years ago and engendered the different races. He also used these observations to justify his medical practice, such as in his essay *Hashish, Its Benefits and Dangers,* in which he shows that he used it in its *dowam meskh* form (Arabic for the "medicine of immortality"), an oily extract with the consistency of green jelly that has invigorating properties. Lastly, Randolph wrote initiatory novels like *Dhoula Bel,* whose hero is a sex vampire; *The Rosicrucian's Story;* and a sequel to the latter, *The Wonderful Story of Ravallete,* which illustrate the ideas of the Rosicrucians.

In addition he was also a militant advocate of human emancipation, as he proved during the Civil War. He played a leading role in the National Convention of Colored Men held in Syracuse, New York, in 1864, and was sent a month later to New Orleans by his "personal friend" Abraham Lincoln to assist Captain J. H. Ingraham, commander of the Union regiment of Creole blacks. He caught everyone's attention with his rousing speeches in favor of the equality of the black and white races. He contributed to the creation of schools for black children, and fought against the superstitions of the Louisiana Voodoo cults in a series of lectures. After Lincoln's assassination on March 14, 1865, he continued the action inaugurated by the president. He became the principal of the Lloyd Garrison School in New Orleans where he had 373 black students. He also started a national subscription for the founding of a teachers' college to train black teachers. Because of this work, he earned the praise of General Howard and was invited to the White House by the new president, Andrew Johnson. Randolph was also responsible for organizing the political pilgrimage in September and October 1866 to Abraham Lincoln's tomb in Springfield, Illinois.

On his return to Boston at the end of 1867, Randolph became the director of the Rosicrucian Rooms, an establishment whose owner, Mary P. Crook, ran a magic shop that sold magic mirrors, talismans, horoscopes, and oracles. Randolph oversaw it without betraying his principles, even when on Wednesday meetings he made public predictions while invoking the soul of Raymond Lull. But his essential teachings still centered on sex magic. These endeavors were audacious but not at all immoral. He was so upright in this respect that he even criticized his patron, the rich and eccentric Andrew Bay, for wishing, at the age of eighty-six ("one-third man and two-thirds ghost"), to wed a fifteen-year-old girl. Randolph took the opportunity to condemn the vast network of pedophiles that existed in America at this time by raising medical objections against their proclivities. An adolescent girl cannot sexually love an old man, he said; consequently, she will not provide him with "the neuro-aura transfusion" in bed that could regenerate him.

Although it would be hypocritical to accuse him of corrupting morals, jealous rivals did accuse Randolph of "obscenity" in February 1872. He spent two nights in jail before hearing the prosecutor say in front of a Boston court "that he was the most dangerous man and author on American soil." He presented his defense in a file on himself, *Curious Life,* but this incident would be the starting point of what was called the "Great Free-Love Trial," which would ultimately lead to a government crackdown on sexual reformers. To get past this incident, Randolph moved to Toledo, Ohio, in 1873, a city where many fans of "radical spiritualism" made their homes. He opened a consultation office there on Vance Street and a laboratory for manufacturing his latest medication: protozone. He also launched a spiritist circle in which two mediums, a man and woman, questioned a spirit that appeared in the midst of a shower of sparks and phosphorescent vapor.

Randolph wished to start a "School of Sexual Science for adults (in brains, as well as years)," and to prepare a bible of erotology, *Sexagyma*, to help couples through all their hardships. As this was not something he could pursue in a government institution, he decided to complete this project within the context of an initiatory society (the Brotherhood of Eulis), which he founded in Nashville, Tennessee in March 1874. He took the name of Eulis from *eolis*, a derivative of the Greek word for dawn, *eos*. Randolph said the Eulis meant the Gate of Dawn. His fraternity was dissolved in June 1874 because of discord among its members, but he revived it the following December in San Francisco (during a lecture tour in California) in a larger format: The Triplicate Order Rosicruciae, Pythianae, and Eulis, whose charter he published. The Great Lodge of San Francisco, directed by eight dignitaries (from the Supreme Hierarch to the Supreme Grand Master of the Supreme Grand Dome), was expected to have branches in other cities. Its adherents, in return for dues of two hundred and fifty dollars, could pursue an education there through three degrees: the first in self-mastery, the second in clairvoyance and the use of magic mirrors, and the third in sexual magic.

Randolph's magic doctrine culminated in his *Casca Llana* (1872), the "Second Revelation on Sex"; *Eulis* (1873), "Third Revelation on the Soul and Sex"; and *The Ansairetic Mystery* (1873), the "Fourth Revelation on Sex." The adjective Ansairetic comes from Ansaireh, designating the Muslim community of the Nasayris (akin to the Druze and Ismailis), who lived in the mountains of northwest Syria. Randolph had been given information on them from his friend, the defrocked Jesuit priest, William G. Palgrave, who had recently published a book on his travels in the Middle East. The Nasayris offered their wives and daughters to their guests, but it was not this sexual custom that caught Randolph's attention. He sought in their "conjugal communion" a cosmic ecstasy that allowed them to establish contact with the invisible.

Randolph redefined the goals of sex magic in accordance with the cult of the Nasayris. He reiterated: "All absolute power, knowledge, energy, force exists in the Sakwalas or spiritual spheres." He also confirmed:

> None of these [powers] spring up from within us, but all are reachable by us, and flow into us in our highest moments . . . and it or they enter the soul *only* in the moment, at the very instant, of the holy, full, mutual, and pure orgasm, or ejection of the three fluids and two auras [in other words the prostatic secretion of sperm and the female *lochia*] and the dual magnetism evolved.[18]

After analyzing these principles, Randolph draws up a list of the 122 possibilities a person can achieve thanks to them: "to attach to oneself innumerable aethric, aerial, invisible assistants," "to impel a specific love-energy to a far-off person," "Forecasting events in the lives of others," "to increase the dynamic force and power of any bodily organ," "the art of adding specific energy to neutral substances" (for example, a powder), as well as giving a woman the ability to avoid an unwanted childbirth through an act of will instead of abortion, and so forth.

In more moderate fashion as a "humble professor of sexual common sense," in Randolph's last book on sex, *The Mysteries of Eulis* (1874), he introduced the method of Mahi-caligna (a term meaning "science of old age"), which allowed a couple to use their sexuality for the seven goals that form the "crowning glory of the system of Eulis":

    I. For purposes of increasing the brain and body power of the unborn child

    II. Influencing one's wife or husband, and magnetically controlling them

    III. Regaining youthful beauty, energy, vivacity, affectional and magnetic power

    IV. Prolonging the life of either the subject or the actor, or either at will

V. Attainment of Supreme white magic of will, Affection or Love

VI. Furtherance of financial interest, schemes, Lotteries, etc.

VII. The attainment of the loftiest insight possible to the earthly soul.[19]

Naturally, many other successes could be achieved through the Mahi-caligna: "If a man has an intelligent and loving wife, with whom he is in full and complete accord, he can work out the problems by her aid. . . . The rite is a prayer in all cases, and the most powerful earthly beings can employ."[20] The woman will not bend to his will out of simple complacency. She shall not be the wife of another, a virgin, a minor, a prostitute, or a vulgar debauchee. She and her husband should maintain perfect cleanliness by washing daily. Their food should be natural with no excess of liquid. Twice a week they will take an "airbath" while totally naked, in the sunshine if possible. They should breathe slowly in order not only to absorb the air essential to life, but the Æeth containing the invisible entities, as well. Their bed should be hard with its head to the north and their room cool and well ventilated.

The Mahi-caligna is a sex ceremony that lasts forty-nine days. On the first seven days, the man will be satisfied by meditating alone in his room, and preparing there the perfume corresponding to the planetary force he wishes to attract. The "Table of Planetary Correspondences" in *Magia Sexualis* provides the metal, number, musical note, color, perfume, and stone of each planet. Recipes are supplied for crafting *force extracts* with the flowers and plants dedicated to each of them, and even "personal melodies" by using "the sound, which it evokes, by analogy of vibrations." On the eighth day, the woman enters the chamber illuminated by a light of the planet's color (green for Venus, red for Mars, multicolored for Mercury, and so on) and the man, having perfumed his palms and solar plexus with the astral perfume, begins the sexual union. It is necessary for both partners to be excited and have orgasms: "The man should never touch a woman who is not excited, and he must not leave her before both orgasms have passed."[21]

The operation will be repeated every three days; during the two days in between, the man will commence again with his task of solitary meditation. The protocol is simple:

> Formulate the desire and keep it in mind during the whole period and especially when making the nuptive prayer, during which no word may be spoken, but the thing desired be strongly thought.[22]

This "nuptive prayer" is not the recital of a *Paternoster* or an *Ave Maria* but the act of coitus itself, performed religiously, under the protection of the "female side of God." For God is androgynous, He and She, and it is his She part that confers upon the sex act its magical scope. Randolph concludes: "If everything has been done correctly, the faculty, sense, or force that you have wished for will have been acquired in your mental makeup."[23]

Sexual operations for charging a volt or magic ring are less complicated. In order to have any effect on someone, "to cure them of a sickness" or "to cast good or ill fortune upon them," a figurine is made representing "the entire silhouette, or the part of the subject's body that is to be influenced." It is covered with the color and perfume corresponding to the subject's horoscope and then "one should work sexually a single time, that is to say, on the eighth day only." The couple must concentrate on the targeted individual: "The statuette that will be the 'volt' must be placed in the room where you operate in such a way that you may see it during the operational coitus." Afterward it will be placed inside a hermetically sealed vessel for protection. When you wish to annul the volt, the statuette should be placed inside a hot bath for three whole days.[24]

To create a magic ring that brings visions to its wearer, it will be necessary to create a "fluid condenser"—solid or liquid—that will be placed in the reservoir of the ring beneath the stone chosen in accordance with the subject's horoscope. "A few moments before the first sex-magic operation, add to the liquid fluid condenser, duly prepared, a drop of blood taken from the monthly discharge of your collaborator. This drop is to be kept in the vessel until this moment."[25] On the finger of a nervous individual, the ring will inspire the medium-like vision of the scene with which it has been charged. On a strong individual, it will give him while he sleeps a dream that he will later take as a reality he truly experienced.

P. B. Randolph obviously put his theories into practice in his personal life. One day at the theater, during the intermission, a friend asked him if it was true that he could dominate any woman by his will. "Yes," said Randolph, "every woman whom I call must come. Every time. At once." To prove this Randolph told his friend to pick out a woman in the audience. Randolph went rigid, closed his eyes, and concentrated: barely two minutes later, the young blonde woman stood up like a sleepwalker and appeared to be looking for him. In a panic his friend asked him to halt the experiment immediately and the unknown woman returned to her seat. Gustav Meyrink recorded the foregoing anecdote in the preface to his German translation of *Ravalette*. However, Randolph's power did not prevent him from suffering some setbacks. His wife Mary Jane left him in 1860 because she attributed her nervous troubles and scrofula* to the magic experiments her husband had performed on her. It was Randolph's free love adversaries that instilled her with that notion. Randolph remarried in 1865, but during the summer of 1867, he took a trip leaving his second wife alone at home. A traveling free-love propagandist, Jamieson, took advantage of his absence to seduce her and break up his marriage. Randolph then had liaisons with Carrie Chute, who financed the publication of his book, *Love and Its Hidden History,* in 1869, and Blondette, "a thin-lipped, blue-eyed affectional sorceress," for whom he wrote *Casca Llana* in 1871.

In May 1873, when his left arm had suddenly become paralyzed, Randolph seduced a young nineteen-year-old girl, Kate Corson, who would become his third wife. On March 30, 1874, she bore him a son whom he named Osiris Budh, convinced that through his method he had created a demigod. But he was soon tormented by thoughts that his new companion was unfaithful to him, and he drowned his grief in alcohol. Violent when drunk, to the point of threatening to kill the little Osiris Budh after claiming Kate had conceived him with another man,

---

*[Tuberculous infection of the lymph nodes. —*Ed.*]

he would become sweet again when he sobered up. On July 29, 1875, he could take it no longer and committed suicide by shooting himself. The Toledo newspaper reported that earlier that day he had warned a neighbor: "in less than two hours, I shall be a dead man." The article stated: "it is most generally conceded that jealousy was the main cause."[26]

An end like this, motivated by a crisis of passion, does not nullify the validity of Randolph's sex magic. One might think that he had not been successful in influencing his young wife by his special procedures. In fact, Kate Corson remained faithful and devoted to his memory, republishing his books until the end of the century in the Randolph Publishing Company, and continuing to manufacture his elixirs (protozone, chlorylle, barosmyn, and a Lucina cordial). Osiris Randolph, who he had wished to make a "superior child," would later become a renowned surgeon. And it was female rather than male admirers who would strive to spread the doctrine of the Supreme Hierarch of Eulis. Two California mediums, Luna Hutchinson and Fanny Green, claimed Randolph's soul appeared to them regularly and revealed his remarks in *Beyond the Veil* (1878). In France, Maria de Naglowska, before even founding her Brotherhood of the Golden Arrow, had partially translated Randolph's teachings under the title of *Magia Sexualis*. This book remains a standard reference because the other works by this major forerunner in the field of sexual magic are practically inaccessible.

3

The High Science
of Sacred Sexuality

A path has been laid that allows the spiritual teachers of our time to incorporate sex magic into their teaching and to instruct their disciples on how to use sex to go beyond pleasure and toward individual omnipotence. This is not an official practice, as our governments are nowhere close to accepting Randolph's dream of a School of Sexual Science. The professors of this science were therefore philosophers leading "initiatory organizations," which René Guenon advised us to carefully distinguish from the "sects" that are the small heretical offshoots of a religion. The schools of Gnosis, the Kabbalah, the Cathars, the Templars, the Freemasons, and the Rosicrucians were "initiatory organizations," and it was inspired by these models that the adepts of magical eroticism blended rituals into their sexual practice, in order for it to be a mystic quest of the sacred nature of the flesh—not simple libertinism.

Randolph's ideas were not continued by his successors, who transferred the Brotherhood of Eulis to Salem, but by a German industrialist and member of the Rite of Memphis and Misraim in Berlin, Carl Kellner, when he founded the Ordo Templi Orientis (O.T.O.) in 1902, which included an initiation into sex magic. Kellner, who was a seasoned traveler, attributed his knowledge in this domain to three experts with whom he had spent time: an Arab and two Hindus. Nonetheless it is obvious he had read the reprints of Randolph's books published by his widow. However, Kellner died in 1905 without having had the time to perfect his organization. The O.T.O. would only prosper under its new Outer Head of the Order, Theodor Reuss, who had initiated adepts in England, France, and Denmark. A former music hall singer, Theodor Reuss had been a spy for the Prussian secret police, in charge of keeping tabs on the German socialist exiles in London, particularly the children of Karl Marx. He had joined the Socialist League (which was Marxist before later leaning toward anarchism) with Marx's daughter, Eleanor Marx Aveling, who got him expelled because she found his activities suspicious. Reuss later became the financial officer of an export-import business and a journalist. He established the newsletter *The Oriflamme* as an organ, making the following declaration in 1912:

> Our Order possesses the KEY which opens up all Masonic and Hermetic secrets, namely the teaching of sexual magic, and this teaching explains, without exception, all the secrets of Freemasonry and all systems of religion.[1]

The O.T.O. had nine grades of initiation, the first six markedly similar to those of classic Craft Freemasonry, dispensing with ritual. In the other three, where the members learned the "royal art" of masturbation and copulation, they received their instructions from written documents. Masturbation was called "the marriage with the gods," as one was expected to masturbate while thinking of the deities of Greece and not real or imaginary people. As for copulation, Francis King, who has seen some of their unpublished writings, says:

> The initiates of the IX° claimed that success in almost any magical operation, from the invocation of a god to "procuring a great treasure" could be achieved by the application of the appropriate sexual technique. Thus to invoke the powers of a god into themselves they mentally concentrated on the god throughout their sexual intercourse, building up the form of the deity in their imaginations and

attempting to imbue it with life. At the moment of orgasm they identified themselves with the imagined form, mentally seeing their own bodies and that of the god blending into one. If they wanted to "charge" a talisman—a magical charm designed to achieve some desired end, such as love or fame—they anointed it with the *Amrita* resulting from their sexual act, during which act they had concentrated on the talisman and its purpose.[2]

Borrowing their vocabulary from alchemy, the members of the O.T.O. named the penis the *athanor,* the vagina the *curcurbite,* semen the *serpent,* and the mixture of semen and vaginal lubrications after ejaculation inside the woman was called the *amrita* or *elixir.* They collected the *amrita* with their fingers from the *curcurbite* of their companion in order to make an offering of it to the god invoked before their coitus—most often this was Pan—or for imbuing with magical power a letter on which they drew the appropriate symbol with the end of their index finger moistened by this *elixir:* for example, "if the letter was an application for money, the sigil of the god Jupiter was drawn on the envelope."

Theodor Reuss wrote a book, *Lingam-Yoni,* in order to connect his order to Tantric Yoga, but he was not a good writer. The order undoubtedly would have gone into a decline if Reuss had not decided to establish contact in London with Aleister Crowley, whose paradoxical reputation made him an incomparable recruit.

ALEISTER CROWLEY AND OCCULT HIGH MAGIC

Going far beyond all the attempts of erotic Gnosis made before him and influencing all those that have been made following his death up to the present, Aleister Crowley incontestably remains the preeminent master of twentieth-century High Sexual Magic (which he called the High Magick Art). He added a *k* to the English word "magic" because this was the initial letter of the Greek *ktéis* (vagina), and this altered spelling symbolized the importance of sex in operative magic. Born in 1875 Crowley was above all an English Victorian dandy who described himself as a "gentleman of Cambridge" when he published his philosophical poem "Aceldama" in 1896. He was a man so perverse and scandalous that he made Oscar Wilde, whom he admired, look like a choirboy. From early on Aleister Crowley presented himself as the Antichrist, nicknaming himself defiantly the Great Beast 666, in reference to the Book of Revelation. He displayed a raucous eccentricity both in his personal life and in his many books containing poems, stories, plays, religious rituals, and treatises on occultism.

In the study that I devoted to him, I referred to Aleister Crowley as "a metaphysical Don Juan" and exposed in detail his extraordinary experiments in sexual magic. This was something that no one had yet dared to do in France up until that point.[3] Like the "catalog" of women seduced by Mozart's Don Giovanni, Crowley certainly had thousands of lovers during his lifetime—including prostitutes he indoctrinated so thoroughly that some refused to take any payment from him. However, his female conquests were motivated by a mystical ambition for the absolute, and he never made love solely for pleasure. He was aiming for something much higher in the carnal embrace: to establish communion with the eternally living gods of Egypt and Greece and to make a cosmic sacrifice to attract good luck.

In his youth in London, as a member of the Hermetic Order of the Golden Dawn, which drew together writers and artists smitten with alchemy and black magic, and in which he had the name of Frater Perdurabo (in Latin: "I will persevere"), Crowley's relations with women combined libertinism with theosophy. It was during an initiatory journey of two and a half years to Mexico, Hawaii, Japan, Singapore, and France (from 1900 to 1903) that he had adventures proving to him that genius was the product of an exacerbated sexuality. He was variously initiated into yoga in Ceylon; into tantra in the Temple of Shiva in Madura, where he performed the maithuna with two *devadasis* (sacred prostitutes); and into Parisian occultism in the entourage of Rodin and Marcel Schwob. On his return to England, where he divided his time between the Boleskine mansion he had recently purchased in the Scottish Highlands (his parents had left him a large fortune) and his apartment in London, Crowley began distinguishing his own teachings from those of the Golden Dawn, which confined itself to the invocation of angels and demons in accordance with the rituals from *The Book of Enoch* by Queen Elizabeth's astrologer John Dee and *The Book of the Sacred Magic of Abramelin the Mage,* translated by a fifteenth-century Jewish kabbalist.

Crowley's central idea was to create a gnostic religion for the future that would be a synthesis of the beliefs and dogmas of Hinduism, Taoism, the Eleusinian Mysteries of Greece, Egyptian religion as revealed by Iamblichus, and esoteric Christianity. He claimed that this religion had been foreseen in John of Patmos's *Apocalypse* in the form of two monstrous beasts. One, which had seven heads and ten horns, represented the old religion to be fought, and the other, which resembled a dragon and corresponded to the number 666 and was ridden by a woman clad in purple and covered with jewels who is called "Babylon." Descended from a family of fanatical Christians, Crowley turned the Apocalypse into an erudite gloss that would have made his uncle, Tom Bond Bishop (who taught Bible classes to children in London), nauseous. He declared that he himself was the dragon 666 and that Babylon should actually be read as Babalon, the feminine principle of the universe. The woman dressed in purple, the embodiment of the "Great Whore," was the one who guided the dragon so he would prevail in his battle against puritanical prejudices.

Crowley then began fervently praying to Babalon as the supreme goddess, by whose grace there is no forbidden pleasure, and oriented his sexuality in search of a Scarlet Woman, comparable to the one in the Apocalypse, who, he planned, would inspire him in his apostolate of the Great Beast 666. His first Scarlet Woman (there were officially eight of them between the years of 1903 and 1930, not counting his mistresses) was a young widow, Rose Kelly, whom he married in July 1903 and used as a medium to interrogate the spirits of the invisible world. This was how, during their honeymoon in Egypt, she was contacted in Cairo by

Crowley's guardian angel, who declared his name as Aiwass and dictated *The Book of the Law* in three days. This book said that the god Horus and Queen Nuit had charged Crowley—as the reincarnation of a Twenty-Sixth-dynasty Theban priest, Ankh-af-na-khonsu—with the task of establishing the religion of the Thelemites who heeded but one rule: "Do what thou wilt."*

At this time Crowley broke with the Golden Dawn and created his own order: the Astrum Argentinum,† based on this revelation from the *Book of the Law:* "Every man and every woman is a star." He also founded *The Equinox,* a "Review of Scientific Illuminism," which came out twice a year, on the spring equinox and fall equinox.

When Rose no longer had the morale and health to perform her role as the Scarlet Woman, Crowley divorced her and formed other liaisons, including a homosexual relationship with a twenty-five-year-old poet, Victor Neuburg, who accompanied him to Algeria to make a Great Magical Retirement for invoking the angels in the desert. His second Scarlet Woman, in 1910, was the young violinist Leila Waddell, whom he named secretary of the Astrum Argentinum. His third Scarlet Woman appeared in 1911; she was the dancer Mary d'Este, known as Sister Virakam, who had visions of the magician Ab-ul-Diz when they were making love. The audible and visual hallucinations his partners experienced owed much to his power of suggestion, multiplied tenfold by the stimulants he took (for example, he smoked rum-soaked tobacco in his pipe). He also resorted to drugs, which in his time were not illegal. Cocaine was considered to be medicine, opium had been given credence by the officers of the Indian Army, and Conan Doyle's readers found it completely natural that Sherlock Homes sometimes gave him-

---

*His three previous lives (including that of the Theban priest) had already been revealed to him when he was admitted into the grade of Philosophus in the Golden Dawn. Crowley had already displayed his admiration for Rabelais (who provided the inspiration for Crowley's cult of Thelema) in his first poems in the book *White Stains.*

†["Silver Star," variously spelled Astrum Argentinum or Astrum Argentum. In his writings Crowley only referred to the order by its initials, never revealing the actual name. —*Trans.*]

self morphine injections. Crowley's drug abuse should not be judged by today's standards, especially as he had the ability to stop taking them at will.

Theodor Reuss visited him in London in the spring of 1912 and asked him to become the Grand Master of the O.T.O. for England and Ireland and to direct the English branch to be baptized "Mysteria Mystica Maxima." Crowley accepted and became a member of the Order under the name of Brother Baphomet (an allusion to the Templar idol) and undertook the perfection of its erotic ritual. In the preceding period, his sex magic consisted of over-stimulating nervous women and using them as mediums. Their nights of love resembled spiritualist séances. With the help of drink, they would go into a trance where they believed they could see and hear an elementary spirit, whose message they conveyed. Now, in conformity with the ideal of the O.T.O., he began making coitus a sacrificial offering to a god of Antiquity while asking him for help and assistance.

Crowley labored diligently to prepare the necessary ceremony. He wholeheartedly believed in what he was doing; even his worst enemies acknowledged that he was neither a crank nor a hoaxer. This humanist—who was able to read texts in Sanskrit, Greek, Latin, and Hebrew—was striving to create a true form of gnostic worship through his extensive study of the history of religions. His fourteen "holy books" of class A (he divided his books into five classes), are those of an inspired high priest.

Crowley therefore wrote a "secret instruction of the IX°," the *Liber Agape,* to teach the English members of the O.T.O. the practice of magical coitus: "it is said that perfection in it [the sex act] as both art and science requires no less study than the most abstruse of philosophies." He first describes in detail the benefits that can be drawn from it and specifies that the results are more or less fitting. Suppose that someone makes love in order to obtain a large sum of money; that sum could arrive within forty-eight hours, but it could also be less or replaced by the promise of future gain. If the operation fails, it should not be repeated: "A Single Act implieth perfection, and full faith in the Adept."

It may turn out, however, that the sought-after goal requires "a series of Sacraments . . . arranged beforehand and carried out regularly." For the male or female operator, "a full meal must be taken not less than three hours before the beginning of the Ceremony." There are no criteria to heed for choosing one's partner: "it seems to Us not unreasonable to allow full sway to the Caprice of the Moment. For this caprice so-called is in truth perhaps the Voice of the Sub-Conscious, that is the deliberate choice of the Holy Phallus itself."[4]

The ceremony will take place in a "temple," which can be any room provided it contains a bed in the east and a table in the west for the god to be invoked. The fire and censer will be in the south, and a square stone in the center of the room holds the sword, the bell, and the oil of Abamelin. The woman, taking her place in the north, is purified by a ritual aspersing. She then takes off her dress while saying: "*Per sanctum mysterium.*" She asperses the man in turn and adorns him with his insignia, and after the rites of censing and dedication, the "sacrifice" is performed on the bed. While penetrating the woman, the adept recites a phrase honoring the god presiding over the act. At the moment of ejaculation, the adept strives to practice *samayama* (intense concentration on the object of a meditation). When the coitus is finished, the priestess will say a blessing in Latin while the man collects the *amrita* from her vagina, in order to offer it to the god whose support he seeks to win. The *Liber Agape* says this blend of sperm and vaginal fluid is the highest of sacraments and that swallowing it is good for one's health: "of this perfect medicine a single dewdrop sufficeth."

While entrusting its members with "the supreme secret of the O.T.O.," Crowley was not remiss in also telling them about magical masturbation. Only initiates of the IX° had the right to masturbate while thinking of Babalon; those of the VIII° could do so while imagining they were embracing Isis, Venus, or Astarte; those of the VII° would have no contact except with Artemis, Vesta, or Mary; and those of the lower degrees had to be satisfied with having an orgasm while thinking of nymphs. He added that female adepts should use the corresponding male gods. There is nothing crude or laughable in these recommendations. Crowley supplemented them with a "Book of Uniting Himself to a particular Deity," the *Liber Astarte vel Berylli,* which describes devotional exercises in a biblical style of great beauty.

The *Liber Agape* was followed by a commentary, *De Arte magica,* in which he presented the method of "Erotocomatose Lucidity," an initiatory ordeal perfected by the lay-sister Ida Nelidoff that made it possible to attain spiritual ecstasy through sexual excess. The candidate was prepared like an athlete and strengthened with a special diet:

> On the appointed day he is attended by one or more chosen and experienced attendants whose duty is (a) to exhaust him sexually by every known means (b) to rouse him sexually by every known means.[5]

Even artificial stimulants were used to achieve this such as strychnine syrup (prescribed by doctors for treating impotence at this time), applications of ether on the abdominal muscles, rubbing cognac along the penis, and so on. When he was no longer able to orgasm, the candidate fell into a deep sleep similar to a coma. It was then necessary to rouse him from this sleep through sexual stimulation or music, which would immediately stop once he awoke. He would be allowed to fall back asleep and reawaken indefinitely until he enters a state that is neither sleeping nor waking and has extrasensory perceptions and communes with the beyond. The ordeal is passed when "ultimate waking is followed by a final performance of the sexual act." This is an erotic variation of the "sleep of Sialam," that P. B. Randolph achieved for himself by setting up a magic mirror in the midst of sleep-inducing clouds of incense.

Aleister Crowley counseled his adepts to each keep a journal of their sexual magic operations. He kept one himself and is moreover the only one to have written a book of this nature, *Rex de Arte regia,* a monument of sacred eroticism in which he never lapses, even momentarily, from maintaining the serious tone suitable to a hierophant. Each experience, called an Opus, is noted down in a report indicating the place, the time, the position of the stars and planets, the god invoked, the physique and age of his partner, the copulative technique used, and the quality and quantity of the *elixir* produced by the orgasm. Also noted was the purpose of the session (later Crowley would add remarks indicating whether it was successful or not). On September 3, 1914, in his Victoria Street temple in London, Crowley made his Opus 1 with Marie Maddingley, a "respectable married woman," in which he asked for "sex-force and sex-attraction," that is to say increased sexual magnetism and vigor. He noted the Operation was "highly orgiastic, and Elixir was first rate quality." He was convinced he had acquired the energy he requested for the success of his next experiments. On September 6 a twenty-six-year-old Picadilly prostitute, Christine Rosalie Byrne, was so impressed by the religious ceremony she refused to take any gift or money. Object: "Knowledge of the Mysteries of the IX°." Result: He wrote four texts on this topic after that session.[6]

It was in the United States, where he stayed during the First World War, that Crowley did the bulk of the Opuses described in his journal. Following his Opus 4 on November 7, 1914, in New York—a masturbation by the left hand while invoking Babalon, for her to ensure his success in this city—he resorted ceaselessly to prostitutes, who were greatly alarmed by his incantations before an altar laden with his ritual instruments, almost always for the object: "Money." The results varied: Sometimes he received a check for eight hundred pounds sterling two days later, sometimes nothing came of it and he started over with another, which attracted a letter containing seventy-two dollars to him. Soon women of high society became his sexual magic partners, like Lola Grunbacher, the widow of an English aristocrat, on January 26, 1915. She enjoyed it so much she returned on January 29, when she performed fellatio on him and swallowed his semen, which had not been foreseen on the program and caused the Opus to fail.

The fifty-year-old Aimée Gouraud, his "thrice holy, thrice illuminated, thrice illustrious soror," was also unleashed (he even found her "Kteis . . . prehensile to an astonishing degree!") before being replaced by the singer Ranta Devi, the poet Jane Foster, the artist Helen Hollis, and many others. The gods to whom he most often directed an appeal were Hermes, Thoth (the Egyptian god of wisdom), and Pan. The purposes of the séances varied: "wisdom," "health," "success at my lecture tomorrow," "magic power." A veritable alchemist of sexuality, Crowley did the *work in black* by using enormous black prostitutes, who enthusiastically served his wishes, like Grace Harris and Anna Grey ("big fat negress, very passionate"), whom he employed several times in order to acquire "health" or "sex-force." On November 7, 1915, he noted: "Operation: excellent. Elixir: the same. Result: marvellous." He sodomized Anna Grey the following time with the objective "help for Soror Leila Waddell," who was experiencing difficulties. Result: "Immediate success."

Worn out from his travels through the cities of the West Coast in 1916, Crowley performed a series of operations with the prostitute Alice Robertson, then with lesbian Gerda von Kothek with an eye to achieving the result: "Youth." He claimed this had rejuvenated him internally to sixteen years old. On his return to New York, he formed an attachment with two Scarlet Women simultaneously, the married laboratory assistant Roddie Minor and the unwed Anna Miller (who bore a strong resemblance to the jackal god Anubis). It is his reports concerning these two partners, who he coupled with in alternation, that he most often includes the indications *per vas nefandum* (by the forbidden vessel) and *per os* (by the mouth). Sodomy and fellatio were called upon for achieving the objective of "Io Pan!" which is for a show of grace toward the god of vital energy without requesting anything of him. But he also sodomized Roddie Minor on October 16 and 17 with a "general Invocation to Demeter," while making this wish: "Prosperity." He coupled with these women even when they had their periods, because this corresponded with the *red elixir* that allowed the alchemists to transform lead into gold. He therefore began his forty-fourth Opus in search of a large fortune by coitus with Anna Miller in January and February of 1918, when she was menstruating. But his desires were not always materialistic, as he had possessed her earlier while evoking "Divine Knowledge."

Crowley returned to London in January 1919 with his seventh

Scarlet Woman, Leah Hirsig, whose angelic face masked a thoroughly diabolical temperament. They wanted to live in Fontainebleau, France, where she gave birth to a daughter, but things did not work out. It was through using the divination method of the I Ching that Crowley chose to move to Cefalù in Sicily, where he founded the Abbey of Thelema. He arrived there with his two concubines, Leah (known as Sister Alostrael) and Ninette Shumway (Sister Cypris), the nurse of his infant daughter, who competed with one another for the role of favorite. Thelema Abbey was a large farm at the foot of Santa Barbara Mountain, where Crowley constantly received the visits of disciples and performed gnostic masses with them in either the central chamber known as the sanctum sanctorum, or celebrated ancient mysteries in the olive tree-covered grounds. Of all the Scarlet Women, Leah was undoubtedly the most unrestrained. She incited him to establish "the Law of C.C.C. and other things" at Thelema. These three Cs stood for Cognac, Cunt, and Cocaine. Crowley's magic diary in Cefalù describes these excesses, but his considered commentary on them shows how sincerely religious he was in his debauches: "I won't use the absurd word Love, but say Agape, 93, if needs must,"* he admitted. In "Babalon and the Beast conjoined," which they achieved on August 12, 1920, in a glorious paroxysm, Leah experienced trances that put her in contact with an invisible cosmic entity, and instead of sexual pleasure, Crowley felt a mystical state: "I am locally tired in Ajna and Muladhara, having lived there for so long" (Ajna is the chakra of Will and Muladhara the chakra of sexual energy).[7]

While at the Abbey of Thelema, Crowley wrote his novel *Diary of a Drug Fiend,* in which he maintained the thesis that to free people from drugs, the latter should not be prohibited, but allowed to induce disgust of them in their users in due course. His hero Peter Pendragon and his companion Lou, addicted to cocaine, are rescued by King Lamus who states:

---

*Agape is the Christian notion of "love your neighbor"; 93 was the sacred number symbolizing Thelema.

Absinthe, forbidden in France and Switzerland and Italy, is still sold freely in England, and no one ever met an English absinthe fiend.[8]

The 1922 publication of this book in London unleashed a campaign attacking Crowley as a "Satanist" and the author of all kinds of crude depravities. It so happens that his so-called orgies consisted of dramatic rites illustrating "the formula of I.A.O.," which represents the theme: "Isis Nature, ruined by Apophis the Destroyer, and restored to life by the Redeemer Osiris." His book *Magick in Theory in Practice,* also written at the Abbey of Thelema, reveals that his "Satanism" was limited to stating "the Devil does not exist," and, reasoning like an exegete of religions, that "Satan is Saturn, Set, Abrasax, Adad, Adonis, Attis, Adam, Adonai, and so on."[9] Despite the scope of his views, however, the English newspapers continued defaming him, which the Italian press echoed to such an extent that Mussolini's fascist government decided to expel him from Sicily in 1924.

Crowley's magical and amorous career continued with great intensity, but there is no room here to treat it in its entirety. He rid himself of Leah Hirsig by pushing her into the arms of one of his disciples; he was next looked after by a young American, Dorothy Olsen; he traveled to Germany because the O.T.O. members named him their Grand Master, and he reorganized the lodges there; he married a young Nicaraguan aristocrat in 1929 and divorced her soon after; and created some manic Opuses with a German, Hanni Jaeger, who traveled to Portugal with him in August 1930. In 1935, at the age of sixty, he fathered a son with his wife Deirdre Patricia MacAlpine and named him Aleister Ataturk. During this time he initiated several English political figures into the Astrum Argentinum such as Lady Frieda Harris (wife of a Liberal party leader) and Tom Driberg (future director of the Worker's Party). At the beginning of the Second World War when Crowley was living in London and writing patriotic poems as the Luftwaffe bombarded the city, it was he who suggested to the Foreign Office to use the "V for Victory" sign.

In June 1940, at the age of sixty-five, Crowley had some unexpected difficulties getting erections, about which he complained in his journal.

No longer able to find German medications for his asthma, he turned back to heroin and cocaine, although he had long been off drugs. At seventy, while living in retirement at a family pension on Netherwood Hill in Hastings, he began writing *Magick without Tears,* eighty letters to admirers that summed up his teachings. This is where his encyclical "Artemis iota" appears, a solemn incitation to sexual freedom: "Be strong, o man! lust, enjoy all things of sense and rapture: fear not that any God shall deny thee for this." Above all, however, is his demand for spiritual perfection:

> Be not animal; refine thy rapture. If thou drink, drink by the eight and ninety rules of art: if thou love, exceed by delicacy; and if thou do ought joyous, let there be subtlety therein. But exceed! exceed![10]

Crowley was outraged that his audacious experiments of the High Magick Art were condemned as depravities. He filed two defamation suits, one in 1933 against a bookseller who described his work as "indecent and shocking," and one in 1934 against the publisher of a book that described the goings-on at Thelema Abbey in Cefalù as abominations. Even in *Leah Sublime*—a long poem written in 1920 about Leah's vagina, where he exclaims: "Rub all the muck / of your cunt on me Leah"—there is a hidden meaning. As Christian Bouchet points out, the poem is:

> pornographic but not without a magical background, as it includes 156 lines and 666 words, the numbers in the Crowley Kabbalah of the Beast and the Scarlet Woman.[11]

Crowley's High Magick Art is not a method that all can practice. First it involves the use of alcohol and drugs, because he wanted his partners to have visual hallucinations. Their health suffered from it: Rose Kelly and Mary d'Este ended up in mental asylums because of their excessive drinking. It is not healthy to mix large quantities of cocaine, opium, peyote, or brandy at magic ceremonies. By contrast the bacchantes of the cult of Dionysus only drank water or pure milk and their trances and mystical exaltation were entirely self-induced. Furthermore, since the appearance of AIDS, Crowley would not have been able to have sexual relations with everyone he wished without a condom as he continuously did during his life, as it was an essential part of the Opus to offer the invoked god a sacrifice of *amrita:* the sperm diluted by the vaginal fluid removed from the woman's vagina. Today this rite could only be practiced with a faithful spouse, provided the latter's conduct was beyond reproach.

Despite all the reservations one may have regarding Crowley's exceptional temperament, the fact remains that his concept of sex as a magical key to the visible and invisible world is unique. It managed to be utterly new while still retaining a basis in the tradition. Aleister Crowley died in Hastings of a heart attack on December 1, 1946, and during his cremation in Brighton following the funeral service, all his faithful chanted: "Love is the Law, Love under Will!"

THE HERETICS OF THE ORDO TEMPLI ORIENTIS

During Crowley's lifetime there were dissidents who left the O.T.O to form rival groups that still advocated sex magic, albeit in a form different from his. One of these groups was the Brotherhood of Saturn in 1928. Their practice is known as Saturn-Gnosis. The group's leader was the Berlin bookseller Eugen Grosche, alias Gregor A. Gregorius, who was inspired by the Pansophia of Frater Recnartus (Heinrich Tränker). These renegades combined various forms of sexuality with the use of narcotics and the study of astral configurations. In his book *Sexuality, Magic and Perversion,* Francis King provides a complete translation of their teaching on "Astrological Aspects as a Secret Symbolism for Coital Positions." In this text Frater Recnartus first defines Saturnian coitus:

> The fertilisation of the woman is not the aim of such sexual acts as these, for they are of a purely religious nature or used to create so-called psychogones, which are easily aroused by such sexual intoxication. Thus the position of the body becomes an important part of this religio-magical practice.[12]

As the purpose of this coitus was the "creation of thought-forms" or the "attraction daemonic beings," this explains why they resorted to drugs. And if one wished to receive celestial impulses, it was natural to turn to the astral bodies to assign the best sexual positions under this relationship. Frater Recnartus notes:

> The squares* between the planets especially important in the sexual spheres (i.e., Venus, Mars, Neptune, and the Moon) are particularly vital and advantageous. . . .
>
> It is said, among other things, that in squares of Venus and Mars sexual intercourse should be carried out in a sitting position, the exact nature of which should vary with the strength of the planets in the Sign of the Zodiac where they are situated. If Venus is stronger, the female partner should be on top, if Mars is stronger the male should be on top. . . . A square Moon and Moon is said to be most suitable for Lesbian sexuality, a square of Mars and Mars for male homosexuality. Where Neptune is part of the square, it is advised to use drugs. . . . If there is opposition between the above-mentioned planets, no sexual act should be carried out . . . All conjunctions are to be used in a similar way to squares because a conjunction means a concentration of forces.[13]

Finally Frater Recnartus does not dismiss the possibility of making a child by these means, for he states:

> Trine formations between these planets obviously provide favourable conditions for the fertilisation of the woman, should this be desired.[14]

Regarding the sexual magic of these Saturnian brethren, Francis King makes the ironic observation:

---

*A "square" exists between two planets when they form a 90° angle to one another in the zodiac.

Any tendencies they may have had to promiscuity were checked by the necessity of looking up the planetary positions in an ephemeris before retiring to bed![15]

However, similar sorts of recommendations were also made by various doctors of the Middle Ages and the Renaissance. The secret document of the Brotherhood of Saturn he cites also includes prescriptions that transform the lover into a veritable mage:

Defensive symbols must be employed together with protective fumes such as incense. The use of erotically effective ingredients is advisable as is the wearing or precious stones appropriate to the planets.[16]

One of Aleister Crowley's disciples at the Abbey of Thelema, Cecil Frederick Russell, parted ways with him and set up a similar fraternity in the United States in 1932. He called this brotherhood the G.B.G. without ever saying what these initials stood for. He denied that they were for the "Great Brotherhood of God," as is often assumed. He managed to recruit numerous adepts in Chicago, Denver, Los Angeles, and other large American cities. His initiates were called "Neighborhood Primates," and one of them, Louis T. Culling, revealed in his autobiography the principles and experiments of this community. The first initiatory degree, Alphaism, "was nothing more than observation of complete chastity in thought, word, and deed." Following this period of purification, the neophyte was accepted into the second degree, Dianism: "prolonged sexual intercourse not culminating in orgasm." Semen retention is what distinguishes Cecil F. Russell's magic from that of Aleister Crowley, and is closer to Tantra and the *karezza* advocated by earlier Free Love authors. Aside from this distinction, however, the practitioners had the same psychic motive: "during copulation [they] built up 'magical images' in their imagination and invoked the gods." Once they had mastered Dianism, the initiates could move up to the "Qadosh degree" (this word means "holy") after passing an examination of their sexual capacities. Francis King stressed: "candidates for the

Qadosh degree were submitted to severe testing." For example, for the Dianism test that he had to undergo before obtaining this degree, Louis T. Culling had to pay the expenses for his examiner from the G.B.G. headquarters in Chicago to travel to San Diego. "I am glad to be able to report that he passed his test with flying colors, engaging (according to his own account) in uninterrupted copulation with his examiner for three hours without orgasm." The G.B.G. was dissolved after six years, leaving behind the memory of a collective experiment that was interesting but did not supplant the O.T.O. doctrine. Cecil F. Russell published his memoirs in 1970 under the bizarre title *Znuz Is Znees.* This memoir, together with Culling's 1971 book *A Manual of Sex Magick,* are the sources to consult for information on this organization.

Another original Crowleyan dissident was the engineer and explosives expert, Jack Parsons, who was attached to the California Institute of Technology and worked for both the federal government and in private enterprises. In 1941 Parsons and his wife Helen became members of the O.T.O, as members of the Agape Lodge founded by Wilfred T. Smith in California. The following year Helen left him to live with Smith; as compensation Parsons was named head of the Agape Lodge. In 1943, probably to guard against another conjugal unpleasantness, Parsons took two companions at once: his sister-in-law Betty Northrup and the sculptor Marjorie Cameron, whose work once enjoyed some success on the West Coast. He decided to perform "the work of Babalon" with Marjorie, that is to say, performing a series of sexual magic acts with her with an eye to creating a *homunculus,* a "moonchild" that would serve him as the perfect assistant. It was Aleister Crowley in his novel *Moonchild* who indicated how a sublunar spirit could incarnate in a woman's gestating embryo, if submitted to the appropriate rites.

Jack Parsons wanted to keep a diary of his magical experiments and for this reason hired a secretary who was none other than L. Ron Hubbard, the future founder of Scientology. After meeting Marjorie on January 18, 1946, he began the operations during the first three days of March, as recounted by Francis King: "Parsons was High Priest and had sexual intercourse with the girl, while Hubbard who was present acted as skryer, seer, or clairvoyant and described what was supposed to be happening on the astral plane."[17] Hubbard later seduced Betty, Parsons's second companion, and ran away with her and the association's money. His misadventures did not dampen Parsons's enthusiasm. During special séances he evoked Babalon, who he believed imparted a personal teaching to him, from which Parsons wrote a gospel, *The Book of Babalon.* When Crowley learned of this, he expelled Parsons from the O.T.O.

Jack Parsons then tried to lead an autonomous Gnostic Church in accordance with the inspiration of his sexual illuminism. On October 31, 1948, he had a vision of Babalon who revealed that in his previous lives he had been Simon Magus, Gilles de Rais, and the Count de Cagliostro. Considering himself a prophet, he changed his name to Belarion Armiluss Al Dajjal Antichrist. He parodied Crowley's excesses, but lacked his vast philosophical refinement and poetic genius. He had barely time to develop his doctrine because he died in an explosion of his laboratory in 1952. Twenty years after his death, the International Astronomical Union, in homage to his research, named a crater on the moon after him. The man who had tried to create a "moonchild" with Marjorie Cameron, found himself projected onto this astral body as a posthumous effect of his sex magic!

A no less curious figure from the various circles practicing the O.T.O.'s brand of sex magic is Austin Osman Spare. Born in London in 1888 and precociously gifted as a painter, he gained notoriety at nineteen for a collection of drawings, *Earth Inferno,* in which he condemned "the inferno of the normal" and described the "Universal Woman" haunting the human unconscious. He had been initiated into magic at the age of seven by an old fortune-teller, Mrs. Paterson, who claimed descent from Salem witches. Spare was convinced he had seen her transform into a ravishing, sensual young woman to give him his first lessons in love. He was obsessed with sex, as indicated by his *Self-Portrait at Eighteen,* depicting only an erect penis. On September 4, 1911, Spare married Lily Shaw but also immediately fell in love with a music hall actress—a friend of his wife, who subsequently caught the two in bed. Enthused by Crowley he joined the Astrum Argentinum around 1909 and collaborated on *The Equinox*. But Spare soon sought to establish himself as a rival to his teacher by advancing his own system of "New Sexuality." The gospel for this was *The Book of Pleasure,* published in 1913, which he illustrated with figures of his "alphabet of desire." In his writing Spare proclaimed the "eclectic path between ecstasies; that precarious funambulatory way." Its deity was the "All-Prevailing Woman"; its creed, "The Living Flesh (Zos)"; its sacraments, "The Sacred Inbetweeness Concepts"; its word, "Does Not Matter— Need Not Be"; and its law, "To Trespass all Laws."

Austin Osman Spare was primarily a painter and had difficulty establishing himself because of puritanical objections, as Massimo Introvigne points out:

He asserted himself as an artist in the years 1919–1921 but his success was short-lived. The intensely magical eroticism of his canvasses aroused the disapproval of numerous critics, who viewed them as a reflection of his scandalous and immoral personal life.[18]

The illustrations in his book *The Focus of Life* in 1921, were of nudes in symbolic situations accompanied by his "Moralities of Shadow" (aphorisms), proclamations, and "Mutterings of Aãos" (himself, based on his initials) during sleep and his dreams.

In 1927 Spare published *The Anathema of Zos,* a "sermon to the hypocrites" in which he lashed out at the art patrons and dealers who rejected his work: "Ye deny sexuality with tinsel ethics, live by slaughter—pray to greater idiots—that all things may be possible to ye who are impossible." He ended his text with a list of the thirty-seven works he planned to exhibit, all of which bore provocative titles such as: *I have traveled the disastrous aberrations of transitory sex.* He withdrew into the cult of Zos Kia, the two life principles: Kia was "the *Atmospheric 'I,'* or Cosmic Self, which manifests through Zos, "the body considered as a whole." These two principles need to be balanced: "In the individual, Zos and Kia are artificially divided, primarily because of reason; magic power is born of the reunion of these two principles." The purpose of the sexual act is therefore the reunification of Zos and Kia in the being who performs it.

Spare's "sigil method" does not resemble those of his predecessors and consists of focusing on an ideogram that represents the desire or plan one wishes to see succeed. Christian Bouchet says:

> The sigil is a program sent to the unconscious. It uses the letters of the alphabet that have been simplified and blended together in such a way to create a symbolic image. The letters used are those defining the desire to be achieved.[19]

In fact, once the sigil has been created, it must be visualized inside the mind while lying down in the "death posture" (*savasana*), without thinking of anything else. Spare believed that we possess several unconscious minds that overlap with one another: those of our previous lives and that of our current life. If a sigil symbolizing a particular desire was repressed to the deepest depth of these unconscious minds, a psychic energy coming from the depth of ages would make this desire achievable. During intercourse, the mage would not have to formulate a wish but simply let come into his mind the symbol corresponding to what he wanted. So that aesthetic details would not cause any diversion from transcendence, he would only make love with aged women or those of repellant ugliness, with succubi, with the atmosphere, or with himself.

Austin Osman Spare invented an extraordinary protocol for masturbation, *urning,* in which he ejaculated into urns in the shape of "earthenware virgins," on the bottom of which he had placed a sigil. He would then bury these urns containing the "sealed desire" at midnight. When his biographer Kenneth Grant claims that Spare successfully had intercourse with eighteen women in one single night, we need not find that especially impressive—they probably were imaginary women inspired by his masturbatory asceticism. Spare died in poverty in 1956, but his ideas continued to live on, inspiring Chaos Magic and its offshoots.

THE ABSOLUTE SEXUAL INDIVIDUAL
ACCORDING TO JULIUS EVOLA

The man we will now consider, not as a rival to Aleister Crowley but as his equal in esoteric erudition, was an Italian scholar. Julius Evola, born in 1898, first appeared as a poet and painter connected to Futurism and Dadaism. His "poem for four voices," *Le Parole Oscure du Paysage Interieur* (The Dark Word of the Inner Landscape) was published in 1920 under the auspices of the Collection Dada in Zurich. Shortly thereafter he became the theoretician of "magic idealism" with three books: *The Yoga of Power* (1926), *Teoria dell'Individuo Assoluto* (Theory of the Absolute Individual; 1927), and *Imperialismo Pagano* (Pagan Imperialism; 1928), which earned the admiration of René Guénon. As Evola described his work to Pierre Pascal: "There are abrupt books that do not spare the reader, books that are barely Italian, for they are frozen fire."[20]

Evola was an advocate for the pure Ego, the "detached Ego centered around itself," which he did not define as a subject or a thought, but as freedom to act. This distinguished, monocle-wearing philosopher sought to wrest the modern world from its crudeness.

During the years 1927 to 1929, an order formed around Evola called the "Ur Group" (*ur* being an archaic word for fire). They published monthly monographs under this name that dealt with magic as a "science of the Ego." The collaborators remained anonymous, concealing their identities beneath symbolic pseudonyms. The autobiographical and historical Ur texts were later collected into three volumes, titled *Introduction to Magic,* which maintained the anonymity of the contributors. Julius Evola next founded a bimonthly review, *La Torre,* to defend his ideas opposing the Tradition to Christianity and his notion of an organic state versus that of the totalitarian state, but he was forced to suspend publication with the tenth issue because of the hostility of some Fascist officials. He explained:

The Duce came to suspect that certain individuals were planning to exercise a magical influence upon him. . . . Mussolini was not only an easily suggestible character, but also a rather superstitious one. . . . for example, he was genuinely scared of "jinxes," whose very name he forbade to be uttered in his presence.[21]

Evola left to purify himself in the lofty mountains, climbing the northern face of the eastern Lyskamm (Pennine Alps). He became, henceforth, a dedicated mountain climber, a sport he called a discipline that encouraged elevation of the soul. He published several more books as the foremost defender of the "hermetic tradition" and the "doctrine of awakening" in Italy, but the war played havoc with his ongoing plans. In April 1945, in Vienna, Evola was one of the victims of a Soviet bombing raid. His spinal cord was injured and both his legs remained paralyzed from it for the rest of his life. His despair led him to contemplate suicide. He reacted energetically, however, and continued to pursue his work, giving priority to "the exploration of the transcendent significance of sex."

His book *The Metaphysics of Sex* was the first of its kind after the Second World War, and the most important. It is not sexology; it is an examination "of what goes beyond the physical in sex and sexual experiences." Taking metaphysics in the sense of "supraphysical, the invisible side of the human being," Evola begins by rejecting "every finalistic, biological [and psychological] interpretation of eros," refusing to reduce it to a reproduction instinct, a search for a specific pleasure, a hormone theory, or the like. It is in the analysis of the "phenomena of transcendency in profane love" that he seeks an answer to the fundamental question: "Why are man and women attracted to each other?" Through primitive myths, the gods and goddesses of pagan religions, he shows there is a metaphysical Dyad, the absolute Man and absolute Woman who exist as purely as Heaven and Earth, Water and Fire, and are reflected in humanity: "The god and the goddess, the pure male and the pure female, are truly present in every man and woman." It is impossible to attain this ideal individually, however, since every human being is bisexual; there is something of a woman in every man and of a man in every woman: "the picture we get of every normal man and woman is one in which the content of pure male or female varies."[22] Evola studies the "degrees of the sexualization" because not everyone contains the same proportion of this blend. There is an "inner sex" that is more demanding than the "outer sex" defined by the genital organs:

> We are man or woman inwardly before being so externally; the primordial male or female quality penetrates and saturates the whole of our being visibly and invisibly . . . just as color permeates a liquid.[23]

This inner sex aspires to the state of absolute man or absolute woman, and will seek in others the male or female part it is missing and needs to become one of the other.

There is a law of the desire for a complement, a reintegration process that motivates the urge for sex:

> the greatest attraction is aroused between a man and a woman when the masculine and feminine parts in both are added together and the totals obtained are the absolute man and the absolute woman. For instance, a man who is three-quarters man (*yang*) and one-quarter woman (*yin*) will be irresistibly attracted and develop the strongest magnetism with his female complement, a woman who is one-quarter man and three-quarters woman.[24]

The amorous magnetism is then irresistible precisely because the sum of the parts together reestablishes the entire absolute man and the entire absolute woman.

This idea comes from Otto Weininger's *Sex and Character* (which Evola translated into Italian), although the psychoanalyst committed suicide before developing his idea further. Furthermore, Weininger was a "puritan, misogynist, and sexophobe," and did not share Evola's expansive views. Evola's objective analyses of male and female began from the principle that the question of superiority or inferiority of one sex as compared to the other "is lacking in sense," and his concept of Androgyny is the opposite to that of Plato, inasmuch as each individual became One thanks to the Other. The Dyad would appear to be a condemnation of homosexuality, but Evola—who rejected distinctions of "normal" and "abnormal"—stated that it partially justified it:

> This law allows us to grasp the cases when homosexuality is understandable. . . . These are cases when the sex in the two individuals who come together is close to the same. Let's take, for example, a man who is only 55 percent man and 45 percent woman. His natural complement will be an individual who is 45 percent man and 55 percent woman. . . . This individual could easily be a man; it would be the same in the case of a woman.[25]

He admits that this does not explain all cases of homosexuality, as some were a result of a surrender to society's "lower forces" or libidinal transference of the kind studied by psychoanalysis.

In the final part of *The Metaphysics of Sex,* Evola establishes that "by means of sexual intercourse, performed in a determined and established manner, it is possible to create energies that can be used for magical purposes." He provides examples from various traditions and sheds light on the activity of some of his misunderstood contemporaries such as Aleister Crowley and Maria de Naglowska. *The Metaphysics of Sex* is the book that gives sex magic its proper due. Finally a profound and erudite thinker has skillfully weighed in on a matter that official philosophers have not dared to touch, considering it beneath them!

In his subsequent books *The Path of Cinnabar* and *L'Arco e la Clava* (The Bow and the Club), Julius Evola continues to tirelessly wage war against "the sexual and erotic intoxication that the modern era, like all twilight eras, presents in a pandemic form."[26] Looking at the excesses of feminism and group sexuality, he analyzes "the dangers of an unrestricted sexual freedom," by showing it would bring about "an insidious domestication of man through sex and woman, resulting in the decay of any higher virile value and all authentic spirituality." In the name of sacred sexuality, he condemned the frivolity of the use some made of it, in a February 1970 interview in *Playmen:*

We must especially see if one is making love in order to make magic, or if one is making magic (pseudo-magic) in order to make love, or if magic is being used as a pretext to organize orgies and give them a certain exciting context.[27]

Evola, who came up with the liberating expression "Truth is a powerful error; error is a weak truth," cannot be accused of being a dogmatic moralist. His opinion is therefore all the more valuable.

This great theoretician of magical eroticism was quite discreet about his personal experiences. He never alluded to his love life, neither in confessions disguised as novels like P. B. Randolph, nor in personal diaries like Aleister Crowley. However, it would be interesting to know if sex magic helped him overcome the handicap of his disability. Joë Bousquet, like Evola, suffered for an equally long time from paralysis due to a war wound. Bousquet's injury was so severe that he had to be picked up in order to leave his bed, but he still managed to have love affairs that he revealed in his *Cahier noir* (Black Notebook) and in his letters to his mistresses. It is only in reading a text like Bousquet's *Cahier noir* that we see Evolian theory put into practice.

In July 1974, after several years of physical suffering that he endured stoically, Julius Evola died in Rome in the house where he was born. According to his last wishes, confided to his friend the Countess Amalia Baccelli-Rinaldi, he forbade any religious ceremony and any death notice in the newspapers. He was cremated in Spoleto, and in accordance with his wishes, his disciple Renato del Ponte, on a rope with four other climbers and the old guide Eugenio David, placed the urn holding his ashes in a crevasse on Mount Rosa, at 13,880 feet.

4

The Great Work
of the Flesh

Sexual alchemy is what the teachers of esotericism have recommended to lovers. The purpose of the sex act is no longer a specific pleasure that culminates in spasms and a release of general tension, nor does its protocol limit itself to a quest for different poses or other means of renewing this pleasure. Its fertilizing power is not limited to the creation of a child, but should be capable of creating invisible beings and currents of influence. Consequently, I am going to discuss matters here from a different perspective than in my book *The Doctrinal of Amorous Bliss*, in which the chapters on the phenomenology of coitus and the positions for sexual intercourse concerned everyday love that—even if it does retain some sacred implications—has a purely hedonistic motivation. The sexual alchemist is comparable to the genuine medieval alchemist preparing the Great Work that will permit him to find the philosopher's stone to convert imperfect metals into gold or, when placed as a powder in a glass of white wine, is used as the universal medicine. The body of the woman is his athanor (the tower-shaped furnace that holds the "philosophical egg" containing the material to cook); his actions are aimed at carrying the primordial material (in this case it is the flesh of the man and woman) to black, then white, and finally red, starting from the *sublimation* and passing through distillation, solution, and

77

putrefaction. Desire is the equivalent of the "secret fire of the sages" that ensures the cooking until the multiplication, fermentation, and lastly the projection (that of the elixir transforming glass into diamond and lead into gold). The man's sperm and the woman's vaginal secretions (and sometimes her menstruations) are identical to the unctuous sulfur and the mercury of the philosophers, whose alliance is named by the Son of Hermes, the "marriage of the King and Queen." The culmination of this Great Work of the flesh is a "philosophical orgasm," independent of physical orgasm or non-orgasm, which is a state of mental and emotional hyperpotency that increases the fortunes in life for those individuals who have experienced it.

The magical sexual act is not performed to achieve orgasm but to experience what in Tantra is called the *rasa* (the pleasure of tasting the juice of the fruit) and the *maharaga* ("the great emotion," passion concentrated to its utmost level of energy). However, orgasm is not proscribed; it is merely submitted to the discipline of *paravritti* (the redirecting of the energies of the subtle body upward), so that it illuminates the higher psychic center above the crown of the head, described as the "thousand-petaled lotus."

Any couple should be able to perform this activity regardless of their religion or lack of belief; hence it is better to call to permanent cosmic powers and not ancient gods. The best guide is the Tao, with its two universal principles of Yin and Yang (the power of Heaven and power of Earth, respectively). These principles combine in every human being in such a way that every woman has more yin than yang, and every man has much more yang than yin. The purpose of their sexual intercourse is to acquire from the other the yin or yang they are lacking, for no individual is truly happy until a perfect balance of both these forces has been achieved within. This is the reason for the two phenomena that are essential for sacred coitus: *mutual absorption* and the *circulation of energies*.

Mutual absorption is both physical and metaphysical. The man absorbs the feminine effluvia as they are intensely released by the woman in a state of sexual excitement, as if he was drinking an electro-chemico-magnetic fluid (exactly that which P. B. Randolph called *keemlin*); and the woman absorbs the virile effluvia, which is multiplied tenfold when the man has an erection, and becomes saturated by his *gheer* fluid. But human bodies also possess an "inner fluid." This is the term used by Taoists to define all bodily fluids like sperm, vaginal secretions, blood, mother's milk, urine, and their mutual absorption can even involve their consumption at certain moments of the ritual, when this act will be sanctified by a mental prayer. The circulation of energies, meanwhile, is essential because the body has several energy centers—three for Taoism, seven for Tantrism, and four for European occultists—and if one of these accumlates energy to the detriment of the others, an imbalance will result. Intercourse, which brings the lower belly into play, known as the "lower cinnabar field" in Taoism and the *muladhara* chakra in Tantrism, is capable of coordinating all the others, in accordance with its movements and positions. Obviously straightforward copulation—as takes place between a husband and wife, or between a rake and a loose woman—will not have this effect. It must be undertaken as a mystical ascetic act in pursuit of higher spirituality.

Philip Rawson, who describes Tantra as "a cult of ecstasy, focused on a vision of cosmic sexuality,"[1] summed it up perfectly when he said it was neither a belief nor a faith, but a method making it possible to attune sex with the universe: "Tantra has mapped the mechanism of currents of energy through which the creative impulse is distributed at once through man's body being and the world's."[2] Female sexuality skillfully stimulated by male sexuality, serves as a medium in this psychocosmic connection:

Indian tradition has it that on different days of the month a woman's sexual sensitivity, which is related to cosmic movements by her own period, needs to be triggered by special attention to different parts of her body. Diagrams illustrate these trigger points and relate them to the phases of the moon. As well, ritual intercourse is preceded by the anointing of parts of the woman's body with perfumed symbolic oils.[3]

Rawson reveals the extent to which this activity ennobles amorous relations:

> Love is not a reaction, but a carefully nurtured creation. Its meaning is a protracted ecstasy of mind and body, whose fires are continually blown by prolonged engagement and stimulation of the sexual organs, not mutual release.[4]

He confirms what I said earlier about the optional nature of the orgasm:

> In the higher reaches of Indian erotics orgasm becomes merely a punctuation in, and incentive for, the state of continuous intense physical and emotional radiance which lovers can evoke in each other.[5]

However, it was the Taoists who invented the notion of inner alchemy (or *nei-tan*), consisting of ways to transform the ordinary body into a transcendent body, destined for immortality. Its operations are guided by sex, which has become a core force, as noted by Kristofer Schipper:

> Sex is no longer concentrated or confined to the genital organs, nor is it a matter of the heart or the mind; it is *united at the Center* and from this Center it radiates and spreads through the whole body. Love thus engages the body as a whole, merging all the organs and the functions. "One breathes with one's heels" says Chuang Tzu. All the faculties of the senses: our eyes, nose, breasts, hands, come together in total participation.[6]

The sex act, considered to be a practice of Long Life (*hsiu-yang*, meaning to arrange and nurture) takes place in two courses: foreplay and union. The aforementioned Sinologist Schipper, exasperated by the crude interpretations of the sexual Tao—as if it involved an orgy by celibate monks—reminds us that both male and female Taoists were generally married:

> In earlier times, the school of the Heavenly Master conferred the highest level of initiation—the quality of Master—not on individual adepts but on couples. . . . The ritual of ordination of the union of *ch'i* was carried out by the couple under the direction of a senior master.[7]

After fasting the couple made invocations to the Tao in a pure room, accompanied by breathing exercises and visualizations of the Inner World.

> When the cosmic energies were all there, the adepts would undress and loosen their hair. The couples, facing each other, were first seated on floor mats. Later, the rites continued in a standing position and finally the partners moved about together in a very elaborate choreography modeled after the magic square. Each stage and every movement was accompanied by a meditation, which accomplished the corresponding structure inside of the body. In a slow dance, the partners, holding and touching each other in precisely prescribed ways, moved from one point of the magic square to another, invoking each time the *ch'i* corresponding to the Eight Trigrams and the Center.[8]

After these expert preliminaries, the rite became progressively more sexual:

> Then even more difficult movements and gestures began. Taking turns, one of the two partners would lie down, while the other performed a dance around him or her and massaged (with the foot) precise points on the body. Again, this kind of acupressure was performed while visualizing and invoking the gods of the Inner World. At certain moments, sexual organs were involved, and there were

short moments of rhythmic intercourse without, however, interrupting the meditation.[9]

In the early medieval manuscript in which the author found this ritual, he noted:

The ritual was performed in a perfectly symmetrical manner. Each prayer, each gesture by the man found its symmetrical counterpart in a gesture and prayer by the woman. There was no such thing as one active and one passive partner.[10]

The mystical notions of Far Eastern erotology have been adapted in a variety of ways in the United States and Europe. According to Margo Anand, who has attempted to modernize Tantra and to go farther than Randolph: "One of the major rituals intended for sexual magic adepts is the creation of the Magic Circle."[11] Having a liaison with a Los Angeles businessman named Keith, she borrowed a house on the California coast where they could have a sacred sexual experience. This dusty, abandoned "grandmother's house" was quickly transformed by the priestess, especially the chamber:

I began by walking three times around the room, circling to the left, a ritual movement designed to remove all negative or unwanted energies. [I then made three circles to the right] ringing bells, singing, and chanting, looking toward the center of the circle and inviting all kinds of positive energies to present themselves.[12]

She next performed invocations to the four cardinal points, and in return for these preliminary actions, she experienced several days of amorous bliss with Keith.

This is why she recommends making a circle in the room with several long scarves of different colors, arranged end to end on the floor around the bed, mattress, or carpet used for the sexual operations. Four stones picked up during a stroll will indicate the four cardinal points.

Her opinion is justified: the word templum, of Etruscan origin, means "circle." A room can only become a temple if it is made sacred by the ancient rite of circumambulation and the equivalent of the magicians' chalk circle. It requires an altar, covered by a red-and-white cloth on which the "power objects" (talismans, pentacles, and so forth), are placed, a candle that will be lit at the start of each exercise, and a crystal to amplify and receive energy. Margo Anand recounts:

> For me, the crystal egg has been a powerful symbol of female sexual energy. Following an ancient Taoist teaching, I practiced placing a crystal egg inside my vagina, contracting and expanding my genital muscles around it for several minutes.[13]

Naturally, an object like this pulled back out of her vagina will retain a bioelectrical radiation that affects those who look at it. She goes on to say:

> Later, I held the egg in my hand while giving public lectures and interviews, and I felt very much empowered by this symbol of female strength.[14]

Margo Anand, taking inspiration from the gurus who were her "teacher-lovers," established a preparatory ritual for the couple that wanted to open "the door to High Sex." The man will ask the woman's vulva questions, who will answer him from that lower mouth: "Now you are going to give Yoni your voice, allowing her to speak through you as if she were a real person." The woman will then ask questions of the penis, who will answer with the man's voice. Next they will attempt to laugh with their pelvis for three minutes. Margo Anand tells the woman: "Imagine that you have become the goddess Baubo who sees through her nipples and speaks or laughs through her vulva."[15] And to the man, "Imagine for a moment that you have become the hairy, goat-like male god [Pan]."[16] The couple should then joke obscenely with each other. But next comes a half-hour "Fire Meditation," with music, for "awakening the energy of the Wild Self," which can occur when iden-tifying with a wild animal—bear, wolf, raptor, and so on—going into rut. Such episodes are visualized and then recounted to the other per-son: "Connecting with your wild animal gives you and your partner an expanded sense of freedom and playfulness, widening the parameters of your relationship."[17]

The magical sex act can be used to realize a wish, but for Margo Anand it is not sufficient to formulate it in your head as P. B. Randolph taught: "One of the keys to success in magic is to be able to translate or condense the vision of your desired goal into a symbol."[18] Borrowing Austin Osman Spare's principle, she urges the couple to create a sigil: "to create a magic symbol you can paint or draw a picture of your desired outcome."[19] She shows what hieroglyphs to use for expressing the desire to get a new job, to be invited on a journey, and so on. Once the sigil has been inscribed on a piece of paper, you must contemplate it until it fills your very being.

The man and woman, each wearing a "magical garment" (robe, toga, or kimono), which opens easily in the front, enter the circle, kneel on the bed or carpet, and make the Heart Salutation:

> To do a Heart Salutation with your partner, face each other in the center of your Magic Circle, standing about eighteen inches apart. Bring your hands together in front of your chest, palms pressed lightly together. Bow to your partner, bending slowly forward from the waist, until your foreheads lightly touch. . . . Then slowly straighten your back, returning to the upright position.[20]

The sigil is lying at their feet; they look at it for three minutes before beginning to caress each other.

The first caress, called "the Chakra Wave," is quite original; it lasts for one hour. The woman sits in front of the man with legs crossed in a half lotus, while his legs are spread out. The purpose of this exercise is to activate the sexual fire by going from one chakra to the next. The body has seven chakras (or energy centers) going from the sexual organs to the crown of the head. The man places his left hand on the woman's "mound of Venus" (the site of the *muladhara* chakra), and with his right hand he rubs her *hara* chakra (below the navel) with a circular motion, then goes up to the chakra of the solar plexus, and so on, until he reaches the crown chakra. The woman will move in rhythm with these gestures:

> Let your whole body be involved. Rotate your hips, move your torso, draw circles in the air with your hands to stimulate your visualizations and help the energy circulate.[21]

The man, too, can do "the Chakra Wave," with the woman sitting behind him performing the manipulations. In this way the sexual fire will unfold harmoniously through both of them from crotch to head.

The following activity is a mutual masturbation, but Margo Anand explicitly states: "This is a work of great art." The woman is lying down on cushions with her legs spread and the man is seated right next to her on the left side with his legs crossed. Margo Anand instructs him how to excite his companion's clitoris with "a two-finger basic stroke," a "double stroke," a "rooted stroke," a "three-finger tickle stroke," and finally, direct stimulation. She recommends to the woman being masturbated a "pleasure rating system" to convey her sensations to her partner:

> For example, if you say "three," this tells Shiva that you are mildly aroused. If you say "six," this lets him know that you are really getting turned on, and a "nine" warns him that you are very close to orgasm. A "ten" means that you have gone over the orgasmic edge.[22]

It is then the woman's turn to masturbate the man for ninety minutes using a technique adapted "to men in their fifties, sixties, and seventies." The man is stretched out on the cushions while the woman sits facing him, between his legs. She starts by dipping her fingers in a jar of olive oil and blessing the three primary chakras. She then makes the "twelve-o'clock stroke" on his penis pressed against his abdomen, caressing it with the flat of her hand and her finger tips going from the testicles to the tip in smooth, continuous movements. Next she does the "spiraling the stalk," holding the base of the penis in one hand and turning her other around the shaft winding her way up to the head. In the "carousel" she takes the penis in both hands and rotates them in opposite directions around the shaft, and in "making fire" she provides vertical friction. "Rub your hands backward and forward as if trying to start a fire by rubbing a stick." After this you can play on it like a "small drum," tapping on it "using the whole underside of your fingers, not just your fingertips." Anand calls the classic masturbation technique "stroking without the hood," which will not culminate with ejaculation, reserved for coitus. As a professor of masturbation, Margo Anand is amazing and delectable. She even teaches women to bury their finger in the anus of their partner, in order to produce an "internal stimulation of the prostate," with drawings to help.

When sexual intercourse takes place, it is necessary to not forget that it is being undertaken to ensure the success of a project. The sigil that symbolizes it will be close to the couple:

> When you are both immersed in an enjoyable flow of lovemaking, stop. Pause for a moment. Gaze together at your symbol in a relaxed way . . . close your eyes and see the symbol inside yourself. The let go of the symbol's image and once again move in other pleasure of your lovemaking.[23]

Once the symbol has been internalized, both partners must make it sexual: "Now as you make love, imagine that you are drawing the symbol into your sexual center." When you feel the orgasm approaching, think of the symbol spreading through the cosmos, "feel that the symbol is exploding into a million pieces, flying out into the universe, carried by the explosive power of your orgasmic release."[24]

I have discussed Margo Anand's concept first because she is a remarkable woman who teaches "the art of sexual ecstasy" in lectures and workshops at her SkyDancing Institutes located in Switzerland (Epalinges), Germany (Eggolsheim), and the United States. I am not going to be confined by this concept, but will offer some substantial changes. She advises couples to devote a Saturday afternoon or an entire Sunday to sessions of sexual magic—which, as we have seen, are long, since some of these exercises take an hour or more. This is true only for an operation that is focused upon bringing an event into being.

I will go farther in showing how a twenty-first-century couple can achieve the Great Work of the flesh in accordance with the laws of modern Gnosis. Like the tantric *maithuna,* this is an exceptional magical experiment that is hard to imagine being pursued continuously. It is quite easy to maintain regular sexual activity and devote yourself for a time to the Great Work of the flesh, after which you can again resume your usual sexual lifestyle. Doing this once a year, preferably in spring, or even once in your life, can have a long-lasting influence on your destiny.

THE WEDDING OF
THE KING AND QUEEN

The place and the season, the day and the hour, all count for much in the preparation of the Great Work. Alchemists concur that it should be initiated in the spring, particularly in March when the (reputedly feminine) morning dew was called the *emerald of the philosophers.* This work took place in a laboratory, which was sometimes small and modest, equipped with an athanor and an inexhaustible source of fuel to feed it and the alembics and retorts necessary for mixtures and combinations. Similarly, the room of the sexual operators should be a kind of lab, or it might be more fitting to call it a temple, as Aleister Crowley did. This was where he set up his altar dedicated to the gods he invoked, wore a high priest's robe, and made conjurations. A luxurious setting is not obligatory. A simple hotel room or modest attic room can become a temple-laboratory, if they have been purified and decorated with sacred emblems.

The Great Work of the flesh of modern Gnosis includes judiciously combined principles from Tantric yoga and Taoism. But if Europeans are the practitioners, it should necessarily fit into the context of Western esotericism. First, each of the two partners will draw a Tarot card by chance from a deck containing only the twenty-two major arcana, which has been thoroughly shuffled before them. The two arcana pulled from the deck will be placed on the altar and indicate what the man and woman can hope from their sessions of sacred intercourse. The arcana that predict complete success for operations of the erotic Royal Art are: the High Priestess, the Chariot (the arcanum of Babalon, according to Crowley), Strength, the Lovers, the Star, the Wheel of Fortune, and Death (symbol of the obliteration of difficulties and ascent to a new life). The others are connotative: the Emperor or Empress, the Sun or the Moon, announce that the ritual will favor either the woman or the man. (If the couple draws the Emperor and the Moon, or the Empress and the Sun, it will be highly beneficial to them.) The Hanged Man means they should primarily resort to sodomy; the Hermit, to masturbation; Justice, to a mutual absorption through fellatio and cunnilingus. Temperance advises restraint, while the Magician, to the contrary, urges them to lose control. The Pope or the Tower would be an invitation to strengthen the mystical effusions. The Devil carries a warning that elementary spirits have taken an interest in the couple, and they should be held at bay with censings. Judgment and the World foresee a consolidation of the couple's social standing or good reputation. The Fool recommends the use of the largest variety of sexual fantasies to ensure the efficacy of the magical union.

Other objects on the altar relate to Western magic: abraxas, talismans and pentacles, a banner carrying a verse from the *Song of Songs* in the Vulgate Latin, a copper candleholder inscribed with the gnostic word MOPHAX ("He breathes life into"), a crystal ball, a necklace of little bells (that the woman can wear around her neck for those positions when it is necessary to count the number of penetrations, which the ringing helps the man to do), and a diagram painted on parchment summing up the couple's desire. The bed in the center of the room shall be surrounded by four circles at the four cardinal points: the east and west circle hold the scientifically rendered horoscopes of the man and woman; in the north the circle holds the sacred words SABIRAUGETA ("You are valiant in the fire"), OSINALTIO ("You have been raised"), and IBLILILIO ("Iblis Lilith"); in the south circle, the name of Hagith, the spirit of the planet Venus. An incense burner or diffuser will emit aromatic substances that vary over the course of the sessions.

The wedding of the King and Queen lasts forty days. I have written elsewhere about the initiatory value of this number, and moreover, the "philosophical month" of the alchemists had forty days, just as their year did not begin on January 1, but on the spring equinox. The couple undertakes this work for its regenerative effects. This is not the limited Opus that Crowley performed with a prostitute for a goal like money. During these forty days, the couple will make love thirteen times, on days 3, 6, 9, 12, 15, 18, 21, 27, 30, 33, 36, and 39 of the cycle, with two-day interludes to prepare the following operation and by spending the fortieth day as a common day of grace.

The first two days of the Great Work of the flesh are a prelude. The initial act of the couple is a paired meditation, forehead to forehead, kneeling on the bed before each other, each visualizing the object of their desire. The visualization, during which the entire mind is focused on an imaginary scene, is a traditional mystical procedure. A Taoist treatise on inner alchemy, in its technique for purifying the body, recommends that the practitioner exhale while making the sound "ho," to rub his face with both hands, and to make this visualization: "Imagine a shower of pearls and jade that falls upon the ground like dew or raindrops; imagine a vast wave that swallows up the rivers."[25] Similarly, at certain times while they are embracing, caressing, kissing, or having intercourse, the couple should visualize images of sacred eroticism. They follow a gradation from the first to the fortieth day: here the woman might imagine a gigantic phallus sticking up like a greased pole that she must shinny up to the top while naked; while the man imagine a vulva of a sleeping giant that he enters to explore as if it were a cave.

Next it is necessary to perform a rite similar to the *nyasa*, which consists of touching the various parts of the other person's body while reciting a mantra that places them beneath divine protection. A mantra is a syllable or a group of syllables, which allow the concentration of cosmic and psychic energies, just as a yantra is a diagram symbolizing these same energies. Rawson says:

> The bodies of man and woman can be marked with symbolic designs that have the force of a yantra. These may be done freehand or with stamps dipped in coloured paste.[26]

It would be incongruous for a Westerner to repeat the mantra EM KLIM while placing his hand on his love partner. It would be more appropriate to compose a litany in which is listed the divine qualities of her eyes, nose, mouth, breasts, arms, legs, and so on, while lightly touching them with his fingertips. Similarly, it would be hardly effective to daub one another with paint unless both partners fully grasped the nature of the magical signs they were using.

The purpose of these preparations is to bring the partners into perfect agreement; they will put themselves fully into all possible caresses until they feel "like a stream of music flowing."[27] Mantak Chia, who has brought Taoism to Americans at his Healing Tao Center in New York, advises them to caress a woman by working their way from the periphery to the center: "Begin at the outer edges and don't go straight to her genitals. Caress and kiss her hands and wrists, her feet and ankles."[28] Emphasis is placed on the meridians or energy channels along the spinal columns, the kidneys, on the nape of the neck, the ears, on the inner arms, and inner thighs. The caresses on the chest should be circular:

> When you approach her breasts, make spiral movements around them, in increasingly smaller circles, until you gradually reach her nipples . . . on the other hand do not forget to rub your thumbs and index fingers together to generate more chi. Finally touch her nipples by lightly rolling them between your two heated fingers. (You can touch both breasts or concentrate on one of them)."[29]

It is also good to make circles with your tongue here that end with sucking the nipples. This method arouses female sexual energy. To increase it further, you can press the *huiyin,* the aphrosdisiacal point on the perineum between the anus and the vagina. You only need to apply pressure to this point with your thumb (make sure your thumbnail is clipped short), then relax it without breaking contact, and to continue doing this alternation for two minutes. The woman will meanwhile continue caressing the man using a revitalizing technique, but they should both take care not to take their dual sexual tension to the point of climax.

On the third day, the rite of phallic penetration begins. Mantak Chia recommends that the lover avoid a monotonous back-and-forth movement.

> When most men make love, they only stimulate a small part of their partner's vagina. This is why sexual kung fu recommends spiraling movements rather than linear ones.[30]

This author prescribes the higher art of the screw: "Instead of pushing back and forth, the ideal is to make a 'screwing' movement with your hips or sacrum, first in one direction, then the other."[31] He announces this law of coital dynamism: "The person moving (generally the one on top) gives more energy to the other,"[32] and emphasizes that this does not imply submission:

> In the West, we think that the person on top is in the dominant position. The Taoists interpret it differently. In fact, the person on top is in service to the one beneath, because he or she is sending out more healing energy. Passion and health, not power, are the primary concerns of a Taoist.[33]

In the frenzy of pleasure, the couple moves on to the shared "great inhalation,'" which Mantak Chia describes in the following way to his male students:

Clench your anus and mentally inhale the energy upward from the
tip of your penis through the perineum, coccyx, and spinal column
up to the head. . . . You will transform your genital bliss into a gen-
eralized climax of the entire body.[34]

The man should imagine he is sucking up the cold energy of the
vagina to transport it to the crown of his head, while breathing in
deeply:

Next, exhale and allow the energy to descend from the top of your
head by the median line between the eyebrows along your face and
through the tongue, and if your tongues are touching, you are able
to exchange energies by the mouth.[35]

For her part the woman should imagine she is sucking in the hot
energy of the penis with her vagina and make upward "thrusts" using
her diaphragm muscles in order to move the energy from her genital
region to her brain. To help the sexual energy climb, each of the partners holds the buttock of the other with their right hand and with
the left applies pressure to the various "energy points" along the back
from the kidneys to the occiput. The energy is exchanged through the
eyes, nose, and tongue, as women are instructed by Chia's former wife,
Maneewan:

Rub your nose against your partner's nose. Feel a spark of energy
jump from one to the other. Move your tongue into your partner's
mouth. Touch his tongue and massage it with your tongue. Feel the
sparkling energy pass from your tongue to your partner's tongue.[36]

"Dual cultivation" includes expansion (all forms of stimulation),
embracing (the two partners lie one atop the other in a comfortable
embrace, staring deeply into each other's eyes), circulation and exchange
of energies, but also coordination of the couple's breathing, which is
done as follows:

In a chest-to-chest position, each partner places an ear near the other's nose. In this position you can easily feel your partner's breathing. In the act of love, the breathing cycles stimulate and harmonize all of life's processes. Physically breathing together unifies the two partners and focuses the rhythm of all of their energies. [This can include breathing as one or establishing a rhythm where one person exhales while the other inhales.][37]

This session can end either in orgasm or by holding it back in order to have a stronger climax in the next session. Orgasm—which is only a "little death" in formication—has wonderful effects when achieved with a mystical sensibility. Pierre V. Piobb, who sought to restore the cult of Venus, goddess of the force of attraction, who makes her home in Libra ("Venus is the Sun of Libra"), said:

The spasm is one of those phenomena that escapes physiology, strictly speaking. . . . one part travels into the fluid body, a vibrational milieu capable of receiving and transmitting cosmic vibrations.[38]

The spasm occurs when "the entire body, oversaturated with energy flow, abruptly relaxes" and spills electromagnetism into the higher planes of earthly life.

The soul, in a frenzy, falls short for a minute into the infinite regions of attraction. It is a moment of unconsciousness during which nothing exists anymore! It is a divine dive into nothingness![39]

But the spasm, which is "for man the highest expression of his cosmic affinities," only possesses the virtue of propelling him beyond his human limitations when it is a "sacrament" at the end of the love act "that takes on the appearance of a rite." Thus, the religion of Venus modernized by Piobb concurs with what the Chinese and Indian authors are saying.

During the thirty-seven days that follow, an alternating schedule of sexual intercourse and interludes prevails, with variations. During these interludes, the man and the woman take care of each other as if they were athletes preparing for a competition. They could practice the exercises of Heng Cheng (pseudonym of two Taoist teachers from Taibei), like "urinating on the tips of the feet" to strengthen the kidneys, and "keeping your waist straight while clenching your teeth," which can cure impotence and frigidity (especially if the woman presses her toes firmly against the ground). Absorption of lunar energy is undertaken by remaining clothed, so as not to attract negative energies:

> Stand facing the moon as it rises in the evening. Breathe in gently, imagining that you are swallowing the nectar of its rays. At this same time swallow your own saliva, imagining that it contains the sap of the moon's yin energy.[40]

The woman should repeat this absorption thirty-six times, the man only six. The absorption of the sun's energy at daybreak should be done six times by the man and nine times by the woman. Exercising the vaginal muscles by contracting and relaxing them regularly while breathing evenly is a simpler process:

> Place your tongue against the palate and inhale through your nose while contracting the muscles of the anus and vagina. Then let your tongue fall back into the bottom of your mouth and breathe out through your mouth while relaxing your anus and vaginal muscles. This method can be practiced anywhere, whether while walking or standing on a bus.[41]

Heng Cheng adds:

> The Chinese believe that massaging the ears can increase salivation and facilitate digestion; similarly, if a woman massages her ears and eyes while performing her vaginal exercises, she will increase her sexual capacities considerably.[42]

The primary concerns of the interludes are love massages, a topic we will return to later. One can use several postures described by London acupuncturist Connie Dunne Kirby and Hatha Yoga teacher Geraldine Ross in *Yoga for Lovers*. The *sukhasana* posture is so suited to encouraging amorous understanding that a couple on the brink of divorce will fall back in love by practicing it together. The partners sit back to back, their legs crossed and their palms facing upward. Both put their hands behind themselves to grasp the other's knees; then they twist their backs from right to left. Next, the man lies over the woman who leans forward until, making a reverse motion, she comes back to lie on top of him. This posture teaches lovers that turning their backs to each other can provide the opportunity for a voluptuous union. The use of shiatsu, a Japanese finger-pressure massage that always takes place on the ground, is particularly indicated here as it makes it possible to stimulate erogenous zones of the body that are not habitually caressed. This is not for the sake of competing with professionals but for safely applying stimulating techniques. Shiatsu also uses elbows, forearms, and feet to massage, which allows the woman to perform some very compelling actions on the man. When he is lying flat on his stomach, she can massage his whole body with her bare foot, applying pressure to his buttocks, thighs, legs, and outstretched arms.

From the sixth session of sacred intercourse to the thirty-ninth, the couple should feel like they are going through the twelve stages of the Way of Sex. The mutual absorptions are multiplied in order to intensify the exchanges of yin and yang. During sexual congress Taoism commands the man to swallow the woman's saliva, which under his tongue becomes a "jade elixir" (jade is a symbol of immortality), when she is in the plateau phase of the orgasm. Incense and camphor should also be burning near the bed as this provokes salivation by stimulating the cerebral cortex. It does no good for the woman to swallow the man's saliva, but absorbing several drops of his sweat while they copulate is beneficial. During fellatio and cunnilingus, the complete absorption of sperm and vaginal secretions are powerfully energetic. The delicate persistent sucking of the woman's breasts is essential for both partners, because this releases "subtle effluvia" that is present in excessive amounts and which will hamper the woman's vitality. The relief she feels from being freed of this surplus is equal to the well-being of the man sucking her nipples. In the sex act there is a way of taking that is the best way of giving.

It should also be known, inasmuch as the Great Work of the flesh should ensure the health and eternal youth of its practitioners, that there are four fundamental positions ("the positions of the dragon") that have therapeutic properties. Taoists, in their standard sexual practice, even have exercises to be repeated daily. To tone sexual energy, the woman lies on her side, with her thighs spread as far as possible. The man stretches out beside her and penetrates her eighteen times, then stops. This position is practiced two times a day for fifteen days. To stimulate the five vital organs (liver, heart, spleen, lungs, and kidneys) she lies down on a large pillow that has been folded back in a way to hold her vulva up high, in reach of the man kneeling between her thighs. He gives her twenty-seven strokes with his penis and then remains still. This should be done three times a day for twenty days. To treat anemia, poor circulation, and low blood pressure, the woman sits astride the man and remains practically still. The man lifts and lowers his pelvis, as the sole active participant. To stimulate the digestive organs, circulate energy into the joints, and alleviate pain, the woman lies down and encircles the man around his thighs (not at the level of the kidneys), with her legs. These, too, are exercises to be performed in a series for a period of two to three weeks.

In the case when a dragon position is used in a single session, it involves the heavenly number of $9 \times 9 = 81$ short (yin) and long (yang) penetrations in the vagina. Here penetration does not simply consist of "screwing" in the manner Mantak Chia described earlier. It has a regenerative effect if, like a kind of rhythmic massage, it is performed with an alternation between short and long strokes. "The man starts with nine light shallow strokes, followed by one deeper penetration. He then makes eight light stokes, followed by two deeper ones, and so on." Counting the penetrations gives rhythm to the breathing and delays ejaculation. The American Taoist Nik Douglas explains:

It is important that love strokes not be counted out loud or in the mind. Rather, they should be measured against a rhythm, such as background music or recorded by the use of rosary beads. . . . Love strokes can easily be recorded on the fingers without actually counting.[43]

The woman will inevitably have her period during this forty-day period, which makes her similar to a Hindu Tantric initiate who is taken while menstruating so that the sexual relations she has with her partner are a marriage of the White and the Red, in other words Water and Fire. About this Jean Varenne reveals:

The two partners are recommended to introduce their fingers in the woman's vagina to collect the blend of sperm and blood inside, and then paint their faces with it. There is nothing unusual about this rite in Hinduism where it is customary at the end of the puja to take some ash from the sacrificial hearth and mark one's forehead with it. Here it is the yoni that plays the role of hearth.[44]

Westerners can dispense with this face painting, but it is still a good idea to recover this sacred mixture to use as an ink for writing your signature at the bottom of a love pact placed on the altar.

On the fortieth day, the couple will engage in a series of operations to glorify what they just did. The forehead-to-forehead meditation will accompany visualizations of the naked king and queen strolling in a park surrounded by their equally nude subjects who honor them by touching their genitals. The *nyasa* consists of thanking each part of the other's body for being so delectable during intercourse. Eating and drinking from mouth to mouth completes the cycle of mutual absorptions; each food will be chewed by one and given to the other to swallow; each will regurgitate what they drink for the other to ingest. The culmination is the prayer for two, in which the couple sits back to back with their chests perfectly straight. This ensures that their spinal columns remain completely in contact with each other. Believers will pray to the God of their religion (for no God can look askance at the sexual act performed religiously); Gnostics can invoke the "unknown God" (who is above the Gods of all religions); and atheists can address the World Soul of the Neo-Pythagorians. Kabbalists can give thanks to Metatron Sar ha-Panim (prince of light), the head of the souls on Earth.

All the foreseeable objections against the Great Work of the flesh can be easily dismissed. One might say it is excessive to perform it for forty days each year and to devote all these nights to it. But haven't people been observing the forty-day periods of Lent and Ramadan for centuries? Isn't it preferable to devote the evenings of this period to sex magic instead of watching debilitating programs on television? One might also say that it is impossible for the impotent and elderly to practice this, but that is incorrect. It is not necessary to have stable erections to practice sex magic; it is enough to rub the male sex organ, even when it is not tumescent, against that of the woman. Bioelectrical contact will be established immediately and allow for an exchange of energies. One could also say that homosexuals and lesbians are excluded from an undertaking like this that equally exalts Virility and Femininity, the phallus and the kteis.

To the contrary special rituals could benefit homosexuals and lesbians by bringing yin to those who lack it due to their abstinence of women, and yang to those whose lack of it stems from their refusal to give themselves to men. It is not my place to describe these rituals, but they should necessarily include mutual flagellations during the interludes, in order to dispel, by a symbolic act of self-punishment, the guilt that is inherent to homosexuality. In order to compensate the absence of the other sex, it is also necessary for a statue of the goddess to be placed on the altar of homosexuals and a statue of the god on the lesbians' altar.

Moreover, a homosexual Great Work of the flesh was achieved by Aleister Crowley and Victor Neuburg in a twenty-four session cycle invoking Jupiter and Mercury, which took place in Paris in January and February 1914. Neuburg performed the duties of priest and had personally sculpted the wax phallus on the altar. A Latin liturgy preceded the sodomistic relations, starting after the word *Accendat* (he shines) and ending with the offering of *haud secus* (the semen of both partners) to the god. Their friend Eleanor Mezdrow, an opium addict, brought them opium on several occasions, which gave them visions. Crowley had a vision of his previous life as a sacred prostitute in the temple of Agrigente. Neuburg saw a white elephant and heard a voice demanding blood in sacrifice. Aleister Crowley cut a number 4, Jupiter's number, in Neuburg's chest, and the blood that flowed out was given to the king of the gods as an offering. Neuburg next performed a dance around Crowley, who was seated in the posture of the *shivasana*. All kinds of incidents of this nature occurred during this experience they called "The Paris Working." But this type of episode cannot be used as a model, any more than can the erotic-mystical scenes from Joséphin Péladan's novel *La Gynandre,* in which all the lesbians of Paris take a cruise on the yacht *Sappho,* and the mage Tammuz organizes a ceremony including a phallic hymn to inspire these enemies of men toward "the coming reconciliation of the sexes."

Whatever the nature of the couple who undertakes it, the Great Work of the flesh, if performed with a religious sense of pleasure, ensures them the acquisition of a lucky streak beneficial to their health, fortune, ability to resolve difficulties tranquilly, and to transform the evolution of their future life together into an unflagging understanding.

SEXUAL VAMPIRISM

By the same token that mutual absorption is beneficial in a couple, unilateral absorption is malevolent. In such cases one of the partners takes the inner elixir and energies of the other without giving him or her anything in exchange. This is vampirism—not the sort found in horror novels (in which Dracula and his emulators are living-dead monsters who bite their victims' necks to greedily suck their blood), but that of the occult villain who feeds on the corporeal effluvia, physiological fluids, and most intimate thoughts of another until the victim has been drained of his or her psychosomatic resources. I am not referring to the murderers found in the annals of psychiatry: the archetypal case being Vincent Verzeni (studied by Krafft-Ebing), who drank the blood of women by biting their thighs and then genital organs before disemboweling them; or the most horrible such example, Peter Kurten, the vampire of Dusseldorf, who was executed in 1931 after committing numerous murders for the purpose of drinking blood, like an insatiable drunkard. The love vampire is a different beast from the blood vampire: he sucks out the psyche and vitality of his prey and strives to leave nothing behind.

Sexual vampirism has been better described in the Far East than in the West. Alexandra David-Neel, who traveled in Tibet accompanied by the lama Yongden, knew the rites for driving evil spirits away. The Tibetans she met in the Gayrong revealed to her the sex magic of the Bon sorcerers: "The energy that sustains and feeds all forms of life can be absorbed during sexual relations, at the woman's expense." This is an ontological vampirism that is more sophisticated than one dependent upon the absorption of blood:

> This is a prodigious secret that the criminal initiates use, claiming many victims, for the women who become their prey die soon after.[45]

However, only tough men can sustain the effort necessary for this action to succeed: "For the purpose of this rite to be achieved, the person practicing it must be capable of remaining completely impassive and able to overcome any desire to taste sensual pleasure." The moment they succumb to sensuality will be their ruin: "The vitality they have stolen from others escapes from every pore of their body and they soon perish, miserably."

Many women today have been involved with a sexual vampire without realizing it, for he is often a man of banal appearance with nothing of the diabolical look of Nosferatu or the characters in Roman Polanski's *Fearless Vampire Killers*. She can recognize one by the fact—pointed out by the Tibetan Buddhists—that during intercourse he remains cold and insensitive whereas a normal lover is expansive, welcoming, quivering.

The vampire cannot be like this since he is concentrating totally on the aspiration of his partner's energies. Furthermore, the woman who has been subjected to a vampiric embrace will suffer migraines after orgasm and retain a more or less conscious sensation of having been *emptied*. This sensation is unusual in female sexuality, in which the culmination of the act normally results in a sense of fullness. Even the fatigue of excessively repeated relations does not remove this impression of being emptied: his climax has filled her and it is the excess of this filling that wearies her in such a case.

In my own circle I have recently seen examples of young women who have been terribly diminished by their liaisons with vampires. The most depressing case is that of a twenty-two-year-old collaborator of mine with brilliant literary talents. I had published one of her texts and she was preparing to write more when she fell in love with a young man who clung to her like a leech. She complained to me that she felt like "she had run dry" and begged me to find her subjects for articles and books. She was incapable of dealing with any of my suggestions. Once, from a distance, she pointed out her seedy boyfriend to me. He was poorly shaved but swollen up with all the vital juices he had sucked from her. In a temporary moment of lucidity, she told me that this man was a germ of which she could not rid herself. On another occasion she called me to ask for advice because he was singing the praises of all the pretty women they met because they would make him happier than she could. In fact, the tactic of the vampire is to make his victim feel so inferior that, out of guilt, she will feel obliged to give him even more of herself. I have no more news about this poor girl, but since she is young, perhaps another love may free her from this hold that has inflicted such great intellectual anemia on her for several years.

There are magical methods that will allow a woman to protect herself from a man she suspects of being a sexual vampire. If he shows no emotion during the sex act, it is because he is busy draining her being. When she is under him, she should put her arms in a cross to ensure a protective magnetism. Long before Christianity the image of the cross was reputed among the Arabs and Egyptians to be the receptacle of a heavenly force that repels invisible threats. The prostitutes and porn movie actresses who wear a chain with a Latin cross or an Egyptian tau cross are protected from the vampires they will inevitably encounter among their numerous partners. If the intended victim cannot cross her arms (because the alleged vampire is taking her from the side or doggy style), she should conceal her thumbs by wrapping her other fingers around them—this will free her from harmful influences, according to the counsel of the chiromancer Desbarolles.

Pierre V. Piobb has provided the definition of this sexual magic infraction:

> When an individual (human or pseudo-human) sucks up the vital fluid of another human being, it is vampirism. This vampirism can be conscious or unconscious, selfish or altruistic (when the vampire is working on behalf of a third party).[46]

He also indicates defense methods such as the following, which is akin to what I mentioned above:

> You can protect yourself against vampirism by closing your fists around your thumbs, and by removing your feet from the vicinity of the person suspected of being a vampire.[47]

He also recommends making the sign of the horns, although not just in a random way:

> The hand making the sign of the horns, in order to be a particularly effective protection, must be held over the chest at the level of the sympathetic nerve.[48]

Dion Fortune accused a group of English theosophists of being vampires who had constructed "a reservoir of astral force to be used for magical purposes" by employing the following method:

This reservoir appears to be supplied by inducing women to concentrate their emotions on the leader of the group by telling them they have a link with him in their past lives.[49]

Other theosophical vampires tried to hypnotize their prey in order to steal their astral force while they slept, although there is a simple method for deflecting this: "The unwilling victim has merely to put his thumb to his nose and the would-be Dark Initiator is completely floored."[50] Aleister Crowley also condemned the activity of vampires (he was scared of them) in his *Liber Agape* and even claimed that the "late Oscar Wilde" was one.

Marie-Thérése des Brosses asked Raymond Abellio: "Do you vampirize women?" Indeed, this author was an apologist for vampirism in his novels, notably *La Fosse de Babel,* in which he made his heroes Drameille and Pirenne incarnations of Lucifer and Satan, and where he divided the female species into two types: "the original woman," that is to say "the quasi-animal woman, endowed with a love of an immediate receptivity"; and the "ultimate woman" who, without being an intellectual, is "a woman whose femininity is as intense as possible, but accompanied by a keen awareness."

The man is a full vampire with the first woman, and is both predator and prey with the second. As Abellio explains:

In physical love, it is the ultimate woman who can absorb a man's energies in an instant; the man is thus compelled, in order to regenerate, to turn to original woman with whom the exchange takes the opposite direction. These latter are inexhaustible.[51]

He reveals that this is his own case: "My own life has long been an alternation between two kinds of women: original and ultimate.[52] Abellio gives a good alibi for vampires by claiming he can treat himself endlessly to the delicious meal of an original woman and go the end with an ultimate woman. "She seems to vampirize you in an instant, and you appear to vampirize her over the long term."[53] His interviewer had good reason to be concerned! I refute, based on my own experience, Abellio's conception, because I do the exact opposite: I do not feed on the strength of a woman, but on her weakness in such a way that she feels twice as strong. My energy increases in proportion to the vitality I give her.

Men also often have dealings with female vampires who lead them to their ruin, but they are not alerted to this in the same way as women who feel the sensation of being "emptied." This sensation is normal after ejaculation, especially during a session where it has occurred three or four times. The warning consists instead in the state of depression that accompanies this "emptying," when it should have seemed like a healthy fatigue following a heroic expenditure. The female vampire is most often identical to a ghoul exhausting a man through repeated acts of fellatio. She transforms an act that ordinarily brings relief and relaxation into a torture and a death sentence.

Here, too, the women that historians have labeled vampires are sadistic criminals like the Countess Elizabeth Báthory in Hungary who bled hundreds of young girls to death in her Csejte castle so she could bathe in their blood. She was a ferocious lesbian whose orgasms were triggered by their suffering. Although her assistant Ilona Joo was an adept of Satanism, her case does not fall into the category of sexual magic. Similarly, the black widow Vera Renczi in Belgrade, who is studied as a vampire because she poisoned two husbands and thirty-two lovers with arsenic over a fifteen-year period, was rather a praying mantis who got pleasure from making love with dying men convulsing under the effects of poison.[54]

In 1868 an old woman living on the rue Rochechouart hired young girls as "living companions" who arrived at her home in good health, but then soon withered away and died. A coachman, whose daughter died under these conditions, alerted the police, but as nothing indicated that the victims had been poisoned or stabbed, they released the old woman. Here is a woman that can be justly suspected of being a true sexual vampire, stealing the vital fluid of her "girl companions" through draining Sapphic caresses.

However, we should not exaggerate the problem of sexual vampirism, as sometimes the victim takes a masochistic pleasure in being vampirized and makes no efforts to get free. In other instances a male vampire will collide with a female vampire, and their relations, through mutual absorption, become like those of a normal couple, only more intense. We must simply remain vigilant with regard to this phenomenon as it can form an obstacle to the Great Work of the flesh.

5
How to Make Love with an Invisible Creature

This chapter title would appear to announce a fictional fantasy. This is not at all the case: since antiquity many men and women, without necessarily being under the influence of hallucinogens or religious hysteria, have experienced the sensation of having loving commerce—and even intercourse—with an entity living in the preternatural universe. In the literature of every land, there are countless tales, inspired by popular fears, that tell of lemurs, striges, empusae, and ghosts who pester humans with their libidinous attentions. I will not draw my examples from folktales, however, but from theological and medicinal treatises. In the early years of Christianity, Saint Augustine stated in his City of God (book XV, chap. 23):

> There is, too, a very general rumor, which many have verified by their own experience, or which trustworthy persons who have heard the experience of others corroborate, that sylvans and fauns, who are commonly called *incubi*, had often made wicked assaults upon women, and satisfied their lust upon them; and that certain devils, called *Duses* by the Gauls, are constantly attempting and effecting this impurity is so generally affirmed, that it were impudent to deny it.[1]

Saint Augustine is mainly speaking here of elementary spirits, to which he assimilates the satyrs of paganism, because the church fathers after him had a different definition for the nature of incubi and succubi.

In addition to the lubricious activity of demons and elementary spirits with human beings, we can add that of undead who have returned with a craving for living flesh—especially in the East. The story of Garab and Detchema, collected by Alexandra David-Neel in Tibet, reveals how a woman was raped by a ghost. Garab became jealous at seeing Detchema moving in her sleep as if abandoning herself to the embrace of an invisible lover. "Had Detchema come to prefer the caresses of her phantom lover to his?" He believed this invisible entity was a yogi "capable of projecting an etheric double that could act like a real person." One night this creature materialized and attacked him before suddenly fading away. Garab went to consult a hermit of Mount Khang Tise, who told him,

> Your father's spirit has become a phantom who still thirsts for the sensations he felt while still alive. . . . He wanted to possess your mistress to steal her own life force and that psychic energy you had given her.[2]

THE SEXUAL ASSAULTS OF INCUBI AND SUCCUBI

The incubus is the male demon that attempts to take his pleasure of a woman, and the succubus is the female demon that lasciviously couples with a man. But how can they do this if they are immaterial? Father Sinistari of Ameno (the Novare diocese), the seventeenth-century Franciscan brother who became an adviser to the Supreme Tribunal of the Holy Inquisition, studied this matter from every angle. To make love with the men or women they desire, the demons create a temporary body or borrow that of a dead person they animate so perfectly that sexual relations with an incubus or succubus is "copulation with a corpse, said corpse having no feeling or movement, and only moves exceptionally through an artifice of the demon." The incubus is so salacious that it will even assault female animals.

> It is not only women he attacks, but mares as well; if they are docile to his desires, he overwhelms them with caresses and braids their manes with an infinite number of inextricable knots; but if they resist, he mistreats them, strikes them, bites them, and finally kills them.[3]

Among the demons with the power to create bodies for themselves, Father Sinistari distinguishes two groups of incubi and succubi. The first group, those who have sworn allegiance to the Devil during ceremonies, he claims to have seen with his own eyes. The second group, which is much harder to fight, includes independent, wandering entities:

> These incubi—which in Italian are called *foletti,* and in Spanish, *denudes,* and in French, *follets*—pay no heed to exorcists and have no fear of exorcisms, no veneration for sacred objects, the approach of which causes them not the slightest fear. They are entirely different in this regard from the demons that torment the possessed.[4]

To convince his readers of the truth of his assertions, Father Sinistari tells the following story that took place in Pavia when he was a professor of theology there. He swears that he has been scrupulous in reporting the details exactly as they happened.

A married woman, Gironima, had ordered a loaf of bread from the oven keeper and he also gave her a biscuit, which she ate. That night when lying in bed with her husband, she heard a hissing voice at her ear asking, "Did you like the cake?" Terrified, she muttered a prayer, but the voice reassured her: "I am smitten by your beauty, and my greatest desire is to take my pleasure in your hugs and kisses." She then felt something kiss her cheek so gently that it felt like being brushed against by feather down. "The temptation lasted almost half an hour, after which the tempter went away." Gironima went to see her confessor the following day, who gave her some relics for protection, but they were useless: "Similar temptations occurred over the following nights, with words and kisses of the same sort." She then decided to have herself exorcised; exorcists blessed her house, room, and bed, and commanded the incubus to cease its importunate solicitations. "The tempter only redoubled his efforts; he claimed he was dying of love, weeping and moaning to soften the woman's resistance."

Despite all of this, Gironima resisted every attempt made by this invisible being to have intercourse with her.

The incubus then ventured an entirely different approach. He appeared to his beauty in the form of a young boy, or little man, who was incredibly handsome with a blond beard shining like gold, eyes blue-green as flax flowers, elegantly clad in Spanish fashion.

He even appeared to her when she was in the company of others, giving her kisses or weeping: "She alone could see and hear him; nobody else could see or hear a thing." Gironima stubbornly refused to surrender to the incubus in her bed: "After several months, the annoyed incubus resorted to a new form of persecution." He stole her jewels, turned everything in the household upside-down, and struck her so cruelly she had bruises that lasted two days. "Sometimes when she was nursing her little daughter, he would snatch the babe off her knees and stick her on the roof by the gutter." One night he appeared in the shape of the little man with the blond beard and tried to rape her, but she repelled him. He left and came back with stones: "Around the bed he built a wall with these stones that was so high it reached the ceiling, and the couple needed a ladder brought to them to get out." During a meal when the couple was hosting eight soldiers, at the moment they sat down to eat, the guests' table vanished along with all the dishes and tableware.

In despair Gironima sought advice from a Bernardine brother of Feltre. Taking heed of his counsel, she made a vow to remain clad in a gray habit cinched with a rope at the waist, like those of the brothers minor of Saint Bernard, for an entire year. The day after she made that decision, on the Feast of Saint Michael, she went to mass at ten o'clock with a crowd of other worshippers.

> The poor girl had no sooner set foot in the parvis of the Church, when all at once all her clothes and adornments fell to the ground where they were carried off by the wind, leaving her naked as a hand.

The incubus played a number of other tricks of this nature on her, to force her through intimidation to surrender in bed to his penetration. "He persisted in tempting her for a number of years, but finally realizing he was wasting his time and energy, he lifted his siege." This is not a superstitious old wives' tale, but a seriously presented example by a priest whose Criminal Code of canon law was most definitive and contained many similar anecdotes on the activity of incubi.

Father Sinistari was outraged at the absurdities spouted by his colleagues, as if he never ventured any himself, and wrote back concerning Vallesius's theory on how incubi impregnated women: "I am amazed that such an enormity has come from the pen of such an erudite figure." Inquisitors claimed that the same demon disguised itself as a succubus to extract the sperm of a sleeping man, causing him to have a wet dream, and then next transformed into an incubus to inject this same sperm into the vagina of a living woman, consenting or not. This sperm had grown cold during this transfer, and she had the sensation of receiving an icy ejaculation in her belly. But it would be hot and endless if the incubus had harvested the sperm of several men and flooded her womb with this mixture. This is how audacious, robust, and proud bastards were born, and a list had been drawn up of historical figures with this constitution because a demon had filled their mother's uterus, with "an abundant, very thick, and very hot sperm, which is highly charged with spirits and exhibits no fluidity": Plato, Alexander the Great, Scipio Africanus, Martin Luther, and so forth. Father Sinistari protests: "I maintain that the demon incubus, in its congress with women, engenders the human fetus with its own sperm." He objects that it is not the quantity of semen that matters in conception, but its quality. In contradiction to other demonologists, he puts forth the notion that incubi and succubi form their own population of invisible beings, midway between demons and angels, and who are "difficult to kill because of the speed with which they escape danger." Their ability to travel through walls comes from "the subtle and delicate corporeality of the beings in question, similar to the substance of liquids." Sinistari of Ameno did not offer his view on an anatomical peculiarity revealed by various theologians, to wit, the incubus had a large, bifurcated penis like a fork, one end of which he stuck in the vagina and the other in the anus of the woman, simultaneously.

There is no shortage of succubi stories in the manuals of the Inquisition, either. In the shape of fluidic women with vampiric manners, they come to the beds of men preparing to go to sleep. The victim may be a bachelor or a married man. They then sit astride him and, with frenzied intercourse, compel him to ejaculate. Sometimes they relentlessly copulate with him the entire night, leaving him exhausted when he gets up. It is possible to maintain a long relationship with a succubus. The most significant case is that of Bernedeto Berno, an octogenarian priest who confessed to the judges of the Inquisition that he had been copulating for forty years with a succubus named Hermoine, who accompanied him everywhere without ever being seen: "He also confessed that he had inhaled the blood of several small children and committed a number of other execrable wickednesses, and was burned alive," says Jean Brosin, who added that there was "yet another priest, seventy years old, who confessed to have had similar copulation with a demon in the guise of a woman, and who was also burned."[5] The dreadful inquisitor Jacob Sprenger reported the case of a German sorcerer of Conflans who had sexual relations with an invisible creature in the presence of his wife and friends. They would see him suddenly throw himself on the ground, open his breeches, and make increasingly stronger thrusts with his pelvis, "as if he was in copulation with a woman, and spurt semen." He was victim to the same kind of autosuggestion that compelled peasant women of that time to go out into the fields naked and lie down on the ground where they thrashed about like girls being raped: "And sometimes husbands would find them mating with devils, who they mistook for men, and when striking them with their swords, would touch nothing."[6]

The history of humanity's sexual harassment at the hands of invisible creatures expanded when Paracelsus, the creator of "spagyric medicine" (which is connected with alchemy and the Kabbalah), in his *Liber de nymphis, sylphis, pygmaeis et salamandris et de caeteris spiritubus* (Book of Nymphs, Sylphs, Pygmies, Salamanders and Other Spirits; published in Basel in 1590, after his death), described the secret peoples inhabiting the four elements of Water, Air, Earth, and Fire, some of whose individual members sought to copulate with humans. This became an article of faith for the Rosicrucian Brotherhood in the seventeenth century and the abbot Montfaucon de Villars, in the *Comte de Gabalis* (1670), reported everything an initiate had revealed to him on this matter, after telling him peremptorily: "You must renounce all carnal congress with women." In fact, no human women could compete with the "invisible mistresses" one could find among the elementary spirits. The nymphs or undines resided in rivers, lakes, and seas: "Few males, and of women there are great number; their beauty is extreme." The upper air is inhabited by the sylphs: "Their women and their daughters are male beauties, like our depictions of Amazons." In the depths of the Earth, in mines or caves, live the gnomes: "The Gnomides, their wives, are small and quite pleasant, and their dress is extremely odd." Finally, fire is the dwelling place of spirits called *salamanders*: "Their wives and daughters are rarely seen."[7] Montfaucon de Villars illustrates his theory with many anecdotes, but they are fables and not adventures concerning actual people.

Another author who wrote on this theme was Jacques Cazotte, after he returned from serving as a chief administrator in Martinique. At the age of fifty-three, he published a book in 1772 titled *Le Diable amoureux* (The Devil in Love), a novel "dreamt in one night and written in one day." Its hero, Alvare, a young captain in Naples, invokes elementary spirits in a cave at the instigation of the necromancer Soberano. He sees a camel appear that transforms into a dog, who he asks to serve him a light meal. The cave changes into a castle room, where a page named Biondetto forms a bond with Alvare. After various trials and tribulations, this page reveals he is a splendid woman, Biondetta, and confesses: "I am a sylph by origin, and one of the highest among them . . . I am allowed to take on a body to associate with a wise man: here I am." An exalted amorous liaison develops between Alvare and his sylph, but after they have made love with infinite climaxes, Biondetta tells him:

> I am the Devil, my dear Alvare, I am the Devil. . . . Tell me finally,
> if possible, but as tenderly as I feel it for you, my dear Belzebuth, I
> adore you.[8]

Alvare flees home to his mother in terror and finds protection from a confessor against this diabolical misadventure.

This novel earned Cazotte a visit from a disciple of Martinez de Pasqually, master of the Order of the Elus-Cohen in Lyon. He was then initiated into Martinism, where he learned that he had misrepresented the sylphs. Gérard de Nerval, in *Les Illuminés* (The Illumined Ones), says that Cazotte blamed himself "for having somewhat defamed these innocent spirits who give life to the middle reaches of the air, by assigning them the dubious personality of a female sprite answering to the name of Belzebuth." As a general rule, everything concerning sylphs and nymphs falls under the heading of folklore or literature. Heinrich Heine spoke of them from a poet's perspective and the ethnographer Karl Grün collected legends concerning them.[9] In this domain there are no historical events that compare with the abundant examples from the witch trials, in which men and women were condemned to be burned alive for confessing they had copulated with succubi and incubi.

Sex with incubi and succubi is not a Christian aberration that no longer occurs. They have modern aspects that René Schwaeblé defined after discussing them with his close friend, the author Joris-Karl Huysmans: "The art of sexual intercourse with incubi and succubi consists of the possibility of possessing at any time any man or woman, living or dead, provided one has a clear image of them." This depends on self-hypnosis, "the art of putting oneself in a trance and causing somnambulistic sleep," that was a subject of experimentation for the doctors from the Salpêtrière Hospital. Schwaeblé mentions the possibility of using an apparatus to help encourage suggestibility, a light source striking the eyelids. "It is necessary before entering the lethargic stage, to clearly determine the individuality of the incubus or succubus personality one desires; one must imagine that she is there in one's bed, and that one is taking her." The experimenter must be in a more or less agitated state from continence; having deprived himself of amorous contact, his obsession conditions him to feel one.

> Later, with habit, the auto-suggestion occurs on its own, so to speak. In this way an individual can parade through his bed celebrities, male and female, who the imagination can inflate even more. With practice, the suggestion becomes so strong and the consequent hallucination becomes so intense that the summoned phantom takes on haunting substance with all the properties of the living individual. One then intensely perceives the color, odor, and sounds that this ghost releases; one can even feel new impressions . . . finally, a veritable individual, a male or female lover, is there—a larva engendered by the incubus or succubus maker.[10]

Before his conversion Huysmans was attacked by succubi and believed much more in their reality than he had let on to René Schwaeblé. In his novel *En Route* (On the Way), the character Durtal has an erotic dream during his first night at the Trappist abbey Notre Dame d'Igny with the "clearcut sensation of a being, a fluidic form vanishing with the sharp sound of a percussion cap or the snap of a whip, nearby, on waking." He even had the impression that the wind caused by its flight had thrown the bed sheet into disarray.

During this same era, there was a case of adultery in which a wife deceived her husband not with real men but with incubi. This happened with the couple MacGregor Mathers (Grand Master of the Order of the Golden Dawn) and his wife Moïna (sister of the philosopher Henri Bergson). In fact, no cheating was involved as he knew and approved of it. He no longer touched her, which she did not find frustrating, because in their conjugal bed Moïna sometimes abandoned herself to the embraces of an incubus invoked by the Abramelin ritual and had fantastic orgasms.

René Schwaeblé was witness to a kind of orgy—this is not too strong a word—between living women and incubi that took place in Batignoles in a deconsecrated chapel on rue Truffault that had belonged to a community of expelled nuns around 1905. "In the evening between five and seven, women and men came to sit in the confessionals or quite simply on sagging, rickety straw chairs." Schwaeblé was drawn there by his writer's curiosity, and noted among its habitués a painter, a theater critic, and a countess ("the famous veiled Lady from the Dreyfus trial"). In the half shadows weakly lit by a lamp on the altar, everyone waited until a voice murmured: "The incubi and succubi are here!" Then, those in attendance "started moving and wiggling like chickens in a sack. Their gestures became lascivious and obscene. Their hips writhed. Sighs were emitted; first they were indistinct and faint, then clearer and more emphatic." Schwaeblé watched this hysteria as best he could: "All at once, they fell still, swooning. They opened their eyes and came out of their trance. The incubus had left . . ." The spectator noted: "That's what I saw. In truth, I couldn't see much of anything!"

To be perfectly sure, Schwaeblé questioned "one of the most gracious regular visitors," who answered him: "You could not see anything because you have not undergone the preparatory training." Which is? "Never eat meat, fast totally two days a week, strive to slow down your breathing, and so on. In fact, it is a matter of purifying your nervous force and being able to concentrate on the exterior object." She told him: "You should not think you can make X or Y show up." First, one should "obtain an object touched by the desired individual, a letter written by him, a lock of his hair." He wanted to know if she could see the incubi that possessed her, but she shook her head: "They generally remain invisible. . . . Sometimes we can see a shadow, a barely perceivable shadow, but finally we can discern it; and in certain cases—very rare cases—we can clearly distinguish a body." He asked her if it was necessary to evoke or expect the incubus. She answered: "Personally, I always evoke the same demons. And once they have served me well, I drive them away without pity." Why did she not form a liaison with just one of them? Her reply is categorical: "You must not let the incubus become the master, under penalty of not being able to get rid of it. It will couple with you night and day, and the nervous expense among other things is so terrible that death will soon follow."[11]

There is nothing implausible about this testimony from the pen of a credible author. This was a time when the "psychic sciences" were in fashion. Worldly women found neurotic pleasure in gathering together in an abandoned chapel to play at being possessed by incubi, watched by voyeurs who paid more attention to their voluptuous contortions than to irruptions of larvae from the astral realm. Among them could be found pretenders, brought to orgasm by the thought of exciting the spectators and by being placed in an unusual situation, as well as hysterics who were genuinely convinced they were being penetrated by an extraordinary lover who had come from outer darkness.

THE LOVERS OF SOPHIA

Never have amorous relations with an invisible woman been more realistic than in the story of Johann-Georg Gichtel and Sophia, which culminated in a collective marriage. Sophia is the highest female figure in the Gnostic belief systems that existed during the earliest period of Christianity. As I said in my book on the *History of Occult Philosophy:*

> It was common knowledge she represented Wisdom, an impalpable aeon, but she inspired such passions that she was transformed into a kind of Christianized Isis. Almost every Gnostic group had its version of her misadventures and made the distinction between the higher Sophia, the Celestial Mother, and the lower Sophia that was sometimes called Sophia Achamot or Sophia Prounicos (lascivious), because in her the desire for light became assimilated with sexual desire.[12]

In the seventeenth century, the great visionary Jacob Boehme restored the cult of Sophia to honor by stating she had been Adam's wife before the creation of Eve, and the mystics of his school began worshipping her more than the Virgin Mary. She was the "Queen of Saints," the sacred Body about whom Boehme said: "This Sophia, who is animated by the Holy Ghost, is of substance, without being corporeal like our bodies."

After reading Jacob Boehme's two books, a man fell madly in love with Sophia: this was Johann-Georg Gichtel. He was born in 1638 in Regensberg of well-to-do Lutheran parents. He made his start by producing a pamphlet against the corrupt clergy of that region, which earned him the wrath of the priests, who caused him to be expelled from his native village and to have all his property confiscated. He took refuge in Holland. Suffering from extreme poverty, he managed to survive because several Amsterdam families took an interest in him due to the dignity of his life, which was animated by an ideal of secular saintliness. The father of a young girl offered him the hand of his daughter (who was the heiress to a fortune) in marriage, but Gichtel declined, thinking he should take a vow of celibacy in order that he might one day deserve the love of Sophia. Next, an extremely wealthy widow fell in love with him and insistently asked him to marry her. Although he felt drawn to her, he postponed acceptance and retired to his home for four weeks to pray to God. The result was negative, as noted by a commentator: "He then gave himself thenceforth utterly to Sophia, who wanted naught of a divided heart; he saw that his vocation was the priesthood in its most elevated sense." In 1672, when the troops of Louis XIV were at the gates of Amsterdam, Gichtel organized prayers to repel them.

His exemplary conduct eventually earned him the love of Sophia. Colonel Kirchberger, in his correspondence with Saint-Martin, described it this way:

Sophia, his dear, his divine Sophia, whom he loved so much and whom he had never seen, came on Christmas Day 1673 to pay him a first visit. He says in this connection that he saw and heard in the Third Principle* that Virgin who was of an amazing and celestial

---

*[In the mystical terminology of Jacob Boehme, the Third Principle refers to the divinely created visible world. — *Trans.*]

beauty. She accepted him as her husband upon this first meeting, and the marriage was consummated in inexpressible delights. She distinctly promised him conjugal fidelity; never to abandon him, neither in adversity nor in poverty, neither in sickness nor in death, and that she would always live with him in the interior luminous depths.[13]

This would indicate that Gichtel most often saw Sophia at the center of his soul, and this inner conversation only manifested itself externally on rare occasions with a fleeting vision before his eyes:

The wedding lasted until the beginning of 1674. He then found more comfortable lodging in a spacious house in Amsterdam whose rent was quite expensive. However, he didn't possess a sou . . .

His heavenly bride carried on constant conversations with him in a "central language, without external words or vibrations in the air." She was an intransigent and chaste lover: "Sophia insinuated that if he wished to enjoy her favors without interruption, he had to abstain from all sexual bliss and all earthly desire—a stipulation he observed religiously."

This union with Sophia gave such assurance and power to Gichtel that all people suffering difficulties came to him for advice and he was able to extricate them from their hardship. A doctor named Raadt appealed to him because he was at his wit's end; Gichtel taught him to pray, and prayed with him to free him of a £24,000 debt, which came to him in a miraculous manner. Raadt then decided to impose upon himself and his wife "spiritual circumcision," meaning complete abstinence from the sex act henceforth. This renunciation was advantageous for him: "Sophia welcomed Raadt, and all those who came to see her husband with good, perfectly clear intentions. . . . She let fall several rays of her image into the earthly qualities of their souls." Soon public rumor ran wild with this supernatural information, and Gichtel found himself welcoming all manner of visitors keen to obtain the benefits of Sophia.

Once their number swelled to thirty, they formed the Society of Thirty. The Society's members made a commitment to practice sexual abstinence with their wives, as Sophia wished them to be pure of all carnal contact. Colonel Kirchberger remarked that "On this occasion, Gichtel observed in noteworthy fashion how greatly the astral spirit desired to enjoy the nuptial bed of Sophia."

With the help of his new friends, Gichtel decided to undertake an edition of the complete works of Jacob Boehme. A rich magistrate (who was not one of Sophia's lovers) provided the funding. In the beginning they were all utterly convinced of the reality of their amorous congress with this heavenly creature, and this galvanized them. "As long as the Thirty, who were spread through different cities, remained one in spirit, they obtained through their prayers all they desired." Little by little their ardor cooled, either because their wives were unhappy about being abandoned for an invisible rival, or because they did not receive enough visions of Sophia, or because the advantages they had drawn from this relationship failed to satisfy them. The first to leave was Raadt, and he went so far in the opposite direction that he became an enemy of Gichtel. Others also abruptly abandoned him, some even accusing him of being a magician. Despite the defection of the Society of Thirty, Gichtel succeeded in publishing his edition of Boehme's complete works in 1682.

A young Frankfurt bookseller named Ueberfeld asked him for two hundred copies on deposit to sell. This individual was such a fervent admirer of Jacob Boehme that he knelt in deference while reading his work. He received an alert from Sophia, ready to become his wife because of his fervor. He went to visit Gichtel in Amsterdam in 1683, and decided to remain with him: "On his arrival Sophia manifested in the Third Principle to the two friends united in the most glorious manner, and renewed her bonds with them, which lasted until 1685." This is how Sophia, who had promised Gichtel fidelity, had no hesitation about becoming bigamous, after having had thirty lovers: he was simply her preferred husband, and she favored the others in proportion to their service to her. The life of these two "brothers" during their years together, both believing themselves to be Sophia's husband, must have been quite odd. When she vanished for a period of time, they had a vision of Christ (in 1690) as if she was working in the higher spheres for their souls' salvation. "Shortly before Gichtel's death, which occurred in 1710, Sophia appeared to the two friends as she had in 1683 for the first time, and recalled her faithful friend to her side," Kirchberger concludes.

Ueberfeld attempted to publish a six-volume edition of Gichtel's letters, but they were full of gaps.

> Sophia came personally, after her husband's death, to oversee and direct the arrangement of his posthumous letters; she revised several pages that had not been clearly stated in the rough drafts that Gichtel had given his friend Ueberfeld; and as this latter worked on this composition, Sophia guided him personally. She had come to see Ueberfeld several times for this purpose. It was a never-ending feast, during which she communicated to the editor and several faithful friends of the deceased, developments of holy economy.[14]

In the preface to his friend's correspondence, Ueberfeld wrote that "mouth cannot express the lasting, permanent joys that this manifestation afforded them."

This case is thoroughly original, as it involves an angelic creature rather than a diabolical one. Her worshipper perceives her at the center of his soul and outside his body at the same time. She is able to vanish, return, and vanish again for a certain amount of time, and she gives a spiritual pleasure that is even more intense than sensual pleasure, as if she was the inner wife of the inner man.

SPIRITUALIST EROTICISM

The birth of spiritualism in America, which came at the time when the three Fox sisters and their mother invented the turning-table procedure in their Hydesville, New York home in 1848, inaugurated a new style of amorous relations between the living and the dead. In spite of their pragmatism, scholars, businessmen, and jurists were convinced that souls in the beyond could make knocking noises, move furniture, and even completely materialize in their former earthly appearance, through the intermediary of a trance medium. The great significance of this social phenomenon makes it necessary to provide several examples here to show just how far one can go in order to take pleasure from the sight, sound, and touch of a ghost.

The first noteworthy case in this regard is that of Charles F. Livermore, a rich New York banker who was in a state of despair after the death of his wife Estelle. Doctor John F. Gray, who had been treating him, brought him to the home of the medium Kate Fox so she could attempt to make contact with the deceased. During the first séance on January 23, 1861, rapping noises echoed through the room announcing she had appeared; her message was received by counting the number of knocks, since their number varied in accordance with the order of the letters of the alphabet. During the twelfth séance, Estelle said she could make herself visible to her husband, and on January 24 he saw the movement of a clearly outlined human shape. The next evening at Kate Fox's home, once the gaslight was extinguished, raps transmitted this message: "Watch closely, I am here." Gabriel Lalonne goes on to report:

> Immediately a luminous sphere appeared, which made some crackling noises. Several moments later, the sphere took the form of a head wearing a veil. Mr. Livermore instantly *recognized Estelle's features*. Soon a full shape became visible, which was illuminated by phosphorescent or electrical flashes that spread throughout the entire room.[15]

The figure vanished and then returned, as Livermore himself recounted:

> The shape renewed its appearance several times, and each time the *resemblance appeared more exact to me*. At one moment the head pressed against mine, *while its hair covered my face*.

More than three hundred séances followed during which Livermore witnessed Estelle's appearance. Once she stood motionless for an hour and a half, haloed by a gleaming light:

> While we gazed upon the apparition, her hair covered her face, and she pushed it back with several movements of her hand. Her hair was most tastefully adorned with roses and violets. This was her most perfect appearance, she absolutely seemed still alive.

She no longer spoke to him, but dictated letters that Kate Fox transcribed in "reverse writing" (meaning writing that can only be deciphered when held up before a mirror). During one séance Livermore placed two white cards on the table, along with a silver pen:

> I saw a hand holding my pen above one of these cards. This hand proceeded calmly from left to right, and when one line was finished, it went back to the left to start another.

He continued urging his wife to write him directly:

> A card that I had brought personally was removed from my hand and, after several moments, it was visibly returned to me. I read on it a message written in *pure French,* not a word of which Miss Fox could understand.

The dead woman wrote him a hundred notes in French, a language she spoke often—one dated Friday, May 3, 1861—and a graphologist they consulted identified the writing as hers. Livermore asked Mumler, a photographer medium, to take some pictures of his wife in various poses: one of these photos depicted her holding an armful of flowers over her husband's head. This was in the 388th séance, in which Estelle appeared for the last time to Livermore; but witnesses stated he subsequently received more discreet signs of her affectionate presence.

Again in America spiritualists experienced eroticism from beyond the grave without going through illusion-dealers like the Fox sisters in their Rochester dispensary. For example, P. B. Randolph mentioned his super-terrestrial love affair with the ghost of Cynthia Temple, a friend who died in 1856, who haunted him for two years in a most unique manner. She did not appear to him, but rather she was him: "I had an invincible conviction that I was Cynthia for the time being, instead of who and what I am. . . . for I was myself and Cynthia—never simultaneously, as is asserted to be the case with many of the people called 'Mediums'—but in separate instants—now her, then myself."[16] These transmutations were, at first, several minutes then lasting for three or four hours. When Cynthia replaced him, where did he go? "We are two in one, but the stronger rules the hour," he answered. *The Two-in-One* would be the very title given the book that his friend Thomas Lake Harris devoted in 1876 to his amorous relations with an invisible spirit, Lily Queen, with whom he boasted he had made a child in the spiritual world. The method was probably the same: periodic mergings of two souls in the individual concerned.

It was believed that for a dead person to materialize, he or she needed to borrow its substance from the fluidic body of the sleeping medium. Elaborate theories were constructed on this basis, which people sought to verify through experiments of "psychic science." The scientist Sir William Crookes performed an experiment on April 21, 1872, with Florence Cook at her parents' home. She was fifteen years old. There he saw "a shape calling itself Katie King partially materialize for the first time." With his friends Crookes decided to study this phenomenon; one of them even offered Florence Cook a large sum of money so that she would always make herself available at their disposition. The séance room included a cabinet in which the medium went into a trance. She had to be isolated in order for the materialization to take place. Katie first appeared against the curtains, silhouetted by the phosphorus lamp. William Crookes says:

For a long time, she only allowed a weak light when she materialized. Her head was always surrounded by white veils for she never formed completely, in order to use less fluid. After a good number of séances, Katie managed to appear in full light, with her face, arms, and hands uncovered.

When questioned she answered: "I disincarnated at the age of twenty-three; I lived during the end of the reign of Charles I. . . . I remember the large pointed hats of Cromwell's time quite well." The scientist was mocked for his gullibility, with his detractors maintaining that Florence Cook disguised herself to play the role of Katie King. In a letter to *The Spiritualist* on February 3, 1874, he responded that Miss Cook was bound in the office and that while Katie was before him, he "distinctly heard a sobbing moaning sound" behind the curtain.

Wearing a white dress and turban, Katie King stupefied him during a séance in Hackney:

> For nearly two hours she walked about the room, conversing familiarly with those present. On several occasions she took my arm when walking, and the impression conveyed to my mind that it was a living woman by my side instead of a visitor from the other world, was so strong . . .[17]

This long-bearded bespectacled chemist and physicist seemed to be in love with this dead woman who carried herself so well: "I asked her permission to clasp her in my arms. . . . Permission was graciously given and I accordingly did—well as any gentleman would do under the circumstances." It should be pointed out that Crookes's wife and two young daughters sometimes attended the séances. Experts made the objection that Katie King was the "externalized double" of Florence Cook; in the spiritualist milieu this projection of the self was believed possible. Furious, Crookes noted all the differences between them:

> Katie's neck was bare last night; the skin was perfectly smooth to touch and sight, whilst on Miss Cook's neck is a large blister, which under similar circumstances is distinctly visible and rough to the

touch. . . . Katie's complexion is very fair while that of Miss Cook is quite dark.[18]

He even goes so far as to take their pulse: "On applying my ear to Katie's chest, I could hear a heart beating rhythmically inside, and pulsating even more steadily than Miss Cook's heart did."[19]

Unappeased, his detractors then said that Katie was the "transfigured double" of Florence Cook. At that time it was accepted that a medium could externally project their fluidic body, which did not resemble them and was called a "transfiguration." But Crookes was unshakeable, exhibiting as proof to the contrary a lock of chestnut hair that the materialized phantom had allowed him to cut from her tresses. For three years the scientist and his friends maintained that Katie King was a dead woman who appeared when Florence Cook was lying on the floor behind the curtain with her head on a pillow, in a trance. Photographs were taken of Katie King, alone or with Crookes, who said: "But photography is as inadequate to depict the perfect beauty of Katie's face, as words are powerless to describe her charms of manner."[20]

The relations between the scientist and the ghost became increasingly tender: "For some time past, she has given me permission to do what I like, to touch her, and to enter and leave the cabinet almost whenever I pleased."[21] Was it because she felt he was on the edge of committing adultery with her that Katie King decided to return to the other world, while saying: "my work is done." Their last séance was full of pathos: "When the time came for Katie to take her farewell I asked that she would let me see the last of her."[22] But Florence Cook tearfully begged the apparition to remain on Earth: "I then came forward to support Miss Cook, who was falling on to the floor, sobbing hysterically. I looked round, but the white-robed Katie had gone."[23]

With the validation of a scientific figure like William Crookes (and in spite of all the fraudulent spiritualists who were then being exposed) many observers thought: "It is from the medium's own substance that the ghost constructs itself," and found it completely natural to see a vapor, a cloud from which a face emerged, or a "fluid hand" over the head of an entranced woman, which proved that the ghost did not have enough ectoplasm to fully form. Juliette Bisson had a series of experiences with her medium Eva Carrière from February 16, 1911, to June 17, 1913, which were intensely erotic and Sapphic in nature. They were the basis for accounts like the following:

> September 26, 1911. Madame B. is alone with Eva in a trance. She undresses herself and is naked. A head then forms next to hers and from it emerges a mass of a substance that spreads over her throat and each side of her bust; the curtains are open; Eva's hands are on her knees.[24]

> October 21, 1911. Madame B. is alone. Eva truly wishes to give her a séance while naked. Almost immediately a patch of gray substance appears on her belly, coming out of her navel. It emerges and falls back on itself like Vaseline coming out of a tube. A hand forms in the middle of this substance, then it is all reabsorbed back into the navel.[25]

All these ectoplasmic emissions have an air of sexual provocation:

> December 8, 1911. Eva is in a trance. Madame B. sees a substance emerging from her lower abdomen. This substance climbs up to her throat, it then moves back down to the navel where it is reabsorbed. It soon reappears, again emerging from the lower abdomen, crawling snake-like over the medium's body, rearing up like a living animal, then abruptly entering the mouth, which absorbs it entirely.[26]

There are often spectators, like Professor Schrenk, which adds an element of voyeurism to the latent lesbianism:

> January 5, 1913. Madame B. undresses Eva; she strips her naked down to the waist. A substance emerges from her navel, which forms into a mass before spreading and crawling upward. It is joined on her

chest by a ray of substance that is emerging from her mouth. A photograph is taken. After the magnesium flash, the substance appears to be gushing out of the medium's body. It is coming out of the tips of her breasts, her navel, her underbelly: it crawls, slides, and moves about before forming into a rounded mass again next to her navel.[27]

When Eva becomes the prey of the ghost of a bearded man who is squeezed out of this substance, the scene gets wild:

February 23, 1913. Barely seated, Eva falls into a trance: she is possessed immediately. She makes sharp cries that in no way resemble her usual wheezes and moans. She says that something is taking strength from her breasts and head, and she does not know where she is being taken . . . Eva makes a writhing movement, rises up several inches above the floor, and Madame B. sees an entire apparition projected on the back of the cabinet. . . . A photograph is taken. Following the magnesium flash, the ghost vanishes. All at once the medium is lifted up like before; her arms are in the air and she is writhing as she did before the apparition and gives the impression she is being jabbed in the back; she takes refuge in the left-hand corner of the cabinet, the ghost follows her.[28]

On April 23, 1913, Eva behaved as if the bearded man was an otherworldly lover who wished to wrest her away from Juliette.

At eleven in the morning, Eva started spitting blood; her throat was contracted and she complained of suffocating. While Madame B. made passes to release her, she went into a trance and announced that the ghost "worked her" and that he would return.[29]

At eight that evening, the experimental séance began:

Hardly had Eva gone into a hypnotic state, when she let out the strident cry that had already been heard under similar circumstances.

Madame B., believing that the great manifestation was about to appear, undressed Eva; the latter immediately was possessed by the writhing movements witnessed earlier; she rose up, sat back down, complained she hurt, and claimed she was being jabbed in the back; in fact, at the level of the sacrum a thick fluid somewhat like glycerin covered her back. With her two arms stretched forward, she made gestures for help and, at the same time, Madame B. saw, in full light, the ghost appear directly behind Eva.[30]

These two women shared a close friendship as Juliette was letting Eva live in her apartment on the rue George-Sand. "In January 1912, she moved in completely with me, sharing my life." Juliette believed in the substance released by Eva although a skeptic had told her,

The medium has a rubber tube that he swallows; this tube has a hand or fingers at its other end, which are also made of rubber. By blowing into the tube, whose free end the medium retains in her mouth, she can prompt movements similar to those of the fingers of a glove that has been filled with air.[31]

It would appear that Eva also put this tube in her vagina, because analysis of the substance revealed cells typical of the vagina's mucus membrane. Juliette also believed in the ghost of the bearded man although he appears to be a flat paper image in the photos. All the spiritualist experiments of this period have this illusionary character, but they nonetheless reflect a truly singular notion about the way a phantom can materialize out of a woman's body.

THE FRATERNITY OF MYRIAM

The strangest attempt of a group of initiates to benefit from the favors of an invisible woman was that of the Fraternity of Myriam at the beginning of the twentieth century. This brotherhood was founded by Giuliano Kremmerz (pseudonym of Ciro Formisano, born in 1861 in Portici near Naples, and died in 1930 at Beausoleil on the French Riviera). He was first a professor of history and geography at an Alvito high school (in the province of Caserta), but he always lived in his mother's house in Portici, which also had an occultist lodger. This individual introduced him to a dignitary of Grand Orient Freemasonry, Giustiniano Lebano, who put him in contact with Leone Caetini, prince of Teano. This prince was a politician, orientalist, and teacher of alchemy and sex magic to a small circle of disciples. In 1897 Formisano left Portici for an unknown destination; when he returned in 1893, he had become Giuliano Kremmerz, healer and esoteric specialist. In 1897 he created the magazine *Il Mondo secreto* (The Secret World), in which he explained his doctrine. Two years later he followed this with another journal, *La Medicina ermetica* (Hermetic Medicine).

Kremmerz's main goal was the healing of patients with magic. The full name of his organization was "The Therapeutic and Magic Fraternity of Myriam." To achieve this healing, he and his adepts joined wills to form a "magical chain" to influence the case being treated. Myriam was both the Divine Woman whose possibilities they deployed, as well as the chain itself. Kremmerz writes:

> The Myriam of the therapists is a wave of love emanating from an impulse center of unknown origins, a man, or a chain of souls. The allegory is mystical in appearance; it has the name of a woman—who was the first and most sublime of all female magicians—a receptacle, a pure treasure of love.[32]

The secret of the regenerative Myriam was the power to love, for, he said: "Love is material like heat, magnetism, light, electricity, radioactivity." The life-giving power of this material is a universal remedy, provided that those who apply it have previously purified themselves through rigorous asceticism.

Kremmerz established an inflexible educational system so that the Myriam healers would be true mages. He taught them that every human being has four bodies: the Saturnian body (physical), the Lunar body (etheric), the Mercurial body (soul), and the Solar body (spirit). If one wishes to acquire the ability to heal magically, one must gradually transition from the Saturnian body to the Solar body through practices like fasting, chastity, and contact with the beyond by any means (vision, audition, intuition, manipulation of graphic signs). The healing takes place "in a state of extra-normal exaltation" that the adept learns to amplify and control.

> He enters into the *Mag* field, a state of being that remains incomprehensible to anyone who has not experienced it . . . *Mag* is the power of active trance. . . . It is a state of shadowy, volatile, automatic trance, in all its deployments and achievements.

For long-distance healing of patients (telelurgy), the will must also be trained. "Whoever wishes and does not understand how to wish is not a mage and will never become one. Wishing is not desiring. To destroy any magic work, it is enough to desire without wishing."[33]

Myriam is not an already existing goddess to be supplicated; she is a feminine power that is created permanently either by a group or a couple or by oneself. Julius Evola explains:

> Every man has his own Myriam or "woman," who is the fluidic essence or living double of his own being. Myriam is also the collective chain or fluidic life force of the organization, invoked as a being or a higher spiritual influence by every participant for his own spiritual and operational integration and for the purpose of enlightenment.[34]

Kremmerz attached great importance to the cooperation of man and woman, on condition their relationship was one of pure love, serving to maintain the *Pyr*, or magic Fire, as noted, again by Evola:

> Other references to a path of Venus in Kremmerz's writings seem to be restricted to the lighting of a psychic fire (fire magic) between a man and a woman in a non-physical relationship.

Then, citing this observation from a Kremmerz monograph: "You must desire the soul, the being of the woman, just as her body can be desired," he analyzes it as follows:

> Eros propitiates in you the fluidic contact, and in its turn the fluidic state enhances eros. Thus an intensity of dizziness can be brought about which is unimaginable in the normal man and woman.[35]

The fluidic embrace, which scorns intercourse as an activity of the Saturnian body, travels on into the level of the lunar bodies of the two sexes, and lifts them toward their solar bodies.

Because of the discretion of Kremmerz's initiates, we have no detailed confessions at our disposal regarding their relationships with Myriam. She was not a polygamous spouse like the Sophia of the Society of Thirty, nor did she encourage their love affairs like the Babalon of the Astrum Argentinum. This abstract woman only existed when they went into a *Mag* state, and they experienced bliss from the very act that brought her into existence. Kremmerz said:

> It is neither self-hypnosis nor religious ecstasy; there is no word in modern languages to describe this state. The operator is plunged into a state of special ecstasy, in which he is not only submitted to their manifestations, but guides them by giving them strength.[36]

At the same time, Myriam was the fluidic woman that the man carries within himself, analogous to Jung's anima, and fire magic made it possible to bring her outside. The real woman also had a Myriam, who her lover strove to strip bare. The document cited by Evola supports this: magic truly begins when the man "staying in the most unlikely intensity of the *Pyr*, or magic fire, actually sees in his lover a being proper to the level he has attained." This same document assigns this objective to the Fraternity: how to keep the magic fire perpetually lit, what foods to feed it, and finally "how to unite with the being in question using Solomon's Seal." It was in order to take their pleasure from Myriam that the lovers long refused coitus, indulging only in "fluidic embraces" with each other. When they subsequently reached the point of performing the sex act, they operated in an isolated spot in the greatest mystery, in obedience to magic rites for preserving their subtle elements that were at risk of being lost during such an act.

In 1907, to escape the hassles of the police (who accused him of illegally practicing medicine), Kremmerz left the Naples region and settled in Vintimille, then Camogli, where, in 1910, he founded his review *Commentarium*. In veiled terms he revealed the sexual alchemy in use by the Fraternity of Myriam, which prompted Prince Caetani to break with him, accusing him of betraying the secrets of the initiation. These secrets were those of the Egyptian Grand Orient, which Caetani had introduced into the Myriam under Kremmerz's supervision. These were masturbation practices of a most unappetizing nature, requiring a masochistic mentality. In the first degree, the man performed a cycle of forty masturbations every nine days (the short cycle) or seventy-two over more than two years (the long cycle), each time swallowing drops of his own sperm. The woman masturbated during her period thirteen times in eighteen months (short cycle) or thirty-three times in two and a half years (long cycle) and swallowed drops of her menstrual blood after she reached orgasm. These operations ended in a ritual fast and by the ingestion of sperm (for the men) and menstrual blood (for the women), blended with an animal ferment, the "ortosvodum," the egg of an unspecified bird.

In the second degree, the man and woman masturbated facing each other, and ingested their sexual secretions blended together and also including the ortosvodum. "Contemporary schools also add salt and vinegar to this," says Massimo Introvigne. I will let him describe what follows:

> The secret of the third degree corresponds with three sex magic practices for couples—"black," "white," and "red" (sodomy, intercourse without ejaculation of semen, and intercourse while the woman is menstruating).[37]

These sexual relations are preceded and followed by ingestion of the second-degree mixture. Lastly there are the initiates five "retreats into darkness," each time during which the initiate remains in the darkness for seven days, periodically masturbating as in the first degree. Through these operations of sexual alchemy it is possible to "separate the subtle from the dense" and create an immortal "light body." Abstention from coitus was a requirement for years, except in the third degree (the protocol of which was ascetic). With regard to this regimen, Massimo Introvigne notes:

> An old follower of Kremmerz that I interviewed told me he did not think the young men and women of today would be capable of practicing this system, which in addition to the operations, presumes a total chastity at the level not only of actions but of ideas.[38]

Toward the end of his life, when he was living on the French Riviera, Kremmerz met his disciples in Monaco; it was said that "he won the money for his living expenses at the casino every day." Since his death in 1930, a dozen or so groups have taken him as their model and sought to continue his legacy. One of the main groups, which is headquartered in Messina, is mainly concerned with healing the sick. Another, the Ceur (the acronym for Casa Editrice Universale di Roma) has taken responsibility for ensuring the publication of Kremmerzian texts including an edition of their teacher's collected works. Others are more interested in his sexual alchemy than his fire magic, like Marco Massai, founder of the Lilith Group in Florence, which published *The Secrets of Sexual Magic* in 1991. However, Kremmerz's best work remains his notion of Myriam, a female entity who emerges from communal magical activity and ends up having a presence as tutelary as that of Isis.

6

The Art of
Riding the Tiger

It would be erroneous to think that sexual magic only draws its effects and powers from active operations performed with sex, in couples or groups in ritual ceremonies, and that those who practice it must indulge in endless copulations. To the contrary it also requires long periods of chastity, but a singular form of chastity that, far from resulting from a physical shortage of means for orgasmic activity, or the impossibility of finding available partners, falls more under the heading of a sovereign mastery of the senses and is practiced in a way that galvanizes the whole being. The mystics of the Far East call this state "riding the tiger": the act of bringing the instinct (in this instance, the sexual instinct) to the height of its force so as to benefit from its energy, and to hold it in check rather than satisfy it, by knowing how to control it and orient it away from its objective of climaxing, in order to attain with neutralized enthusiasm some spiritual purpose.

"All the true adepts have been independent even amidst torture, sober and chaste till death,"[1] says Eliphas Levi. This notion is based on the many recommendations to abstain from the sex act that can be found in religious and initiatory writings. Even alchemical treatises prescribe that the *filius sapientiae* (Child of Wisdom) should not sleep with his wife during the span of time he works in quest of the philosopher's stone. Sensual pleasure seems to be a solvent for the will, and when a person makes sex a priority, it has a fatal attraction that diverts the mind from its creative ideal. Continence is a means of accumulating the forces that are lost in orgasm, in order to employ them for a more urgent activity. This principle is not a byproduct of the Christian theory of sin, as one might think, since ethnologists have discovered such applications among primitive peoples.

As James Frazer explains in his study *The Golden Bough*, all hunting and fishing expeditions involved a temporary renunciation of sexuality:

Thus the Indians of Nootka Sound prepared themselves for catching whales by observing a fast for a week. . . . They were likewise required to abstain from any commerce with their women for the like period. . . . A chief who failed to catch a whale has been known to attribute his failure to a breach of chastity on the part of his men.[2]

The whalers of Madagascar and those of the southern coast of Alaska impose the same sexual taboo. In New Guinea, Oceania, Africa, and South America, groups of hunters feel so compelled to be continent that some isolate themselves in "men's houses." Others refuse to eat any food cooked by a woman or to look any individual of that sex in the face, not even their mother or sister. Warriors must also be chaste, as well as travelers: the Akamba and Akikuyus of East Africa refuse any sexual pleasure during a journey, even if their wives are with them in the caravan. A community undertaking demands abstinence from everyone:

Among the Ba-Pedi and Ba-Thonga tribes of South Africa, when the site of a new village has been chosen and the houses are building, all the married people are forbidden to have conjugal relations with each other. If it were discovered that any couple had broken this rule, the work of building would immediately be stopped, and another site chosen for the village.[3]

The priest kings of Africa earned their high positions through the same asceticism as King Kikulu, who did not have the right to touch a woman or leave his house. In the kingdom of the Congo, the supreme pontiff Chitome, regarded as a god, could leave his residence, but when he did so "all married people had to observe strict continence the whole time he was out, for it was supposed that any act of incontinence would prove fatal to him."[4] This is sympathetic magic: the waves from this act would make him assume, despite himself, a state of impurity against which he should guard himself in order to exercise his power. The ban also applied to adolescent masturbation. In the Humbe kingdom of Angola, the incontinence of young people under the age of puberty used to be a capital crime, because it was believed to entail the death of the king within the year.

The belief that continence has energetic virtues has been so strenuously advocated in all times and all places that it seems almost banal when we hear the following from Papus at the end of the nineteenth century: "The most rigorous rites impose fifty days of abstinence before the magic operation to the best trained practitioners."[5]

George Gurdjieff, whose teaching does not include any method of sexual magic, considered the "abuse of sex" as the greatest evil and the "chief form of slavery." However, Gurdjieff was not describing sexual excesses or perversions. His teaching refers

> to the wrong work of the centers and to the role of the sex center in this work. He spoke a great deal about how all centers rob the sex center of its energy and produce with this energy quite wrong work full of useless excitement and, in return, give to the sex center energy with which it is unable to work.[6]

For Gurdjieff man is a machine moved by "psychic centers" (there are seven, each divided into three parts or three *stages*), which function with particular hydrogens (that of sex is hydrogen 12). There should be no mixing: "Neither the thinking, nor the emotional, nor the moving centers can ever create anything *useful* with the energy of the sex center." In Gurdjieff's system—based on the "work" through which everyone transforms their physical body into an astral body—continence is optional, although it remains important. "Sexual abstinence is necessary for transmutation only in certain cases, that is, for certain types of people. For others it is not at all necessary."[7]

RED CHASTITY

It is easy to be chaste and abstain from sexual relations when you do not desire them in the first place. However, to remain chaste when confronted by desire, or even by intense desires, is so difficult that all religions from Christianity to Buddhism have seen this as a victory of the mind over the body—a victory that earns salvation in the next world. So there have been mystics and ascetics who have sought to put their chastity to the test of desire, going into the presence of a naked woman like a starving man to a banquet table, where he contemplates all the succulent dishes to the point of drooling, but refrains from touching any of them. It would obviously be absurd to do this for no good reason. An adept of High Magic practices this kind of abstinence to obtain a super-concentration of his intellectual faculties and to acquire a superior power of dominating the tangible world. We could call this a "red chastity," animated as it is by the fire of the passions, as opposed to a "white chastity" that is devoid of all passion (and which is the chastity recommended in the books of devotion).

Esoteric Christianity has taught red chastity, as have Hinduism and Taoism. The authoritative example is that of King David, who at the age of seventy would go to bed each night with a young girl, Abishag, without having sexual relations with her. The king's rabbis had selected her from among the most beautiful of Shunem. The Book of Kings does not say what exactly took place between King David and Abishag when they were wrapped up in the same blanket (as was the custom for couples sleeping together at that time), but the medico-magical principles of the time allow us to guess. The young girl was naked and pressed her body against that of the ailing monarch in order to transmit the vital heat of her youth and health to him. If he experienced an erection during this arrangement, she did not use it to satisfy her sexual needs: it was simply evidence that his forces were being restored at the contact with female flesh.*

In sanctioning such a precedent, the religious authorities adopted the custom of sleeping with a woman without touching her, and even the innocent contemplation of nudity. In the third and fourth centuries, virgins called *agapetes* (meaning "darlings" or "beloveds") would become attached to Christian priests. Abuses soon followed, which led the Council of Antioch in 269 to depose that city's patriarch, Paul, who was living with two *agapetes* after having gotten rid of another. The letter of dismissal said: "When it would be granted him that he would do nothing dishonorable, he should at least have feared the suspicion such conduct would produce out of fear of scandalizing someone or setting a bad example." In 314 the Council of Ancyra stipulated to the clergy: "We forbid that any cohabitate with virgins living with them as sisters." It was at this time that Saint Cyprian, Bishop of Carthage, wrote a treatise on this subject: "It is not permitted for churchmen, they who profess the most perfect continence, to lodge with virgins."

His arguments show how numerous and subtle were the partisans of red chastity. Syrian priests went so far as to bathe nude with naked women in the public baths, in order to prove they were capable of overcoming any erotic emotion in their presence. Cyprian protested against them:

> None of you did realize that you were thinking and telling yourselves: I wish a subject over which I can be victorious. This would be the same as telling yourself: "I wish to constantly live in the obvious peril of an imminent death." He condemned the paradox of a situation in which one was neither chaste nor depraved:
>
> What a fine sight it is to see these two projects of incontinence and chastity reciprocally supporting and destroying each other! Isn't

---

*"She took care of the king and waited upon him, but he knew her not," says 1 Kings 1:4.

there a great deal of spirit in this procedure of the immodest chaste? To earn themselves the glorious name of continence, they pretend to renounce pleasure, and to enjoy pleasures, they pretend to practice continence.[8]

Saint Cyprian assures his readers that it is impossible, even for an ascetic, to resist feminine appeal: "How many assaults does the man who approaches the immodest woman expose himself! Sins cluster around her like an army of brigands."[9] The pious man who lives with an agapete and takes pride in never touching her, will inevitably suffer turmoil

> when in their domestic duties, sometimes to perform certain tasks more comfortably, she will remove her stockings and roll up her sleeves, sometimes when made uncomfortable by the heat, she will remove some of her clothes, and sometimes when overcome with exhaustion, she will change expressions and postures a thousand times.[10]

While he might be able to resist a temptress like this, it may be impossible to prevent her from being tempted by him: "You have your own flesh to subdue, which gives you never a moment's peace! How is it that you think you are able to fight against the flesh of another?"[11] And even if the priest and agapete succeed in mastering their temptations, the Devil will make them victims of their affection.

> He pushes the continent man and the continent woman to live together, so that after they are bound by the indissoluble knots of reciprocal comfort and consolation, he can corrupt them using the same means they had sought to use to retain their purity.[12]

Saint Cyprian's exhortations did not curb the spread of red chastity. Aldhelm, a bishop in England in the late seventh century, had such strong sexual desires he was obliged to plunge into cold water up to his neck, even in winter, to extinguish them. But he decided that his merit would be all the greater if he was able to recite the entire Psalter next to a completely naked woman sharing his bed.

> He fled not women when he felt tempted; to the contrary, he chose one and slept alongside her until the temptation had passed and nature had restored his calm. He caused the Devil great wrath with this great victory; because this did not divert him from singing the Psalms and he sent back the woman without any prejudice to her honor.[13]

During the era of Courtly Love, this mystical technique became the rite of the *asag* (trial) in Provence, in which the lady verified through a trial if her servant was a sincere lover. To quote one of my earlier books:

> It was necessary to know if he was capable of the self-control essential for courtesy. The lady therefore invited her friend to share her bed; they remained naked all night with the permission to caress, but without ever doing the "deed." In the case where the man surrendered to temptation, this was proof he did not love her enough. He was expelled and declared unworthy of the *fin amor*.[14]

In the opposite case, she would reserve for him a repeat visit in which he would possess her carnally, because he knew how to do so differently than a beast satisfying its genetic needs.

The most remarkable case of a medieval Christian "riding the tiger" (though it might be more exact to say "riding the wolf" as this took place in France and at that time people called the penis the "wolf") was that of the monk Robert of Arbrissel "who several accused of sharing the beds of his nuns, though in truth not for taking his pleasure of them, but in order to contend with the strongest temptations," as the seventeenth-century lexicographer Pierre Bayle would later explain. After teaching theology in Angers and starting a college of regular canons in 1094, Pope Urban II named Robert of Arbrissel an apostolic missionary because of his eloquence. He chose to be an itinerant preacher, and traveled across France to preach the gospel, preferably to women.

> He walked barefoot through the streets and squares, in order to urge the girls of ill repute to repent, and he even went into the brothel to make his exhortations. One day he entered Rouen and there went by a fire to warm his feet. He found himself soon surrounded by women convinced he had come there to enjoy venereal pleasures, but he spoke to them of something entirely different: he announced to them the word on the life and mercy of the Son of God.

They cast themselves at his feet and promised to repent. "He took advantage of this good turn and, taking them all out of the city, led them to his retreat in the wilderness."[15]

By populating his hermit's lair this way, Robert of Arbrissel was able to found a monastery in the forest of Fontevrault at the end of two years of this apostolate; he would always return here after one of his preaching tours. He exclusively concerned himself with nuns, among whom were soon found daughters of the nobility like Pétronille of Chemillé, who became the first abbess of the Order of Fontevrault (a papal bull confirmed these privileges in 1113). Every time Robert of Arbrissel returned to Fontevrault, he slept in Pétronille's bed, without ever committing the sex act, in order to prove that carnal temptations could not defeat his virtue. This was insufficient, and other nuns were summoned to share the preacher monk's bed. According to Father Raynaud, Robert was quite harsh to ugly nuns but very gracious with the others: "Théophile Raynaud stated that Robert chose all the prettiest nuns when he wished to expose himself to temptation by sleeping with a woman."

His conduct was revealed when the letters of protest he received from the Abbot Geoffrey of Vendôme and Bishop Marbod of Rennes were published in 1610, with commentary by Ménage. Robert of Arbrissel eventually had numerous women accompany him on his preaching tours, probably sleeping with each of them in turn. "The priest of Mainferme, a cleric of Fontevrault, published three apologetic volumes in which he took great pains to justify his patriarch," by only admitting "that this holy man sometimes took Pétronille, abbess of the Order, and Angardis, prior of Fontevrault, on his journeys."[16] This seems to indicate that Robert had no hesitation about sleeping between two nude or semi-clad nuns. When he realized he was dying in 1115, he decided that the Order of Fontevrault would always be headed by a woman, something that had never been seen before in the history of monasticism. It was a fitting sign of his gratitude to the female body, which he had made into the instrument of his spiritual salvation.

Pierre Bayle compares monks like this sleeping with nuns to scientists performing an experiment:

> The secret they seek is inside a vase of which they can only touch the edges; all their movement around it, all their comings and goings are in vain, everywhere they find the circumference of the circle and never reach the center. This is the emblem of Robert, except—unlike them—he did not wish to penetrate to the heart of the mystery.[17]

This is a clever metaphor for accusing Robert of Ardrissel of not being contented by sleeping next to a naked woman, but of placing his hand on her underbelly to increase the desire to be held in check. "It is unbelievable how many heretics can be found who while professing to forbid marriage and full sexual bliss, still sleep with women and hug and kiss them, overlooking no manner of foreplay,"[18] says Bayle, who doubts the sincerity of the majority of these disciples of a chastity exposed to sexual tests.

> This is how these devoted adventurers, these hunters of hot opportunities, these hermits who leap into the beds young girls in order to demonstrate the courage of their continence, are only pouring oil on a fire hidden beneath the ashes. Are they not responsible for the desires they kindle? There is much to show that these men are not seeking a total victory.[19]

However, the behavior became customary in sixteenth-century society. Medical justification for it could even be found as it was alleged that contact with a woman's naked breasts would reinvigorate old men. In 1555 François de Billon wrote:

> Doctors cannot conceal the fact that the breast of a young woman, pressed against the stomach of an elderly individual, will vivify the natural warmth of life, and maintain and increase it. This was not unknown to the royal prophet David who chose the beautiful Shunammite to warm the chill of his old age in this way. A likely example of this is Monsieur d'Albret, grandfather of the last deceased king of Navarre. At the age of 120 he kept two beautiful young women for this purpose, whose milk he lived long on without any other substance; he slept in their midst and for this they were honored like princesses in his house.[20]

This fortunate old man therefore slept between two naked women during the last years of his life, after having nursed on their breasts. But they were not able to provide a continual supply of milk, without having children, so he was obliged to find more wet nurses. In any case female breasts, even when they are not lactating, release "subtle effluvia" that feed male energy. An old Taoist text cites the case of a monk who lived until the age of 107 because he was in the habit of sucking the breasts every morning of a young girl or woman who had not yet had a child. Candidates for this were numerous because the woman who had her breasts sucked by a sage rather than a baby also extended her own life.

For people outside the religious community, red chastity consisted of "sleeping together without orgasm" and was established by some Christians who did not wish to admit to their confessor any but the minor sins of lust. As an example, in a true story in *The Heptameron,* a woman permitted a young man to spend the night with her several times: "She consented to talk with him in bed, both lying there in their shirts as long as he asked no more of her beyond kisses and tender words."[21] He always managed to contain himself. In the debate following this story, an interlocutor says: "By keeping his promise to his lady, he made her suffer as much as himself or more." Montaigne revealed that he also practiced this form of libertine continence: "I do not consider it a miracle ... nor for a thing of extreme difficulty, to pass whole nights, where a man has all the convenience and liberty he can desire, with a long-coveted mistress, and yet be true to the pledge first given to satisfy himself with kisses and suchlike endearments, without pressing any further."[22]

I could go on forever if I wanted to list all the examples of machinations of this sort, which sometimes ended in tragedy. For example, Madaleine Bavent, one of the possessed nuns of Louviers, admitted in her general confession in Rouen, in 1602, what she had seen in the Louviers Convent, which she had entered at the age of sixteen. She was given a confessor and spiritual guide professing the following doctrine:

> He said we slay sin by a return to innocence and resemble our first parents, who went naked and unashamed before the fall. And beneath this apparently pious speech, how much filth and obscenity did he not utter? The nuns passed for being most holy, perfect, and virtuous, yet stripped and danced naked in the choir and went naked into the garden. That's not all: we were encouraged to touch each other immodestly: and do things I dare not say aloud that were infamous sins against nature. . . . Horrors! I have seen circumcision made on a figure that looked like paste to me, that others prayed to afterward to do as they wished.[23]

This is a resurgence of the doctrine of the Adamites, as described by Walter Schubart:

> The Gnostic sect of the Adamites in the second century adopted a fairly original form of fighting against sexual temptation: instead of fleeing it, they courageously faced it—man and women performed their divine worship in complete nudity.[24]

This Adamist tradition endured for a long time, so long that in an Inquisition trial in Toulouse, whose details were published in Amsterdam in 1692, a sect was punished because its members said: "We all strip nude amongst each other and atop one another, we kiss and tickle each other; this is how we show proof of our spiritual strength."

The notion of red chastity has continued to live on into the modern age. In his book *Le Vice Suprême* (The Supreme Vice), Joséphin Péladan, the "occult novelist" and founder of Catholic Rosicrucianism, drew a portrait of the mage Merodack who resembles him like a brother. Seeking to attain "metaphysical prowess" in Paris during the time of the Third Republic, this character strives to overcome the seven mortal sins within himself: pride, laziness, gluttony, and so forth. "It is of imperious necessity to tame Lust, this vice that is so universal and active that the psychologist has the right to make the Animal a character of his studies of the passions." To achieve this he throws himself into lust as a way to protect himself from it:

> Merodack saw naked women, and he was not tempted; he contrived ways to watch them undressing, at their toilet, when they rose and went to bed, when they kissed, and while they slumbered. He read all the literature of the flesh . . . he looked at all obscene art.[25]

He would go straight from frequenting hookers in their dives to spending time with the high society women of Saint Germain.

> He was proof against the shameless magic of the pelvis. . . . He would sit upon the sofa of excitation but only rise from it to flee. Behind him rose the insults spawned by the injured pride of the woman with whose desire he had toyed." He also focused his assaults on popular courtesans: "He went to those ugly, often stupid women who had been voluptuously magnetized by the vice of many men. This was the final effort of his prophylaxis of Mithridates."[26]

By exposing himself this way to aphrodisiacal promptings and never surrendering, Merodack strengthened his psychic faculties.

> The Beast was vanquished in all its many forms; it had to be hunted down. He went through several days of delirium and fever, and for a full two months was obsessed by lubricious phantoms that he finally purged from his astral field.[27]

When Merodack attained "absolute continence," his self-initiation was complete: "An ineffable sense of well-being flooded through him; he felt invested by boundless power. As a master of himself, so he would be of others, whenever he wished." The perverse Princess d'Este, who tried to rattle him by undressing in front of him, felt an electrical shock from his cold, hypnotic eyes. He became a living force, whose will could be transmitted by a simple handshake.

In the twentieth century, Mahatma Gandhi was the most perfect representative of this tendency that consists of obtaining powerful mental energy by exacerbating your sexual energy and then sublimating it. The psychoanalyst Erik H. Erikson explained his behavior to those who told him, "You know, of course, that Gandhi had naked girls sleep with him when he was an old man." Gandhi had once led a sexually precocious life, accompanied by moral scruples, and when he left to pursue his studies in England, he swore an oath before his mother that he would abstain from wine, meat, and women. He kept his word, although he was a hearty eater, and became a steady customer of *The Center*, London's vegetarian restaurant.

When he returned to India as a lawyer and a married man with a family, Gandhi made *Satyâgraha* (passive resistance) the core principle of his political activity, by using vows of abstention as symbolic weapons. For example, "he would not drink milk because of the cruelties inflicted on cows." Not only did he fast from eating, he fasted from sex. In 1906, at the age of thirty-seven, Gandhi made public his vow of chastity, the *bramacharya*, which included "purity not only of the body but that of thought and speech." He told his wife Kasturba: "We are tried friends, the one no longer regarding the other as an object of lust." His continence was a means of action, for he thought violence could only be overcome by "sexual self-disarmament." Accordingly, he tried to inculcate his fellow citizens with the same self-respect. He fasted for a week to show three libertines (a young girl and two boys who had fornicated together) that their bad behavior caused him suffering. The young girl wept, fasted with him, and shaved her head. His ideal, Gandhi explained in a telegram to Winston Churchill, was "to be as naked as possible." This physical and moral nakedness was based on red chastity.

In fact, it was the practice of sexual fasting that trained him for his political fasts like that of Ahmedabad, when he decided he would not take any nourishment until the textile factory workers got a raise. "The fast, begun on March 15, 1918, was the first of seventeen fasts 'to the death' which Gandhi was to undertake throughout his long life. In later years, all of India would hold its breath while the Mahatama fasted, and whole cities would leave their lamps unlit in the evening in order to be near him in the dark."[28] It is easy to see that if an ascetic like Gandhi had squandered his strength in sexual relations, he would have been less obstinate and had less vigor for overcoming hunger and undernourishment. However, abstaining from intercourse did not mean abstaining from the presence of women, as we shall see. Writing in a newspaper in 1936, Gandhi responded to the English who continually expressed their surprise that he had not ceased being surrounded by women and touching them: "I have never believed that all contact with a woman should be avoided for appropriate observance of *brahmacharya.*"

For example, when his wife Kasturba was on her deathbed, she asked him to take care of her orphan niece Manu, who was fourteen. Gandhi became so attached to her that he had her sleep on a mat at the foot of his bed and later next to him, with both of them naked. Arthur Koestler recounts how the British police surprised Gandhi in bed with a naked young girl and retreated without demanding any explanation. Erikson minimizes the incident by noting: "there were neither beds nor doors in the sleeping arrangements, that nakedness is a relative matter in the tropics, and that the whole matter never was a secret."[29] Gandhi's relationships were more ones of marriage than libertinage, as Manu describes in her 1949 book *Bapu—My Mother*. The sexual magic he was after when he made her sleep naked next to him was therefore not to awaken his virility, or even to overcome it, but to acquire a femininity identifying him with Shakti, goddess of universal energy.

A major crisis occurred in the Hindu leader's political activity, which accentuated his self-defense process.

> This occurred in the very last phase of Gandhi's life when the Mahatma was 77 and 78 years old, and when in Lear-like desperation he wandered among the storms and ruins of communal riots which seemed to mark an end of any hope of a unified India. At night he at times suffered from severe attacks of shivering; and he would ask some of his middle-aged women helpers to "cradle" him between them for bodily warmth.[30]

This was no longer a young girl but three or four fully developed matrons who plopped their heavy breasts on the ascetic's chest, rubbed their generous bellies over his hips and wrapped him in their lavish thighs, took him in their arms in turn to rock him, placed their rumps on top of his frozen feet until his shivering stopped, and his entire body began to get warm again. These were no servants but high-caste women, whose names were whispered in Erikson's ears by Nirmal K. Bose*: "Considering the personages involved, however, I doubt that the story will ever be fully told."[31]

On more than one occasion these arrangements gave the old man an erection, and he proudly proclaimed how he had not taken advantage of it to take his pleasure from one of his "cradlers." As Erickson said:

> Some of his best friends parted ways with him when Gandhi made things immeasurably worse by claiming publicly that by having

---

*This acquaintance of Gandhi was the first author to reveal the Mahatma's sexual magic practices.

(sometimes naked) women near him at night he was testing his ability not to become aroused. This implied, of course, proving to himself by implication that he could be.[32]

Gandhi stated: "If I can master this . . . I can still beat Jinnah," meaning avoid the partition of India advocated by his adversary Jinnah.

This will to avoid orgasm—through which Gandhi fortified his will for nonviolence—is a sexual magic principle that some ascetics observe even during coitus, as I noted above. He abstained from consummating relations with the naked women he had around him, who were readily available for sex, in the same way he abstained from drinking milk or eating meat; and this ability to resist eminently desirable things ensured his ability to be a pacifist combatant.

AUTO-SEXUAL MAGIC

In addition to the red chastity that some have imposed upon themselves in order to increase their moral strength, there is also the solitary satisfaction pursued by masturbating in a specific way called "auto-sexual magic." This revalorization of masturbation is the work of modern practitioners, as no prescriptions for the practice can be found in Tantra or Taoism. P. B. Randolph was entirely hostile toward it, in the name of "spermatic economy," and he accused masturbation of causing "depletion of the vital forces," and a lowering of nervous tone and will. In his book *After Death,* Randolph revealed how he had discovered the horrific consequences of onanism in 1854 and had striven ever since to cure it, either with his elixirs or by making the onanist wear an "electromagnetic disk" on his head or over his body at night to preserve his vital fluid.

The reason that solitary vice is so destructive is because there is no electrical, magnetic, or chemical reciprocation—no natural leverage; all is lost and nothing whatever gained; it is all intensity, no diffusion—and the effects are analogous in the case of either sex, for each alike [is] guilty of this mode of self-murder, and are both rushing down the same declivity to—ruin; and both lose more life and vitality in such a debauch than in *ten* normal intercourses.[33]

This is why he offered his patients—for five dollars—an anti-masturbation disk that would spare them this inconvenience.

Another occult theory, formulated by Paracelsus and based on the Kabbalah, was that elementary spirits were born from Adam's ejaculations when, before the creation of Eve, he masturbated while dreaming of a companion. By virtue of this, the masturbation of a man will also engender larvae in the astral plane or attract those that are already there as they are wild about the odor of sperm. It was therefore difficult for occultists to sing the praises of masturbation, let alone accept it as a legitimate sexual activity, especially since throughout the nineteenth-century harebrained medical notions derived from Samuel Tissot's atrocious book *On Onanism* ran rampant. These theories presented masturbators as the shameful sufferers of an illness that demanded the most radical treatments, including surgery. Paradoxically, it was a priest ("A bad priest but still a priest," as André Breton said about Young, the author of *Night Thoughts*) who was first to attempt to sanctify the autoerotic use of sex.

Mystical masturbation was superlatively developed in the Work of Mercy founded in 1839 by Eugene Vintas in Tilly-sur-Seule, to prepare the reign of the Holy Ghost. This heresiarch was subject to visions and stigmata, and he overstimulated his disciples with fake miracles. Condemned to five years in prison, he left the leadership of his community to his disciple, Abbé Marechal, whose mystical exaltation was of quite another nature:

Starting in the earliest days of July, the Abbé Marechal declared he was inspired and could commune with heaven. He began giving prophetic consultations at night. He would give them while lying in bed in his room with his eyes closed and grimacing with ecstasy. He took care to announce their day and designate those who would be permitted to witness them.[34]

In this state he transmitted what he called the "holy liberty of God's children," a doctrine teaching "as a means of slaying lust, that the acts of the most revolting impurity are acts that are pleasing to God, when one lifts his soul towards him, and when one goes into his holy presence to commit them."

After his revelation masturbation became "the daily bread of some of his penitents—both men and women." They did not masturbate separately in hiding, but in a group while watching each other as if they were praying together. The journalist who exposed their doings wrote:

> To commit this shameful sin, a woman of a more than ripe age, a forty-eight-year-old spinster living in Tilly, a young woman sent on pilgrimage to this valley by her trusting husband, a young girl of sixteen, her thirty-two-year-old brother, a young man of thirty-six whose life had been chaste and pure until this time, and finally the priest, their corruptor. Sometimes they gathered all together in the Cenacle, whose doors they carefully sealed from within, sometimes they shut themselves off in pairs, to indulge themselves without constraint in everything the demon of impurity could suggest to them by way of turpitudes.

It was by listening to the sinners' confessions in the church confessional that Abbé Marechal was able to tell if they had "attained the degree," meaning they were open to his notion "preached only to those men and women he believed capable of tasting it and putting it into practice." He taught them that masturbation was a *sacrifice of love*.

> This sacrifice, according to the priest and adepts, was one of the most pleasing to God that the blessed children of his labor could commit. He recommended that *those who feel sympathy for one another* to often offer it together. *Each time they did it, they were sure to create a spirit in heaven.* Offered alone, it did not have that power.[35]

Abbé Marechal began by seducing the sixteen-year-old girl, Marie. After spending a night masturbating with Marie in her room, he said to the older woman, Josephine: "This child has crossed the barrier; would you like to cross it, too?" She did not have to be asked twice.

> The old maid Josephine, who was forty-eight or forty-nine, enthusiastically accepted this proposition and from this moment became one of the most zealous assistants of the confessional.[36]

Adrien Gozzoli, who knew these details through Marie, recounted:

> I know that the young girl, who by the way is a relative of mine, became quite familiar with all these infamies, which became imperious needs for her. She committed this crime with each of the guilty parties in turn, especially, most habitually, with the priest. She also committed it—my pen shudders as I write this—with her own brother.[37]

The brother even boasted of masturbating with his sister, and claimed he did so more to relieve her than to satisfy himself. "He made this confidence to a believer he sought to drag down into the filth with him." How did this masturbation in pairs or several people take place? They probably sat in chairs facing each other, with their pants down or with their long dresses of the time of Louis Phillipe I bound up around their waist, letting the genitals they were handling be seen by all those present.

Abbé Marechal must have directed these collective masturbations with as much frenzy as he said his masses.

> He celebrated the holy mass while sobbing in the noisiest way. Once the holy sacrifice was over, he hurled himself on all those in attendance, regardless of sex. He gave them never-ending embraces. He yelled out, while still weeping and sobbing, "Love! Love! Love!" and everyone had to repeat this word and imitate him in these tender demonstrations.[38]

It is likely that similar shouts and trances accompanied the masturbators of Tilly-sue-Seule until they reached orgasm.

The young married woman, a native of Sarthe, was so fascinated by the priest that she followed him everywhere like his shadow: "It once happened that she spent twelve whole hours with this corruptor in the room of the Cenacle." In reference to this, one of the priest's acolytes told the faithful: "The father just had twelve hours of ecstasy!" The same woman is notale for her attacks of hysteria: "The sense of this poor creature who had been stimulated and irritated without relief by this shameless priest, threw her into a state of almost permanent feverish agitation." This man was a sexual hypnotist of the first order, as is evident from this anecdote:

Abbé Marechal was sitting at the table used for common meals in the downstairs room that led to the chapel, surrounded by believers of all ages, among which were some travelers who had come from a great distance. There were people to his right and left, and people behind him. A pious woman who felt she was not as close to the good father as she wished, to display her affection as conveniently as the others, she got up on the table in front of him, and half-sitting, half-crouching, she did not confine herself to kissing him. She even went so far, it must be said, as to lick his face from time to time.[39]

The members of the Order of Mercy must also have masturbated each other on occasion, if we can believe the following scene:

One July evening in 1845, Abbé M—, Miss Josephine G—, Mrs. G—, and her daughter Marie, a young peasant girl of Tilly, and two other people were gathered together in the downstairs room of the apartment known as the *chapel room.* They were all conversing. All at once, in the middle of the conversation, under the very eyes of her mother, the young Marie went up to the priest and put her hand on him . . . and inside his clothes."[40]

This scabrous gesture appeared completely natural to everyone present. The priest exclaimed with a smile: "It is the simplicity of childhood!" and the mother approved.

This experiment in religious collective masturbation only lasted a year, for Adrien Gozzoli lodged a complaint against Abbé Marechal, who fled and was replaced as head of this establishment by Abbé Charvoz, who did not share the same principles. The fact remains that this was no example of everyday libertinism, but an audacious attempt to sanctify sex in the name of the Holy Ghost who purifies everything. Abbé Marechal wished for masturbation to no longer be treated as a solitary vice but as a convivial virtue. Strange as this may appear, he found fellow Christians to share his views and to believe they were freeing themselves from sin by giving new value to the act of Onan.

Next, at the beginning of the twentieth century, at the very time Freud and his disciples were taking a stand in their Wednesday meetings against the prejudiced who viewed masturbation as harmful, occult movements were restoring it to honor, as if it were a prayer, an invocation, or a spiritual exercise as venerable as any other. At Theodor Reuss's instigation, the O.T.O. began teaching its adepts the best ways to masturbate (in its Eight Degree instructions), before Aleister Crowley, an innovator on all points of magical eroticism, made auto-sexual magic a branch of the Royal Art.

There are two elements that coordinate in masturbation: the mechanical, repetitive gesture of handling the sex organ until orgasm is achieved; and the "activating fantasy," a series of stimulating images that roll out in the masturbator's mind like a sequence from a pornographic movie. In order for this to have a magical effect, these two elements must undergo a transfiguration. The gesture is not just made at any time or in any manner. It has the nature of a ceremony, and—like sacred intercourse—it will be of greater worth if it takes place in a room that has been transformed into a "temple" through the presence of an altar bearing the image of the person the masturbator wishes to take possession of with this act. The "activating fantasy" will take on cosmic or mythological proportions. One does not masturbate while thinking about someone in one's immediate reality, known or perceived, or an individual one wishes to meet, bedecked in all kinds of libidinous glamours, but by imagining that one is making love with a god or goddess, or a king or queen, for in this way masturbation ennobles the individual performing it.

An act like this has the power to fulfill a wish made at the moment of orgasm. According to Crowley one should not forget to say *"Fiat"* (as in the biblical phrase *Fiat Lux,* "Let there be light"). This Fiat will be followed by the indication of what someone desires to be: a financial return, a trip, a new love affair. As not everyone is capable of translating their wish into Latin, it is enough to say *"Fiat Fortuna"*: "let there be fortune." Fortune in this case can mean good luck, wealth, success, and even that secret power the kabbalists call the "fortune of the soul."

Aleister Crowley, who wrote a treatise on the "secret weddings of gods with men" (*De nuptiis secretis deorum cum hominibus*), advised his disciples to masturbate while imagining they were the partner of a god or goddess. In the Opus that Crowley personally wrote down in his magical record when he masturbated (while specifying "with the left hand" or "full hand"), it was through visualization of the goddess Babalon, and while always considering whether the "elixir" was of good or poor quality. But he also masturbated while invoking aloud Hermes, and while imagining himself in front of the god, or even behind as he sodomized him. This was the case in New York on January 14, 1915, at 11:33. The object of the rite was "Energy," as he felt profoundly depressed. *Hermes per anum manibus,* he wrote, meaning that he had masturbated his anus with one hand and his penis with the other, while convincing himself that the god was penetrating him in an act of anal intercourse.

> The operation was most extraordinary. I figured the God well on the whole, and experienced the complete orgasm without the emission of even a single drop of semen. Erection then failed. I wanted to go on, but the God spake and said: "Thou hast thy will. Depart; write down the record, and make a particularly careful study of the stars." I obey.[41]

Another master of auto-sexual magic was Austin Osman Spare, whom we discussed earlier. Influenced by Mrs. Patterson, the old fortune-teller he regarded as a second mother and who initiated him into "warlock love," Spare was disposed to bizarre sexual experiments. Kenneth Grant says:

> His most memorable adventures were those with a fierce Welsh maiden, a dwarf woman with a flat nose and beetling brow, and a hermaphrodite.[42]

As it was not possible to come across such specimens every day, Spare devoted himself to systematic and skillfully employed masturbation. His imaginary partners were not known or unknown pretty women but horrible witches he evoked by putting himself in a trance and which he finally believed he could see half materializing before him. He called the entity that became visible and often visited his home an "intrusive familiar" like Black Eagle, a birdman who appeared whenever he created automatic drawings. Mrs. Patterson had taught him her method for communicating with the elementals (different from the elementary spirits), which she visualized in the form of animals from the invisible realm who conferred supernatural powers upon man.

Austin Osman Spare did not have the impression that the women who appeared to him when he masturbated came from the remote regions of space. He attributed these apparitions to the deepest layer of his unconscious, and they appeared no less alive to him because of it. A member of the Theosophical Society, he put into practice what Franz Hartmann professed:

> Every emotion that arises in man may combine with the astral forces of nature and create a being, which may be perceived, by persons possessing higher faculties of perception, as an active and living entity.[43]

To convoke his "intrusive familiars," Spare drew a sigil on a card that he placed over his forehead while muttering a charm. He claimed a greenish mist would seep into the room, from which emerged female forms with glowing eyes. He masturbated while believing he was taking part in an orgiastic witches' sabbat with the worst devotees of witchcraft, as he described this way:

> The Witch so engaged is old, grotesque, worldly, and libidinously learned and is sexually attractive as a corpse; yet she becomes the entire vehicle of consummation.[44]

In fact, by binding himself through masturbation with the most seasoned witches of the Middle Ages, Spare intended to give more magical force to the desire he had enclosed in an urn. In his *Zoëtic Grimoire of Zos,* he explained his procedure.

> Now unto this period I had copulated only the atmosphere or rode whores, lined old hags, witches, and bitches of all kinds, there being few virgins. The autotelic wish into heterotelic conception is by concummation through using an urn of correct shape and dimension—which must correlate nearly to that of the lingam used—so that there is sufficient vacuum. At the moment of orgasm the wish must be *imperatively stated*. After ejaculation seal the vase with your sigil and with the secret formula of your desire. Bury same at midnight, the moon being quartered. When the moon wanes, disinter and pour contents as libation into earth with suitable incantation, and re-bury same. This is the most formidable formula known, never fails and is dangerous.[45]

Kenneth Grant adds the following commentary in his book on Spare: "It should not be necessary to add that it is not in the actual sigil that the power resides—this is merely the vehicle of the desire—but in the intention sent into the vase at the moment of spermatic effusion."[46]

Spare's painting and drawings also reflect the visions that fed his auto-sexual magic. His last exhibition in London in 1955 included wooden "*stelae*" with titles like *Desire for Vampires and Succubi,* and "psychic" studies such as *Ghosts I Have Seen,* and *Materializations Witnessed.*

It is possible to proceed in a less morbid manner by choosing historical heroes and heroines as partners for mental masturbation, like Apollinaire did in his short story *The Moon King.* Inside an underground Tyrolean shelter in which King Ludwig II of Bavaria is living, he sees young people lying on the ground near devices to which they are connected by a slowly turning belt:

> The hands of these young men strayed in front of them as if over supple, beloved bodies, and they gave the air amorous kisses. Soon they became more irrepressible and lascivious and wedded themselves to the emptiness. I was taken aback, as if I had witnessed the disturbing games of a college of priapic maniacs.

As the purpose of these devices was to bring back a portion of time, for only a few minutes, and to make its contents visible and palpable, their users believed they were making love with Cleopatra, the Abbess of Gandersheim, Michelangelo, or Lola Montez. The narrator tried one of these devices and experienced their effectiveness: "immediately there materialized before my ravished eyes a naked body which was smiling up at me voluptuously." He quickly grasped that he was making love with Leda, and before leaving, he wrote on a wall: "I have cuckolded the swan"—a reference to Jupiter, who adopted that guise when approaching his lover.[47]

With his poet's intuition, Apollinaire anticipated the "cybernetically assisted masturbation" that I discussed in my book *The Doctrinal of Amorous Bliss,* for it is inevitable that the progress of virtual games and cybersex will induce some adepts of auto-sexual magic to its practice through the twenty-first century using the scientific array of computers, helmets, screens, and consoles. But they would be wise to keep in mind what I also said:

No sophisticated masturbation with the help of instruments resembling medical prostheses or industrial robots will bring a voluptuous sensation superior to that of natural masturbation, the hand caressing the genital organ.[48]

Women can of course cultivate auto-sexual magic just as easily as men. The only difference lies in the specificity of female physiological reactions during masturbation. If this masturbation is performed solely by stimulating the clitoris with the finger, the woman is capable of repeated orgasms with no need for recovery time in between. She has the capability of shouting *"Fiat Fortuna!"* five or six times in one session, and sometimes more. She can also experience so much satisfaction from the rumination of her activating fantasy that she does not even need to have an orgasm. Her climax is a trance occurring during its fabulation because she experiences it in a fever pitch. This was the "erotic daydream" of Belle, the patient of psychoanalyst Robert J. Stoller. She was twenty-four, unmarried, and a Baptist born in the southern United States. Belle could not reach orgasm when she masturbated. But she climaxed within by imagining she was experiencing a situation of this nature:

A cruel man, the Director, a Nazi type, is directing the activity. It consists of Belle being raped by a stallion, which has been aroused to a frenzy by a mare held off at a distance beyond where Belle is placed. In a circle around the periphery stand vaguely perceived men, masturbating while ignoring each other, the Director, and Belle. She is there for the delectation of these men, including the Director, who, although he has an erection, makes no contact with her.[49]

In other erotic daydreams, Belle imagined she was watching men while they urinated on women, or the Queen of the Amazons making her warriors whip young girls. These are the kinds of mental scenarios manufactured by those dedicated to auto-sexual magic. They are so akin that initiatory episodes are mixed in with the obscene excesses: the Nazi

Director of Belle's erotic daydream, for example, would be replaced by the high priest of a pagan cult.

There has not yet been a woman to write a complete theory of auto-sexual magic for her fellow sisters such as Austin Osman Spare did for men. However, Dion Fortune (pseudonym taken by Violet Firth in 1919 when she was a member of the Golden Dawn) would have had the requisite experience and competence. She was considered as "Aleister Crowley's female counterpart" and it is said that she put together a harem of dead historical figures. Her sexual relations with them could only be masturbatory in nature. In 1924 she published *The Esoteric Philosophy of Love and Marriage,* which dealt with spiritualist eroticism. That year was when she first made contact with her earliest teachers from the other world: Melchizadek; Socrates; Lord Thomas Erskine, the lawyer who became chancellor following William Pitt's rule; and David Castres, a young officer killed in Ypres during the First World War. To meet them she made journeys in the astral plane based on her own personal method: "It involves self-hypnosis achieved by means of a symbol. This symbol works like a door giving access to the invisible world." She therefore knew to what sector she was going, instead of wandering in search of adventure.

> These astral journeys are really lucid dreams in which one retains all one's faculties of choice, will-power and judgment. Mine always begin with a curtain of the symbolic colour through whose folds I pass.[50]

In 1927 Dion Fortune married Thomas P. Evans, a doctor who put his residence (3 Queensborough Terrace) at her disposal, which became legendary as the headquarters of the Fraternity of Inner Light, which she founded in 1928. In her novels and essays she developed "a type of magic, called sex magic, even though it was a sexuality expressed in discreet terms," according to Massimo Introvigne. He went on to say: "For Dion Fortune, male sexual energy could not provide magical results unless it was awakened and guided by the analogous energy of the woman."[51] She performed experiments for discovering her previous lives in Atlantis and King Arthur's England, where her husband was the wizard Merlin. Around 1935 she began practicing the rites of Isis with her disciples in a converted Presbyterian church called "The Belfry." She describes these rites in her novel *Moon Magic.* Her husband left her in 1939 for a medical colleague with no interest in magic. Dion Fortune continued until her death in 1946 with her mystical love affairs with the deceased masters of the Tradition. If she climaxed sexually in these relations, it was probably without the use of her hands or any other aid; in a manner similar to Belle who engaged in her erotic daydreaming with such intensity.

Usable scenarios for female auto-sexual magic can be found in Unica Zürn's *Man of Jasmine.* Zürn, although not an esotericist, exploited magical thought excessively during the schizophrenic episodes that led to her internment. In love with Henri Michaux (the "man of jasmine" of the title), she invented "games for two" in order to possess him in dream: the game of extension (she saw him in his room three meters tall), the game of incorporation (he absorbs her into himself), the game of harmony (while she sleeps, he lies down outstretched in her body as if it were a sarcophagus), and others. Imagining the unwinding of these games gave her bliss without orgasms, in contrast to the imaginary intercourse of another resident of Saint Anne's, whom she observes with the feeling that her own auto-eroticism is preferable:

The woman is in the midst of an extremely intense erotic crisis. Her hands are tied; one cannot see her arms. She tosses back her head and pokes out a wiggling tongue. With an enormous exertion she attempts to get close to her imaginary partner. It is clear to see that she in in the throes of intense sexual pleasure. Finally she slumps down on her mattress and rests, trembling. Her face twists into a grimace. Not five minutes later the scene is repeated. Without a male partner or touching herself, she enters into physical rapture more than thirty times in just one hour.[52]

This semi-conscious woman who mimed intercourse also behaved in a way that was fitting for auto-sexual magic, but in a less pure form than that of Unica Zürn, who felt hypnotized from a distance by the man of jasmine, who sent her hallucinations, like that of being inside a room invaded by bird wings—without the birds—flapping and flying about in all directions.

We are only afforded a glimpse of the possibilities for auto-sexual magic in today's world, for we are lacking the accounts that would allow us to draw up a complete picture. However, this form of magic fully exists, and it is only the discretion demanded by initiatory organizations of their members that prevents the latter from popularizing, with public revelations, the principles that enliven their work in this area. It is foreseeable that the practice of auto-sexual magic will evolve over the course of the twenty-first century and find itself illustrated by personal confessions, allowing an author in the year 3000 to write a book like mine based on the countless documents that will then be available for citing on specific points.

7

Magical
Sex Aids

In the beginning of this book, I discussed traditional magic spells—
potions, charms, incantations, the procedures for casting enchantments
and counter-enchantments—examples of which can be found in the
most remote past, such as on the cylinder seals of Sumer and the papyri
of Pharaonic Egypt. I have yet to analyze the magical sex aids that relate
to astral, terrestrial, or animal magnetism, for while they figure in the
above-cited occult methods, their users did not know it yet, for it was
only in the eighteenth century that occurences previously seen as supernatural were defined as natural phenomena.

It is important to keep in mind that the sex aids such as the preparation of a talisman or the execution of a magnetically eroticizing massage—
which belong more or less to ceremonial magic although this may not
be readily apparent—need to be realized with a certain liturgy in order
to have their magical aspect manifest itself. Massimo Introvigne rightly
notes that there is a "profound difference between ceremonial magic and
initiatory magic; although both speak of initiation, in ceremonial magic
the accent is placed on the efficacy of the ceremonies and not on the legit-
imacy of the initiatory chain."[1] The actual or symbolic ceremonies of ceremonial magic, Pierre V. Piobb informs us, can be solemnities, sacrifices,
or supplications. The common rites are: orison, invocation, aspersion,

unction, sealing (in order to connect with the operational forces), which "the operator performs while holding the sword in the left hand and making the signs with the right, while pronouncing the *hieratic words*."

During the century of Louis XIV, when Bousset railed against "the images named talismans, imbued with celestial virtues," it was a Benedictine bishop, Dom Jean Albert Belin, who took up their defense, by stating that the first ones had been crafted by Adam himself: "If this science was Adam's inspiration, it is neither vain nor superstitious." Belin provides the following etymology:

> Although some maintain that the word "talisman" is derived from the Greek *telesma,* which means "perfection," because talismans are the most perfect thing in this world . . . I prefer to believe it came from the Hebrew word *tselem,* which means "image."[2]

Hence his definition:

> A talisman is nothing other than the seal, figure, character, or image of a heavenly sign, planet, or constellation, crafted, imprinted, engraved, or carved on a sympathetic stone or a metal corresponding with the celestial body.[3]

They can also be written on parchment, but in whatever manner they are created, they are objects that allow the owner to benefit from a planetary influence to promote his affairs.

We should first distinguish between the amulet, talisman, and pantacle. It was Pliny the Elder who first introduced the word *amuletum* to designate a natural mineral, plant, or animal object that protected people from certain illnesses or peril. As Henri Meslin says: "The primary difference between the talisman and the amulet is that the first is active and the second only acts as a protector." If someone wants to win the love of another who does not love him or her, a talisman is required; but if an individual only wants to avoid a fiasco during a night of love, brought on by erectile dysfunction or premature ejaculation, an amulet is what one needs. As for the pantacle (which many dictionaries write as pentacle, confusing it with the pentagram or five-branched star), it is a kind of shield against invisible malefic forces, about which Piobb says: "The pantacle is an instrument of protection for the magic worker. It plays the role of *insulator*." He sees this word as derived from the Greek *panta-kléa* (from *pan* meaning "all" and *kleos,* "glorious," in plural form: an object "for all glorious actions"). A pantacle can be lent to a friend, who will receive equal protection from it, whereas a talisman has an individual character and can only be used by the individual for whom it was made.

Georges Muchery, an astrologer who has made many talismans for his clientele, defines each of them as "a fluid capacitor, which must be aided by a personal effort." In fact, a talisman demands to be *sustained,* which means it is not a good luck charm. Its power is also limited to a predetermined action: "It can only help satisfy one single desire, thus in practice there are as many talismans as there are desires."[4] I am only going to examine love talismans here, of course, which were viewed as shameful by MacGregor Mathers, Master of the Golden Dawn, who claimed: "a talisman made for terrestrial love would be sealed with the impress of your own weakness, and even if successful, would react on you in other ways."[5] It would, in fact, be better to find happiness in love through the effect of the individual's sexual magnetism, but if this is deficient, is it at all surprising that desperate people would have recourse to a magical aid?

Henri Meslin has written:

One of the oldest love talismans is the scarab. . . . The Louvre Museum owns a splendid collection of them. And these petrified insects retain a fluidic power that the sensitive can feel through the display glass.[6]

This sex-magic expert thought it could still be used:

The scarab should be prepared following the magic ritual, with the customary consecration. It should be set within a gold, silver, or copper jewel, while evoking the goddess Isis and the angel Anael. It should be worn over the chest, right next to the heart.[7]

But despite what he says, the scarab is an amulet and only works by virtue of the sacred value of this insect in pharaonic Egypt, where it symbolized the future and guaranteed immortality to its owner. The "heart scarab," placed on a mummy, was decorated with a mystical scene.

The talisman is primarily an object that condenses an astral influence, as Belin notes:

> For example, you wish to wear a talisman to inspire terror or love, meaning Mars or Venus; your talisman, strongly imprinted and stamped by the influences of these stars, is in this world like those same stars given body in their own material. Yet they act and give off their virtue like those stars.

Meslin himself gives the recipe for crafting a love talisman: "The talisman of Venus should be carved on a Friday, during the hours of Venus, on a plate of very pure copper that has been carved in a circle and is the size of a medal. Both sides should be polished perfectly."[8] (The hours of Venus are: Friday from noon to one, from seven to eight, from two to three o'clock after midnight, and from nine to ten on the following morning.) Pierre Christian says that on the first face, one should engrave the image of the letter G from the Alphabet of the Magi, enclosed within a pentagram, using a chisel with a diamond point. On the other surface, a dove should be carved in the center of a star with six points surrounded by letters forming the name of Suroth, the planetary spirit of Venus, also in the alphabet of the Magi. One should choose to begin and end this operation on Friday when the course of the moon, which is sacred to Venus on this day, is traveling through the first ten degrees of Taurus or Virgo, and is forming a good aspect with Saturn and Venus.

> It is necessary to draw up the horoscope on the nearest Friday. . . .
> If the aspect of the Moon with Saturn and Venus is contrary, it is necessary to go from Friday to Friday until the good aspect is encountered.[9]

Catherine de Médici wore a talisman that was removed after her death in 1579 in Blois, which was then kept in the office of Abbé Fauval. Made by the queen mother's Florentine astrologer, Cosimo Ruggieri, this talisman was a medal depicting on one side the naked figure of Venus (the carving was said to have been modeled on the body of Catherine de Médici herself), together with the sign of Venus, that of her "house," Libra, and the name of its spirit, Hagiel. On the flipside Jupiter was seated with the eagle of Ganymede while a spirit with the head of Anubis presents him with a magic mirror. On it can be read the names of the angels Hé, Amic, and Oxill, combined with the signs of Jupiter. A book published in London in 1696 reproduced it with this commentary: "It is claimed that the virtue of this talisman was to govern sovereignly and to know the future and that it was made from human blood, goat blood, and several kinds of metal melted together under several specific constellations, which were related to the nativity of this princess." I think instead that this was a dual talisman of Venus and Jupiter, intended to attract both love and political power.

To make a talisman on parchment, Papus prescribes the following: "Under the prevailing influence of the Sun (Saint John's eve), you should purchase a hide of either a stillborn calf or lamb, which should be carefully kept wrapped in white linen after it has been consecrated following the customary ritual."[10] Georges Muchery advises using a sheet of virgin parchment "that has been magnetized for a period of around ten minutes, seven days in a row, at the time the Sun is moving into a sign that is appropriate to the desire pursued."[11] The magnetization is obtained as follows: "One places one's hands on the sheet while strongly projecting, via thought, the image of what one wishes to see realized." Next, the talisman is crafted in accordance with the astrological theme of the subject: "At a time in relation to the desire, draw two concentric circles in Chinese ink, and inscribe the signs of the Zodiac." If the operation is being performed for love, "it is helpful to glue the hairs of the two spouses on the talisman." Once the talisman has been completed, it is sealed within glassine paper in a safe place, but each day, while staring at the colored part, the operator will intensely visualize the image of his desire.

You must formulate the same desire three times, or better yet, you must inscribe this desire very legibly on a sheet of paper, to materialize it yet more strongly. Then for the next three or four minutes, with your back toward the north, stare at this piece of paper while visualizing the exact image of the beloved individual and imagining exactly what you wish of her.[12]

In 1861 Eliphas Levi described thirty-six talismans created based on the Kabbalah, starting from Schemhamphorasch, the incommunicable Name of God, formed from twenty-four points that each have three rays. "It was formed from seventy-two names that are written in pairs on the thirty-six talismans."[13] Each is a circle within a circle ("circular talismans express realizations") and the pair of names that gives it its character confers a specific power upon it. Love bears the names of Leviviah and Jejahel, the arcanum of love, Haajah and Rejahel, and the science of love is brought by Lecabel and Lehahiah. A great moral power can be hoped from them: "Talismans settle the mind, strengthen thought, and serve as sacraments to the will."[14] Eliphas Levi also showed how to create thirty-two talismans with the ten numbers and twenty-two letters of the Hebrew alphabet, in combination with the major keys of the Tarot. These talismans, which do not refer to Venus or other astral bodies, have effects different from the others.

> They serve to repel the illusions and glamours of light. The wandering spirits tremble at their appearance because they are fixed symbols and characters of the Verb, which is by it itself, and commands victoriously over all the spirits.[15]

The kabbalistic talismans therefore attract the protection of the higher and fixed spirits—the purest being the angels—and frighten the lower spirits, the wanderers and mixed entities, whose constant attacks will destabilize the individual who has not been forewarned. It is in a lover's best interest to wear the love talisman of Leviviah and Jehahel, or Lecabel and Lehahiah, if he desires protection from the disruptions that these invisible forces strive to create between him and his beloved.

It is not enough to simply inscribe an image, numbers, or letters on a piece of metal or parchment to make a talisman. It must again be consecrated through hieratic words and gestures, and censings meant to purify it using ritual perfumes (for Venus, benzoin, sandalwood, saffron, and verbena), or by burning plants that are sacred to a planetary deity (again for Venus, roses, violets, hyacinths, and myrtle). Consecration of a talisman confers the qualities of the four elements upon it. It is sprinkled with water seven times (the number of Venus) while saying aloud: "I consecrate this talisman with Water so that it may . . ." (here its purpose is stipulated). Incense is then burned and the love talisman is passed through the smoke seven times while saying: "I consecrate this talisman with Fire so that it may . . ." (the above intention is repeated). Then it is breathed upon seven times while saying: "I consecrate this talisman with Air . . ." and salt is sprinkled on it seven times while saying: "I consecrate this talisman with Earth." In addition, the initiates of the Golden Dawn visualized a luminous ball above the talisman, which gradually shrunk as it descended until it became extremely small and entered the talisman. They also added a drop of blood from pricking the little finger.

"A mage should never use an instrument, nor burn a perfume, nor use fire or water that has not been consecrated," Papus said. He clearly defines just what he means by consecration:

> The consecration is a kind of magnetization of objects by an action combining logos and gesture. The use of the aspergillum in Catholic worship is closely connected to this part of practical magic.[16]

Pierre Christian has provided the final instructions for the love talisman:

> This consecration consists of exposing the talisman to the steam from a perfume made of roses and violets, which has been burned with olive wood in a terracotta cooker that has not been used for anything else and which will be reduced to dust after the operation

and buried in a deserted spot. This talisman is next placed inside a pink or green silk pouch, which is then worn over the chest using ties made from the same fabric that have been interlaced and knotted in the form of a cross.[17]

Opinions differ on the way to use a talisman. Dom Belin said: "The way to use a talisman is to wear it. Some authors claim the people on whom its effect is desired should be touched with it." Eliphas Levi advised the opposite:

The images on talismans can be carved on seven metals or drawn on virgin parchment, then consecrated and magnetized following a very specific intention. In this way one will create focal points of light, they will be perfumed with ritual perfumes and kept in silk or glass boxes so they do not lose their strength.

And he adds this prescription, about which all the authorities agree: "You should neither lend nor give them to another unless they were made for the purposes of that other person and in concert with him or her." Pierre Christian suggests, "If it is possible to make a foe drink water in which a Venus talisman has been steeped, the hatred of this enemy will transform to unfailing affection and devotion." Modern initiates say about a talisman that has been crafted properly: "Forget it." It will work like an accumulator, permanently connecting its owner to a favorable star. In the opinion of Francis King and Stephen Skinner: "The advantage of talismans is that once created and charged they can be left to do their work without further attention."[18]

EROTICIZING MAGNETIC MASSAGES

The best means for maintaining healthy sexuality is couple massage, which is entirely different from the therapeutic massages practiced by trained specialists. Just as you can learn to massage yourself by using easy to learn self-massage techniques from manuals and similar self-help books, it is equally easy to initiate yourself into the art of massaging your partner. There was a time when sexologists organized seminars on the theme of "Mutual Massage" for their clientele and when authors like André de Sambucy wrote books on "family massage." But this activity does not fall into the jurisdiction of sexual magic unless it aims at restoring the subtle body at the same time as the carnal body.

Esalen massage (a variation of Swedish massage, the techniques for which were perfected around 1970 at the Esalen Institute in Big Sur), can be used for erotic-magical purposes. It is practiced on the ground or on a table because, as one of its specialists, George Downing, said: "a bed is the worst possible place you could choose for giving a massage." This is a complete body massage "of about an hour and a half in length." Everyone is capable of devoting themselves to it, as this author intends to show in teaching it as an art "for your mate, your family, and your friends."[19]

Jean-Louis Abrassart has created an excellent guide to floor massage, illustrated with a series of photos in which he performs it on a patient. She is lying down naked with her arms and legs spread and her hands open palms facing upward. He is sitting behind her, near her head, with his body completely straight, focusing his attention on the woman's *hara,* a spot on the abdomen two fingers below the navel. In his initial contact, he simply rests his hands on the top of her thorax, applying no pressure. He remains still until the warmth of his hands is in harmony with that of his partner's body. He then begins the massage with wide casual, superficial movements that cover large areas of her body.

> Your movements should be fluid and continuous, each in sequence with the others. . . . Don't forget to always keep your hands in contact with the body of the person being massaged until the end of the massage, even if you stop your movement to take a break.[20]

He always starts with light pressure that gradually intensifies. His hands are always coated with apricot kernel oil, used in India for skin care, to which he adds rosemary, pine, and summer savory.

There are a certain number of basic hand positions and movements, used sequentially with an eye to their physiological effects. The simplest is effleurage, with which he always begins.

> Effleurage is done with the whole hand applying a light, gentle pressure. The hand glides over the skin, adhering to the body whose contours it has wed. All the fingers are together and the rhythm is regular without any jerkiness, and the pressure remains uniform. . . . When done in all directions, it brings energy back to the surface.[21]

Next comes sliding pressure: "The hand position is identical to that of effleurage, but the pressure is stronger and pushes back the skin, which forms into a slight roll in front of the hands."[22] The gestures are more careful: "Sliding pressure should be slow to respect the speed of blood flow (several inches a minute). It is traditionally applied in the direction of the return circulation, which is to say the blood flowing back toward the heart."[23] There are more specific movements, such as kneading, friction (with the fingertips or thumb), and twisting in which "both hands form a bracelet turning in opposite directions to move like a corkscrew up the limbs."[24]

After the preliminary general effleurage, his massage begins at the chest, which he "opens" by separating his hands toward the armpits and then bringing them back to their starting point, then doing this again several times. The neck is massaged by gentle circular frictions, using the pads of three fingers together. Head massage focuses primarily on the forehead, the multiple tension points of the jaws, and includes kneading the eyebrows. The arms are massaged with both hands starting from the wrists. The belly receives special attention: "Massage the belly with a sweeping circular movement of both hands in a clockwise direction for a good number of times, fairly slowly. . . . You can do it with both hands working in alternation, each drawing a circle with one passing above the other when they cross."[25] Vertical massage of the chest can trigger unexpected reactions.

Slide both hands alternately, or one over the other from the top
of the sternum to the underbelly. . . . When working on the hollow of the belly alternate slow movements with more rapid ones.
Frequently, repressed emotions, fears, anger, anxieties, and so forth,
or suppressed memories will emerge during this massage.[26]

Once he has massaged the legs, "both the front and back," he does a
circular effleurage of the inner and upper thighs, then kneads the inner
and upper muscles (the abductors and quadriceps) with his whole hand.
An important point that can regulate problems affecting female genital
organs is located "on the inner thigh, a hand's width above the crease of
the knee, in a hollow spot right in the center." It merely requires stimulation: "You can apply deep pressure to it perpendicularly to the body,
using the pads of your thumbs."

When the woman turns over on her belly, he places himself behind
her feet in order to massage her back, starting from the top of the buttocks. "Don't touch the spinal column, your pressure should increase
gradually, this is the basic movement of back massage." Here, too, he
"opens" the back with fairly wide V-shaped gestures, which become less
and less open. He kneads the trapezoid muscles around the nape of the
neck between his thumbs and fingers, for it is in this area, known as
"the bison's hump" that fear and anger are headquartered. "Work the
entire zone between the base of the neck, the tip of the shoulder, the
upper edge of the shoulder blade, and the spinal column."

This "Californian massage" ends with light contact (applying no
pressure) from both hands joined together over the entire back of the
body, in a circular movement that gradually becomes slower and finally
comes to a halt at the hollow of the kidneys. What state does the massaged woman find herself in? "Rapid massage produces a stimulation,
slow massage is calming." This method has a semblance of magic: "In
Californian massage, the return movements without pressure can be
incorporated into magnetic passes, with the addition of their mechanical effect of stretching and opening the joints."[27]

George Downing, who teaches how to massage on a table and not on the ground, displays more obvious erotic-magical concerns. He advises the man massaging a naked woman to "try dancing your massage." "Enjoy yourself: dance! Move and sway all you can." He also suggests turning off the lights: "Give an entire massage in complete darkness. Do everything with the sense of touch alone, including finding the oil bottle and putting on oil." He even makes massage a libertine experiment: "have a friend arrange for you to be led in the dark to a waiting subject that you do not know, and have never encountered before." In addition to effleurage with the palm of the wide open hand, his movements over the entire body include: raking from top to bottom; stoking with the heels of the hands; and the "bear walk," in which both hands are flat and follow each other up the body. He also distinguishes himself from his colleagues by teaching ear massage, with the index finger following the contours of the cavities, or with two fingers pinching the lobes, then pressing the head between both hands more and more strongly.

No one has better described buttock massage than George Downing, who provides five ways to give it. The first is this one:

> Begin by kneading the flesh of either buttock exactly as if you were preparing bread for the oven. Lift the flesh and squeeze it between the thumb and the other fingers. Knead rhythmically, alternating hands. First cover one buttock thoroughly and then go on to the other.[28]

The second method is to hold three fingers tightly together to make circular movements a half inch wide or smaller across the buttocks, starting from the waist. Begin again at the bottom as if you were following lateral strips about one inch apart until the base of the tailbone. You can also use the bottom of your palm and vibrate it quickly at this same spot. Continue, covering the entire surface of the buttock, from top to bottom in strips about one inch wide. Here is some good advice he offers his readers: "Now shake your hand lightly but very quickly from side to side, shaking the buttocks beneath at the same time. Looks silly? Just ask your friend how it feels."[29]

George Downing makes a distinction between ordinary massage and erotic massage: "One is sensual, the other sexual. One leaves the body feeling calm, the other leaves it feeling aroused." But he also notes: "The key to erotic massage is not, as you might expect, a detailed massaging of the genitals." Erotic massage has stages, the first of which is simply an ordinary massage: "Next do feather-light stroking with the fingertips all over the body . . . " Repeat this massage "ten, twenty, any number of times more."[30] It is also necessary to concentrate on other erogenous zones besides the genitals.

> These include primarily the pelvic region and the regions immediately joining—the stomach, the insides of the thighs, the buttocks, and the lower back—and the breasts. But also give some attention to the ears, the lips, the back of the neck, the palms, the insides of the elbows, the armpits, the soles of the feet, the big toe, and the backs of the knees.[31]

For erotic foot massage, he only recommends a single stroke: "run one finger slowly all the way in and out between each pair of toes."[32]

Another stage involves placing the hand indirectly in contact with the genitals. "Here the idea is to do strokes which at some point lightly touch or graze the genitals." It is only in the final stage that they become the primary focus: "Pressing lightly with your fingertips, work slowly and with great care over the entire genital region. Cover each surface with tiny circles, outline the contours of each distinct part with one fingertip."[33] He instructs men to massage the edges of their companion's vagina with one thumb tip directly above the other, and women to slide their forefingers along the penis, then over the glans before going back down the other side.

George Downing is so non-dogmatic that he tells amateurs: "making up your own strokes is not hard. The more massage you do, the easier it will become. Your hands, you will find, have tremendous imagination."[34] He even goes so far as to claim: "doing double massage for a friend can be an especially fine experience for a couple."[35]

Erotic-magical massage should obviously be done with essential oils, while knowing that some are revulsive like oregano, thyme, marjoram and risk irritating the skin if they are not highly diluted in sweet almond oil. An English specialist of aromatherapeutic massage, Maggie Tisserand, published a treatise on the subject in 1993, *Essence of Love: Fragrance, Aphrodisiacs, and Aromatherapy for Lovers,* to encourage "holistic sexuality": the combination of the physical (desire), the mental (eroticism), and the emotional (love). Her guide is primarily addressed to women, to whom she says: "You could be improving your own sexual functioning by giving your lover a massage."[36] In fact, it is this self-massage of their thumbs that helps women relieve their problems with menstruation, menopause, and sterility. She begins by offering instructions. "Place a pillow under your partner's ankles and tummy while massaging the back, and under the knees while you are massaging the front."[37] She first places the man on his stomach for the erotic-sensual massage of his back: "When you massage your lover's back, the main difference from the therapeutic massage is that this massage goes down from the nape of the neck to the buttocks and is stimulating rather than relaxing."[38] But a traditional effleurage should set the stage for this downward stroking:

> With palms flat and fingers pointing toward the head, glide smoothly up the spine to the neck, then, drawing your hands away from each other, slide them down to the place you started, at the base of the spine.[39]

This is also an opportune time to rub oil into the skin:

> One of the most important oils is the precious sandalwood. Often used for its erotic properties, it can safely be used (suitably diluted) for massaging even the most intimate parts of the body.[40]

Maggie Tisserand makes a strong case for myrtle, the preeminent Venusian plant:

The goddess Aphrodite arose from the waves and realizing her nakedness, plucked some sprigs from a myrtle bush to cover herself. This is why, it is said, the myrtle plant has leaves shaped like a vagina, the outer lips (labia majora) being likened to "the lips of the myrtle" and the inner (labia minora) to "the fruit of the myrtle."[41]

With such an origin, it is hardly surprising that a tiny dose of its essential oil was an aphrodisiac.

Myrtle is slightly rubefacient, which means it brings heat to wherever it is applied—a little diluted may be applied to the inside of the thighs or to the labia. . . . For the dilution, use no more than 2 or 3 drops to a teaspoon of fatty oil.[42]

Black pepper oil, also diluted in massage oil, is another of her prescriptions for massaging the genitals.

Maggie Tisserand's advantage over the authors cited earlier is that she includes massage of the Chinese acupuncture points on the feet and hands that provide sexual energy.

Two points on the foot are of major importance in the healthy functioning of the sex organs, and are the same for both sexes. The first is the solar plexus area on the sole of the foot, which is located in the center, just below the ball of the foot. . . . Apply pressure to this area using the thumb. . . . The second reflex point is the area on either side of the heel. Massage gently between the thumb and the index finger.[43]

Her ear massage technique is different from Downing's: "Press and massage the entire earlobe between your thumb and index finger. Then use the edge of your fingernail to stimulate specific points."[44] With regard to the buttocks, she advises that the kneading be done only with the lower fleshy part of the palm (called the heal or the Mount of Venus), whereas Downing recommends kneading with the whole hand.

A woman may happen to get "wet" when massaging her lover so sensually. So much the better. "An experiment showing that when a woman's vaginal secretions were applied to her chest she and her partner had sex more often has recently been reported in the *British Journal of Sexual Medicine*."[45] We could conclude from this that it would be a good idea for her to then bury one or two fingers into her vagina, and then rub the secretions she obtains between her breasts. The act will be magical if she draws the circle and cross of the sign of Venus with her moistened index finger. For the final massage, Maggie Tisserand recommends the "full body massage" of the Bangkok brothels:

> With your partner lying face down, straddle their legs and lean forward, placing your hands at either side of their body at waist level (this is one massage where you do *not* use your hands). Slide up and down using your breasts/chest and belly to massage your lover's back. . . . Or have fun and write your name on your lover's back using your chin, nose, or nipple.[46]

Maggie Tisserand says that a massage like this can even replace intercourse and she is entirely correct. Couples that have not become obsessed with the goal of achieving orgasm at any price, as so much useless literature promotes, will find infinite sexual resources in the "eroticism of the surface" and obtain a diffused sexual pleasure from skin contact.

The use of the thumb by these authors is borrowed from the traditional Japanese massage of shiatsu, the name of which derives from shi (finger) and atsu (pressure). This massage is given on the ground, on dry skin, using the thumb or other fingers, but also with the help of the palms, elbows, knees, and feet. The strokes use effleurage, friction, drumming, twisting, stretching, and manipulation of the joints. They are also applied to the acupressure points, which form energy lines or paths called meridians. The primordial center of emotions is the hara, a part of the abdomen between the navel and pubis about which the master Wataru Ohashi said: "The central point of hara where our vital energy is stored is called the dan tien. To locate it exactly, place your palm over your stomach with the thumb folded back and the forefinger right beneath the navel. The dan tien is precisely beneath your ring finger. . . . People who are dissatisfied with their sex lives can find their problems in the dan tien region."[47] Here are the massage strokes he recommends for strengthening sexuality.

> Start the session by massaging and applying shiatsu for ten minutes over the patient's kidneys, at the spot where the torso and thighs meet. . . . Apply pressure to the *dan tien* with your palm, then relax the pressure. Continue this way for ten minutes, going deeper each time while the patient is exhaling.[48]

The use of the hands in shiatsu is restricted to the tip and pad of the thumb; the index and middle finger forming a V; the knuckle of the index finger (with the hand in a fist); the fingertips with all the fingers brought together; one thumb over the other (with both hands flat next to each other). The strokes apply pressure perpendicular to the body, without sliding over the skin. These pressures, which last from three to seven seconds, are made while the patient is exhaling. They are continuous, gradual, and rhythmic; the hand remains in contact with the skin when the pressure is relaxed.

Yuki Rioux, who runs the Centre de Plein Être in Quebec, focuses her attention on sensual awakening through shiatsu, between a giver and a receiver. The giver goes into the *seiza* position (kneeling or sitting over his heels) or into a genuflexion. He applies the pressures with a harmonious swaying of his body, which avoids the use of muscular strength. Yuki Rioux massages the twelve primary meridians (six yang and six yin) identified by the Chinese, as well as the eight extraordinary meridians.

The Master of the Heart [pericardium] vessel is the most erogenous meridian of the human body. It reaches its maximum energy between seven and nine in the evening, every day."[49] This yin meridian has nine points, the first of which is located on the chest at the level of the nipples. The second is on the inner surface of the arm above the crease of the armpit: "The Master of the Heart 2 figures among the most erogenous points of the meridian and has a direct effect on the sex organs."[50] The third is on the inner arm in the middle of the elbow crease, on the tendon of the biceps going toward the body; "it has a tonic effect directly on the sex organs."[51] In the center of the inner surface of the forearm, three centimeters below the wrist in the direction of the elbow, we find point 5, pressure on which works against sexual inadequacy. The seventh point is in the center of the wrist crease, between the two tendons: "Master of the Heart 7 works on the psyche as well as on the sex organs. It is located in a little known erogenous zone."[52] The eighth point is in the center of the palm, aligned with the middle finger. "Master of the Heart 8, like many of the points in this meridian, works directly on the sex organs. Pressure is applied with the thumb here, but elsewhere the tips of the fingers held together are used: To stimulate the sex organs and urinary tract, apply pressure with gentle, sharp drumming movements."[53]

When the receiver lies flat on her stomach with legs spread, the giver massages her with one of his feet. For example, he will work up the body to the armpit, applying pressure with the ends of his toes. For the thighs and calves, he applies pressure with or by vibrating the sole of his right foot from the top of the thigh to the ankle. The giver also uses his forearm to massage:

> Caress each leg with smooth strokes of your forearm. Go down following the direction of the energy meridian until the end of the foot; with your fingertips, lightly scratch the entire yang part of the leg; this stimulates blood circulation and makes the leg surface more receptive to caresses. Linger while scratching the back hollow of the knee, it is a highly erogenous zone.[54]

Shiatsu with the feet is performed as follows: Caress the sole of the foot with your forearm. Gently slip your pinkie between each toe and pull it out with a twisting motion. Pressure on the big toes should be moderate. On the other hand: "applying deep pressure, stimulate the sexual energy point located at the center of where the heel begins."

Shiatsu of the buttocks requires particular attention: a highly erogenous region but with lots of adipose tissue, the buttocks need much deeper pressures applied. The giver kneels to provide a gentle effleurage over the entire area, followed by much deeper work. "With the fleshy part of the hands, massage both buttocks at the same time while following their contours and with a corkscrew movement end at the Ten Shi points where the horizontal projections of bladder 54 and gall bladder 30 intersect."[55] The massage should become increasingly intensive:

> With the help of the elbow and rotary pressures, follow the same movement on each buttock. Apply alternating finger pressure with your thumbs over the full surface of one buttock, then the other. Create gentle vibrations with your hands over the entire buttock region, then apply effleurage down to the ends of the feet. End the massage by blowing gently over the entire dorsal surface.[56]

There are thus a few techniques in the erotic energy massage domain for massaging the buttocks, which can be used by couples on each other. Taoist masseurs teach a different method.

> Place your hands, one on top of the other, in the middle of the right buttock and press down while making circles in a clockwise direction. Do this 36 times. Do the same on the other buttock, but this time the circular movement should be counter-clockwise. Again, do this 36 times.[57]

It is a good idea to create a mixed method that borrows notions from different schools. There are only a few that can be taken from Chinese massage as only trained professionals can execute the *pai* (tapping), *chui* (hammering), and *qia* (pinching). Taoism primarily prescribes individual exercises and self-massage techniques for sexual development, and in one session for couples, its best advice is for finishing the session:

End your massage by drawing an "eight" with your right hand from the nape of the neck to the coccyx, twelve times. To conclude your massage, place your right hand over your coccyx and your left hand on the top of your head to ADJUST your energy flow.[58]

To discuss couple massage in a treatise on sex magic is an innovation; and no other author has yet made this connection. However, the appeal that traditional Eastern medicines (which look at things like stimulating the chakras and balancing yin and yang) now have for many of our contemporaries makes such a development inevitable. The magic inherent in massage is reinforced if it is combined with ceremonial elements, censings, invocations, hieratic signs drawn on the skin with the fingers, and so on. But in any event, for the magnetizing virtue of his manipulations to be assured, it is enough if the mental concentration of the masseur is strong and his touch is closely connected to his psyche.

AMOROUS THERMOPUNCTURE

Between 1949 and 1952, François Suzzarini, a French soldier in South Vietnam, married in accordance with local rites a girl or *con gái*, Thi Ba, who one day treated his back pain using a technique called "mouth moxa." An old mage, Trang Truih, informed him that this was a love technique taught to certain young girls "so they could give more pleasure to their companion of the time." This is a gentle form of moxybustion, which consists of placing a moxa (a small cone of tinder and mugwort) on a specific point of the body and lighting its top end. The patient feels an intensifying impression of heat and vibration. Instead of cones warm air is blown on the treatment points through a piece of wool cloth. This is how the author defines thermopuncture: "It is the treatment of 360 precise points of the human body (acupuncture points) through the radiant heat provided by breath from the mouth."[59]

Here is the protocol:

First you need to obtain a small piece of wool cloth about 2" × 2" in size. This square will be the intermediary between your mouth and the skin in which the point to be treated is located. It also increases the heat provided by the breath.[60]

The giver sets in motion *prana,* the vital breath: "Your thermopuncture obliges you to use your breath as an intense heater and a transmitter of energy between you and your partner." The giver needs to prepare herself for this activity through preliminary breathing exercises: "You shall study the three breaths of amorous thermopuncture and learn how to apply them when and where they are needed." This specialist names three breaths: the breath of passion, the breath of love, and the breath of tenderness.

The breath of passion is made with a four-second inhalation and four-second exhalation: "Some amorous thermopuncture points require a passion breath made with lips open that is violent, strong, and abrupt but of short duration (only four seconds), which is repeated without stopping for four or five minutes." The love breath uses a six-second inhalation followed by an eight-second exhalation: "This should be done for a total of fifteen minutes. Moreover, this technique should be performed two times in a row." The breath of tenderness consists of inhaling for eight seconds and exhaling for twelve seconds: "Some points, though few in number, need the breath of tenderness, lips clenched, light but constant, and repeated without stopping for a total time of ten minutes." The author recommends: "Do not blow too hard; you need to remain aware of your actions." He describes the different "amorous paths" that can be followed over the body while admitting there will be individual variations: "Everyone should be able to draw up their own *erotic cartography.*"

You begin on the face, choosing between the useful or the sensual course (which goes from a point right next to the ear cavity to a point right above the upper lip):

Face your partner and try to identify the eight thermopuncture points on his or her face.

. . . Place the virgin wool square on the precise spot and breathe according to the rhythm and duration prescribed for treating this specific point. While you are breathing, your fingers should not remain inactive. Caress whatever part of your partner's body you please or simply place your palms on his or her shoulders.[61]

There is also a range of postures to choose from: "You can just as easily remain standing face to face, or stretched out with one atop the other."

For the "amorous path of the torso," one partner stretches out on the ground and the other leans over him, or sits at the level of the hips, or they can kneel down facing each other. This path must be covered three or four times in one session. "All the points dealing with sexual fatigue are located below the navel, choose no more than two for one circuit." To follow the "amorous path of the back," the partners should be either standing or kneeling behind one another, or sitting with their legs stretched out.

Do not overlook the wealth of erogenous zones on your partner's back; mainly along the spinal column, the anal area, the neck, and the nape. Note which of your partner's regions are the most receptive to your touch. Compare his back's erotic map with your own.[62]

The amorous path of the back contains seventeen points. "Experience has shown that you should go from the least sensitive point, which you caress briefly, to a more receptive area in a way that puts your partner into a state of expectation for a more acute or voluptuous sensation."

The "amorous paths of the upper limbs" can be traveled while lying next to each other: "For the upper limbs, the sensitive zones are the armpits, the inner surface of the arm and elbow crook, the wrist, the sensitive space between the fingers, and the palm." For "the amorous paths of the lower limbs" the receptive partner should be lying on her belly, then on her back, with the active partner perched over her. Here is a good recommendation: "Each time you or your partner apply the breath of your mouth to a specific point on an amorous path, you should be completely relaxed and free from cares and annoying thoughts." There are points that correspond to an "amorous path of well-being," over which the breath of tenderness is blown: two thumb widths below the wrist crease; midway between the Achilles heel and the anklebone; in the hollow between the anus and the coccyx, and in the center of the perineum, located between the genitals and anus.

François Suzzarini justifies these erotic breath massages by explaining we have an average capacity of three-and-a-half quarts of air in our body, of which we only use one quart, while breathing eleven to fourteen times a minute. Furthermore, our lungs emit electrical currents, as was established by Dr. Atkins of the Medical College of California in 1905. The scientists following in his footsteps found that the air entering the left nostril creates a negative current and a positive current in the right one. Sazzarini states the "repeated breaths have a calming and relaxing effect thanks to the production of alpha waves in your brain, waves you can learn how to create on command."[63] Alpha waves, which have a frequency and duration of around ten seconds, are the waves of rest. Finally, this method can also help establish good conjugal harmony as much as sex magic: "Thermopuncture offers you a good opportunity for foreplay and caresses using your hands and mouth as a prelude to intercourse, and facilitates the creation of a dialogue for your couple."[64]

MAGICAL PERFUMES

The origin of perfumes was for both magical and religious purposes. Perfumes were used not to increase the seductive potential of the human body, but to dispel morbid miasmas, fight off the demons that were essentially drawn by awful smells, or to produce a sorcerous enchantment. They were associated with the rites of pagan temples and the liturgies of monotheistic churches alike, and while they may appear to have become profane by entering into the domain of grooming and hygiene, they remained of divine extraction because the Greeks attributed the invention of perfume to Aphrodite and the revelation of their existence to mortals through the betrayal of one of her servitors, the nymph Oenone. The development of modern aromatherapy, far from being contrary to the magic of perfumes, has added additional possibilities to them. We still need to know, however, what the functions of the substances used in ceremonies were.

The preeminent religious perfume is incense, and not only in regard to the Bible. In Greece "the room where a meal took place is still perfumed either by burning incense or by sprinkling scented water over the furniture."[65] Incense releases aromatic fumes that mask bad odors; its combustion can help to reveal poor ventilation; and it creates acids that neutralize rank, gaseous, or alkaline substances and keep new ones from forming. This is why the early Christians, according to Tertullian, used them to purify their underground catacombs where they held their clandestine meetings. Later, the obnoxious stench caused by burying the dead was dispelled in the churches with the generous use of incense. The incense tree, whose gum resin it was the privilege of the Sabeans to harvest, was not its sole source. Incense could also be made with olibanum, another gum resin found in India from various species of the *Boswellia* genus, and from terebinth. The Phoenicians brought it to the Greeks, who used it in their sacrifices to the gods, in order to dispel the putrid odor of the immolated animals.

Myrhh, cited in the Bible as one of the most exquisite ingredients of holy oil, came from a tree, two species of which were abundant in Abyssinia. The Greeks called it *myrrha,* for they believed it was made from tears of Myrrha, the mother of Adonis, after the gods changed her into a tree. Benzoin, considered a "Far East incense," is harvested from an incision in the tree Styrax benzoin, which is widespread in Siam and the Sunda Islands. The Chinese perfume their houses with it, and it is associated with rites in Hindu and Buddhist temples.

Among the Greeks and Romans, the application of perfumes to the body was in obedience to the desire to strengthen the magical value of anatomical elements:

Each part of the body had its particular perfume: mint was recommended for the arms; palm oil for the jaws and chest; a pomade

made from marjoram was put in the hair and eyebrows; for knees and neck, essence of ground-crawling ivy was used; this latter was reportedly helpful in orgies, as was rose essence.[66]

In England pomanders intended to stave off infection were balls of perfumed paste that were worn around the neck or carried in one's pocket. It was thought that women could cast love spells on men by merely breathing on them with their magic perfumes. This is why an act of Parliament in 1770 stipulated that

> all women, of whatever age, rank, profession, or degree—whether virgins, maids, or widows—who shall, after this act, impose upon, seduce, and betray into matrimony any of his majesty's male subjects, by virtue of scents, paints, cosmetic washes . . . shall incur the penalty of the law now in force against witchcraft and like misdemeanors . . .

Sexual magic uses two kinds of perfumes: tutelary perfumes and coital perfumes. The purpose of the first is to protect the couple against incubi and succubi and gain the favor of the invisible forces. They are intended to conciliate the higher elementary spirits and inspire their active benevolence while repelling the lower elementary spirits, whose malefic activity was condemned by Eliphas Levi: "These demons are mortal and seek to live at our expense; they seek the effluvia of sperm and blood, the fumes from meat, empty envelopes. . . ." Against them we can turn to the sacred substances that have long been used in the great religions and about which R. P. Sabazius (his pseudonym appears to be the cover for an exorcist-priest) says: "White and black benzoin, elemi resin, aloe wood, coriander, incense, styrax, or myrhh." Sabazius notes: "According to Arab tradition, the best perfumes are those that burn and thereby enter, through fire, the subtle planes of the *occultum*."[67]

Incense is the most common tutelary perfume. Sabazius is very strict in this regard: The incense will be liturgical incense, or even better *absolutely pure incense* (little tears from the *Boswellia serrata* found on the Somali coast). Its aromatic vapor drives away those demons that are always eager to meddle in sexual affairs. It has the drawback of calming rather than arousing, so Omer Haleby advises that incense be burned following intercourse and not before. Once that has been done, its fumes will maintain the beatitude of the lovers and dispel all harmful influences around them. Before intercourse, the incense should be blended with a coital perfume. This is why Mohammed recommended perfuming the home with a blend of male olibanum (the incense found in round pieces) and savory.

Among the coital perfumes, the most important is that of musk. Louis Claye says of it:

> Its divisibility is so great, its aroma so penetrating that a single atom is enough to permeate an apartment with its odor for several years.[68]

Few people can tolerate it in its pure state, so it is often blended with amber, which mellows its aroma without masking it. "Before going into combat, the Tartars, to stimulate their courage and strengthen their limbs, rub musk over themselves,"[69] Claye informs us, who also reveals what the people of Greco-Roman Antiquity used as its substitute:

> The ancients were unacquainted with musk; the Greeks and Romans made a valuable perfume from *muria,* a kind of brine made from putrefied fish that likely included octopi and similar creatures that in some cases give off a very musky odor.[70]

Musk is a secretion of the musk deer, which is more abundant during rutting season and is found in a pouch formed of several layers of skin near its navel. The average production in an adult animal is twenty-eight grams of musk. Only the male has a pouch in its execratory hair follicles, and even if it holds no more than three grams of musk, the ability of this odor to spread was so strong that the East India Company prohibited its transport on the same ship carrying tea. "It is the most coital and noble of all perfumes!"[71] exclaimed the *Khôdja* (professor) Omer Haleby, who was born in Algiers and lived in Istanbul, where he died in 1866. He added that Mohammed used it because it was warm, dry, and bracing: "The Prophet perfumed himself with musk and ordered his women to wear this same substance following their menustrations."[72] Mohammed considered the best musk to be that from Khorasan, China, and India. This is the native region for musk deer, along with Siberia and Tibet.

Another coital perfume of animal origin, civet, is secreted in the area of the anus by a carnivore of the marten family that inhabits the equatorial regions of Africa and the Indies. "Some perfumes are never used in their pure state. Civet is one of these; its strong and extremely persistent odor would be intolerable,"[73] says Louis Claye.

In France during the reign of Louis XV, this musky blend was used to encourage sensual pleasure:

> Twelve grains of musk, crushed in a small mortar with a little piece of sugar, then add a small thread of cinnamon essence, an equal amount of clove, and four grains of civet, to make a full blend. It must be picked up with cotton to be placed in an incense burner.[74]

It is placed inside an earthenware vase pierced with holes so that it exhales its coital perfume near the bed; gloves are also dipped in it.

"Coital perfumes can be either simple or complex," says Omer Haleby. The complex ones come from blends like this one:

> If one adds the aroma of pure incense or one mixed with myrtle to musk, the perfume one will obtain from placing these two powders—musk and incense—on hot coals, one will be sure to perform intercourse with great power and singularly facilitate the arrival of the spasm and final ejaculation.[75]

He asserts that "myrtle, tossed onto the hot coals in an incense burner is suitable for vigorously making one predisposed for intercourse." The Arabs claimed that when Adam was exiled from Eden, he brought with him a myrtle bush, date paste, and a blade of wheat: the first among aromas, the first among fruits, and the first among foods. The myrtle was also the first bush Noah planted on leaving the ark.

Omer Haleby disclosed the recipe for the most excellent of all coital perfumes:

In 500 grams of rosewater

Finely powdered olibanum incense	2.50 grams
Finely powdered musk	0.50 grams
Finely powdered myrtle	2.50 grams
Finely powdered camphor	0.50 grams
Savory (flowering tops)	2.50 grams

Macerate this in a hermetically sealed flask and expose it to sunlight for forty-eight hours. Decant it, strain the liquid out by squeezing the solids, filter it, and keep it in the same flask.[76]

He also says that some substances, minus the rosewater, can be blended with gum. Arabic and powdered cascarilla can be rolled into small fatty balls to be burned "around twenty-five minutes before the couple enters the chamber of bliss." Omer Haleby indicates:

They must be spread large as chickpeas over the burning coals of the incense burners, which should be three in number with one in the center, one in the north, and one in the south of the *room for intercourse.*[77]

Another highly regarded coital perfume was the Balm of Gilead, a liquid resin from the amyris tree or shrub that originated in Southern Arabia and was cultivated in Judea and Egypt. It is likely the same as the nard mentioned in the scriptures. The Turkish sultan reserved it solely for his own use, and sent it as a gift to other sovereigns. The beautiful odalisques of his harem used it. Simply dissolving it in alcohol provides a fragrance with the properties of an aphrodisiac.

Two other coital perfumes are ylang ylang, in the form of an essential oil made from the flowers of a tree that originates in the Philippines, and the neroli oil produced from the blossoms of the orange tree (not the sweet orange but the *Bigaradia,* the bitter orange tree).

In the nineteenth century, the English perfumer Septimus Piesse created "the harmony of odors" to show that their magic was identical to music. Each corresponded to a note in an octave: *do* (camphor, rose, pineapple, jasmine, sandalwood, geranium), *re* (lemongrass, bergamot, heliotrope, vanilla), *mi* (verbena, citron, iris, clove), *fa* (civet, ambergris, daffodil, tuberose, musk), *sol* (magnolia, mock orange, orange blossom, frangipani) *la* (lavender, tonka bean, balm of Peru, tolu balsam), *si* (mint, pepper, cinnamon, carnation). Piesse explains: "There are odors that have no sharps or flats, and there are others that make an entire octave by themselves, thanks to their various nuances. The class of odors with the greatest number of varieties is that of the lemon."[78]

It could be possible to compose melodies of perfumes using the laws of musical harmony to arouse amorous sensations. Piesse provides the recipe for a "*fa* bouquet," which is perfect for lovers: "Musk (*fa*), rose (*do*), tuberose (*fa*), tonka bean (*la*), camphor (*do*), and daffodil (*fa*)." The magical range of perfume sounds escapes the majority of musicologists:

> The experienced perfumer sometimes has two hundred odors in his laboratory and knows how to distinguish each one by name. On a keyboard containing two hundred notes what musician can recognize and name the note struck without looking at the instrument?[79]

The use of magical perfumes does not only involve physical ointments or vapors from diffusers but also works through their permeation of a cloth. A handkerchief saturated in a "*fa* bouquet" would have a fine erotic effect. Maggie Tisserand suggests eroticizing the bed itself.

> Scented bedclothes are extremely sensual and very personal. One simple way to scent sheets is to place the bottom sheet on the bed as normal and then to spray it lightly (a plant mister is good for

this) with a mixture of spring water and the essential oils of your choice—neroli and ylang-ylang, for example. Leave exposed to the air for half an hour if the room is warm, longer if the room is cold. Then make the bed in the usual way.[80]

PROPITIATORY JEWELRY

Since the dawn of civilization, jewelry has also been used as a magical aid for all circumstances, and to start with, the great case that has been made about their abilities to arouse, temper, or increase sexuality. With good reason Sabazius says:

> Circular objects like crowns, necklaces, belts, bracelets, and rings are not only the finery and adornments to which modern ignorance has reduced them, or even symbols. They are protective signs, veritable *magic circles* that insulate [the wearer].[81]

Like some of the perfumes we have just considered, such jewelry has the power to keep the demon incubi and succubi at bay from a lover. This round form has been exploited by all religions: "The various Catholic, Arab, and Asian rosaries are nothing else but movable magic circles that can be used with their respective religious rituals,"[82] Sabazius adds, emphasizing that other jewels are particularly effective for sexual activity. "Rings are veritable *volts* of enchantment. The wedding ring is a love spell."[83]

The primary propitiatory jewel is the ring, with or without a precious stone, as long as it is engraved with a hieratic word and has been ritually prepared. Jean Marquès-Rivière states: "The talismanic ring, the pantacular magic circle one wears on their finger, has been used by all peoples since the beginning of antiquity."[84] Pierre V. Piobb did not seem to even wish to consider talismanic medallions and categorically stated: "Talismans are placed on the finger, but on the left not the right hand, for the left hand (the passive hand) is the one used by the operator to perform his magic gestures."[85] It is also necessary to know what finger on which to wear the ring: the thumb belongs to Venus, the index to Jupiter, the middle finger to Saturn, the ring finger to the Sun, and the little finger to Mercury. It was forbidden at one time to wear a ring on the middle finger, called the indecent finger (*digitus impudicus*) because it was the one women used to masturbate. It is appropriate today that some lesbians wear their rings on their middle fingers, sometimes on both hands, to display their predilections and provide a means for others to recognize them. In principle a ring attracting love should be worn on the thumb so it can benefit from the influence of Venus and absorb its fluids.

Grimoires contain countless recipes for manufacturing rings for sex magic. For example, in the Voyer d'Argenson collection in the Arsenal Library: "Make a ring of silver, and carve on its inner part that touches the skin these words and crosses: DABY + DABY + DABY + HUBER + HUBER." Another page reads: "On Thursday before sunrise, make a ring half gold and half silver, and when this is done, you must utter over it this word, LETHONIUS, and carve on the ring the following characters . . . ." These are the two characters of Venus's astral signature in the writing of the Magi.[86]

In the grimoire known as the *Petit Albert,* the recipe includes a charge of personal magnetism:

Take a gold ring with a small diamond that has never been worn since it left the hand of the jeweler: wrap it in a small piece of silk and carry it for nine days and nine nights, between your shirt and skin, opposite your heart. On the ninth day, before sunrise, carve inside the ring with a new awl this word SCHEVA.[87]

But this is not all:

Next you shall have three hairs of the person whose love you would win, and you will couple them with three of your own hairs while saying: "O body! May you love me! And may your design succeed as passionately as mine through the effective virtue of SHEVA!"[88]

After which the hairs should be tied into love laces (corded over each other to form a figure 8) in such a way that the ring is interlaced in the center of the laces.

> Having wrapped it in the silk cloth, you shall then wear it over your heart another six days; and on the seventh you shall free the ring from the love laces, and do what is necessary to ensure the beloved individual receives it.[89]

It is essential that a spell be carved on the inner circle of the ring. Marquès-Rivière says: "The Gnostics made wide use of this means for carrying sacred names. The gnostic ring of Astorga is made of gold and around it is carved in Greek letters "UR-OA-EO-UR-OE-UR-OE-UO-UR-OO." Magical words must always be written in capital letters separate from each other. For my part I recommend carving the gnostic invocation O H ROO (O Eros!) on any piece of jewelry that you wish to have an erotic effect.

Over the centuries many jewels were considered propitiatory because the jewels adorning them seemed to possess the ability to heal certain illnesses. Louis Dieulafait said of kings and church officials: "Their finery consisted of gems arranged in a carefully calculated order to form a truly protective armor that guaranteed health, magnetically averted danger, and conferred physical and moral invulnerability, and magic power on their owners."[90] Stones were believed to be animate male and female entities and only worked if they were flawless. Jean de la Taille stated:

> Stones are not only alive but they are also subject to nourishment, illness, old age, and death. . . . They can sometimes be seen to grow pale, take offense, and fade, until they lose some of their strength and virtue.[91]

Several stones were believed to repress sexuality and a father would give one to his wife or daughter as a means of ensuring their proper behavior. For example, the emerald, also a stone of Venus, did not favor amorous relations: it was said to break when adultery was committed or a virgin was deflowered. According to Gerolamo Cardano, "men know through experience that the emerald is broken by venereal intercourse." He explains this is because it is the most fragile of precious stones and that "the body is much heated in veneral intercourse . . . breathes and sweats much." Sapphire was extolled for its purifying role as follows: "Sapphire makes its wearer chaste and clean." Similarly, Chrysolite "from the star named the Northern Crown . . . received the virtue of maintaining chastity, chilling the ardor of Venus, and giving elation to whomever wears it (if it is touching the skin)."

Among the stones that are propitious for love, we find "the agate makes pleasing to women, a man they do not love," according to the lapidary of Orpheus. The hyacinth (or garnet), in communication with the Sun and Jupiter, conveyed this message to Jean de la Taille: "My use is recommended to several ill-treated lovers so that they will be loved and highly valued by their mistresses."[92] The ruby (then called the carbuncle) was a stimulant: "The particularity of the carbuncle is to stimulate the mind and make it joyous," but not the balas ruby, which "greatly chills the soul of the heat of lust."[93]

Necklaces and bracelets can be propitiatory jewels based on their material, shape, and hierograms. A simple gold link chain hung with a Latin or Tau cross is a means of sexual selection for a woman, driving away the bad lovers and attracting the good. On the horizontal bar of the cross, on the side touching the skin, it is a good idea to carve a gnostic word like AEIA (I am), or RIOTHEOR (Principle of light). A medallion to be worn on a necklace should carry magical signs. A triangle pointing downward is Water and pointing upward is Fire. S repeated three times—the "pluvial waters" in Alchemy—signifies steadfastness and faithfulness. Lovers inscribe it as a sign of their fidelity to their beloved. Z, meaning "life" (Greek *zóé*), is a promise of everlasting love.

A necklace or bracelet can be adorned with a rough cameo: a stone that has been picked up during a stroll outdoors, and on which a figure appears that makes it a natural talisman. Jacques Gaffarel has described cameos that show the crowned head of a king, a fish, and many other images created by chance. He says that if someone is touched by one of these "figured stones," they will be influenced in the direction of the figure that is depicted on it. If the lines on a stone depict a heart, a mouth, a phallus, a vulva, or some other element of sexual desire, it holds a magnetic charge that can lend one an advantage in amorous commerce.

Belts are another form of propitiatory jewelry. Reference is often made to the belt of Venus, who makes anyone who receives one as a gift fall madly in love. This belt was in fact her *subligaculum*—the ancestor of the female thong that leaves the buttocks naked—holding the goddess's *odor de femina*. Margo Anand said: "Belts are important in magic, especially those with a strong metal plate made of steel, iron, or copper that covers the abdomen, the balance center, or *hara* point."[94] She neglects to say what symbol should be carved on it. For a silver belt buckle, the magic square of 15, discovered in China by Emperor Yu on the back of a turtle in the Huang-He river, is recommended against physical pains and sexual impotence.

4	9	2
3	5	7
8	1	6

The diagram above is the *ouifq* of the Arabs, who noted that by replacing the four even numbers of this square, you obtain the word *badoûh*, the equivalent of the Aramaic-Persian word for the planet and goddess Venus: *Bîdukht*. This divine word is a powerful appeal to love, and I have plucked it from the depths of the ages to be the conclusion of this inventory of magical sex aids.

Coda

As I promised at the outset, this handbook of sex magic that I have offered here is resolutely emancipating. Some have expressed their regret that I systematically eliminated all of the folklore on witchcraft and on the excesses of Satanism, which one tends to stumble across when dealing with this subject. For those who are curious, my *History of Occult Philosophy* contains detailed descriptions of "diabolical eroticism" with its possessions, sabbats, and black masses, and recounts many little-known facts from contemporary accounts along with an in-depth analysis. I did not want to repeat myself here, and in any event I feel strongly that it is now necessary to free High Magic from aberrations of this kind.

There are still many individuals and sects today who connect sexuality with the most old-fashioned kind of black magic. The short treatise I have written here is opposed to these retrograde deviations. In order that the readers can judge for themselves, however, I will say a few word on neo-paganism, whose predominant manifestation is Wicca, and on the Church of Satan, which is so prominent in the United States (a scene in Stanley Kubrick's final film, *Eyes Wide Shut* [1999], features a "satanic orgy" inspired by its rituals).

Wicca (a word in Old English for witchcraft) is the pagan religion of the witches, according to a theory maintained by Margaret Murray, and a religion that groups of women in England feel confident they have revived. They first began gathering in covens in Hampshire's New Forest, but the religion has since become widespread. Wicca's true initiator was Gerald B. Gardner, when he retired from the British Civil Service in 1936, after a long career working in the customs department in Malaysia. He retired to New Forest where he frequented with theosophists and occultists, and shared with them an interest in the origins of witchcraft. The first group formed around an extremely wealthy old woman, Dorothy Fortham, together with Dolores North (who took the esoteric name of Dafo) and several others. Gardner explained their notions on witchcraft in two novels and *The Book of Shadows* (1949), a kind of gospel written in an Elizabethan English pastiche, because he attributed it to a sixteenth-century witch. Aleister Crowley, who visited him in 1946 in Hastings, probably helped him. But Gardner imposed his sexual tastes in the rituals of *The Book of Shadows* by recommending *scourging* (the erotic flagellation that "governesses" applied to gentlemen is specialized houses in London).

After Gardner's death in 1964, Wicca fell under the influence of his initiate Doreen Valiente (died September 1, 1999), whom he named priestess of the New Forest coven and who described her relationship with him in *The Rebirth of Witchcraft*. A later Wiccan priest and "King of the Witches," Alex Sanders, claimed to wield authority over 107 groups or covens, each with thirteen members. In 1980 Francis King, counting several thousand members in English Wicca, said:

> Today the witch-cult is split into five or six competing sections, some of them still with a marked bias towards sexuality—one of these has an extraordinary "death-spell" which involves the Priest and Priestess indulging in the no doubt very uncomfortable process of having intercourse through the hole drilled through the middle of an allegedly Neolithic stone relic![1]

From a twenty-three-year-old witch, Marian, whom he interrogated on several occasions, Francis King learned of one Wiccan community devoted to sexual magic based on the principle of "suffering in order to learn." In Marian's coven at her initiation "she had been stripped, tied up so tightly that her circulation had been impeded, and heavily beaten on the back, buttocks, and even breasts by not only the Priest but by each member of the coven." Marian's admission into the third degree was sexually traumatic.

> She had expected to undergo ritual sexual intercourse with the High Priest, but she found that the High Priestess, who seems to have been the dominant figure in this coven, had decided that she herself would "initiate" Marian with the aid of a dildo . . . the dildo used was very old, unlubricated, and made of wood.[2]

The use of whips and dildos indicated to Francis King that the members of Wicca were "simply sado-masochists, using witchcraft as a means of living out their own pathetic fantasies."[3]

However, Wicca prospered after it spread to the United States where feminist movements adopted it as a religion with a female clergy, and where underground groups were attracted to its pagan principles. This tendency is still going strong today. On October 24, 1998, the news reported that a fifteen-year-old high school girl had been expelled from Baltimore's Southwestern School by the disciplinary board because, as a self-proclaimed witch, she had been casting curses during recreational periods. She was the daughter of Colleen Harper, a transsexual enchanter who had become a Wiccan priestess. The following year the American magazine *Green Egg* estimated the number of neo-pagans taking part in ceremonies between three and five million based on the television shows starring witches (*Sabrina, Charmed*), and concluded that books on paganism, Wicca, and witchcraft were so successful that the *New York Times* considered this the fastest-growing and most profitable sector of the publishing industry.[4] Even better is a *Washington Post* article by Hanna Rosin (republished in the *Courrier International* of June 17, 1999), who reports that the army had recently authorized Fort Hood, the largest army base in the country, to allow an official Wicca group to form. They established their sanctuary in a clearing. "They trade in their Army fatigues for hooded robes, chant to the lead of their chosen high priestess and dance around a fire well into the night."

At the same time, there are contemporary groups that cultivate Satanism, taking as reference the most characteristic of these efforts: the Church of Satan. Its founder, Anton Szandor LaVey, born in 1930, worked in the circus for seventeen years as a lion tamer in training, then as a musician in a Los Angeles dance hall, where he allegedly had a brief affair with Marilyn Monroe. In 1948 he moved to San Francisco where he married and obtained a job as a police photographer, responsible for photographing murder victims, and the organist for a nightclub. His friendship with famed Hollywood filmmaker and Crowley fan Kenneth Anger inspired him to read John Symond's biography of the Beast. In 1954 Anger shot his first Crowley-inspired film, *Inauguration of the Pleasure Dome,* in which Marjorie Cameron played a "scarlet woman." Later he made *Invocation of my Demon Brother,* which has a soundtrack by Mick Jagger and features LaVey in the role of Satan.

With his collection of torture instruments, horror novels, and photos of famous criminals, LaVey moved into his notorious house at 6114 California Street in 1956. In the former nineteenth-century brothel with secret passages, he had all its rooms painted black and he kept a lion there whose roaring alarmed the entire neighborhood. He organized lucrative lectures with slide projections on vampires, werewolves, and psychopaths, sometimes causing scandals over his outrageous behavior. For example, the newspapers claimed that following a lecture on cannibalism, his wife had served the audience the body of a forty-two-year-old woman who died in the hospital (a doctor friend had supplied the body). The flesh had been marinated in cognac, grenadine, and covered with both flambéed bananas and jellies, as if it were a cannibal meal in the Fiji Islands.

In 1961 LaVey created the Magic Circle, where the regular attendees of his lectures met to practice rituals led by Kenneth Anger. The Church of Satan was founded on April 30, 1966 (on Walpurgis Night). Clad in black and his head shaved, LaVey announced 1966 would be "the year of Satan." Various celebrities from Hollywood were there. In October the blond and buxom Jayne Mansfield became an adept of the Church of Satan and had herself photographed with LaVey wearing a devil costume. Every member had to sign a credo on a yellow sheet of paper containing the "Nine Satanic Statements" that they swore to uphold. In 1967 LaVey invited the media to cover the first satanic marriage in history, that of newsman John Raymond and Judith Case, a rich New York heiress. Massimo Introvigne writes:

> The official photos—with a prone naked woman serving as an altar (this was Lois Murgenstrumm, one of the first adepts), in the background—were taken by Joe Rosenthal, known for his famous photo of the Marines raising the flag on Iwo Jima.[5]

A satanic baptism in May of his daughter, Zeena Galatea, and a satanic funeral of one of his followers in December, were further manifestations of his cult.

That same year Jayne Mansfield died in a violent car crash (June 29, 1967) together with her manager, who had had a violent quarrel earlier with LaVey. These two deaths were naturally attributed to his black magic powers, and he was nicknamed the "Black Pope." Anton LaVey continued creating provocations worthy of this title; for example, he organized a "Topless Witches Sabbath" at a San Francisco nightclub. One of his dancing witches, Susan Atkins, later became famous as one of the Manson murderers. At the premiere of Roman Polanski's film, *Rosemary's Baby,* for which he had been a consultant, LaVey caused a sensation by appearing with a black-robed group of his followers. This was where Michael Aquino, a young officer attending the University of California in Santa Barbara and an expert in psychological warfare, met him and decided to become his chief assistant. To regulate the public ceremonies of his group, Anton LaVey published *The Satanic Rituals* (New York: Avon, 1972), although his liturgical black mass manual remained only available for use by his inner circle.

The black mass, performed over a naked woman serving as an altar, opens with an Introit in Latin, followed by the Confiteor in English. Insults were hurled against Jesus during the Gloria, the Epistle, the Gradual, and the Offertory. The desecration (opposite of consecration) "required a consecrated host, which should have been taken from a Roman

Catholic community." (Such a host could not be found for the first black mass and a cracker was substituted instead.) The host is to be introduced into the vagina of the woman who is serving as the altar, and she "should masturbate until she achieves orgasm or be masturbated by the celebrant using the host itself." The celebrant then strips off his clothing and, once naked, masturbates until he ejaculates. His semen is collected in a silver spoon, which is then placed on the woman-altar's belly. During the offertory, the sperm from the spoon, the host—which has been burned and crushed into a powder—will be mixed with wine in the "chalice of ecstasy." This chalice is then passed hand to hand so that all in attendance can drink the "elixir of life." The service ends with a blessing with the sign of the horns: three fingers turned down and two pointing up. It is also indicated that "the ceremony includes several benedictions that bring into play the sperm and urine (feminine) gathered during the rite itself."[6] The author of this ritual was the Catholic priest Wayne F. West, who found his inspiration in the black mass described by Huysmans in his novel *Là-bas* (Down There). According to Introvigne this is "the only black mass that contemporary Satanists (from California to Italy) know and follow practically to the letter."

In 1969 LaVey published *The Satanic Bible,* a summary of his teachings, and in 1971 *The Compleat Witch,* which teaches women how to become a "satanic witch" by turning their sexuality to their advantage. The rites of the Church of Satan took place in a "grotto" in San Francisco. Michael Aquino, who had moved to Kentucky, founded the Ninevah Grotto in Louisville with his wife. Wayne F. West created the Babylon Grotto in Detroit, and Charles Steenbarger (alias Adrian Claude Frazier), director of a mental health clinic, founded the Pluto Grotto in Denver. A former Wiccan priestess, Lilith Sinclair, ran the Lilith Grotto in New York. Seven rituals were performed in these grottoes, including glorifications of the fleshly pleasures (like those of the Khlisty sect) or the "Homage to Tchort." The active members of the Church of Satan barely numbered five hundred—a certain amount of whom were assigned to grottoes—but there were several thousand dues-paying adherents, including personalities like Sammy Davis Jr. of the Rat Pack.

Anton LaVey was forced to retreat into the shadows by the anti-Satanic campaigns that swept through the United States in the 1980s. He sought to protect himself by claiming he did not worship Satan but used him for psychodramas that free Christians of their prejudices. In his five-point program of "pentagonal revisionism," he recommends the creation of "total environments" (which might also be termed "Disneylands for perverts"), where those individuals could act out their fantasies in such a way that they would no longer seek to create them in real life. His argument was so convincing that the authorities regarded the Church of Satan as a group to be consulted for information about satanic activities, and the Black Pope's daughter, Zeena LaVey, became an official spokesperson for Satanism. Anton Szandor LaVey died on October 30, 1997, but the Church of Satan survived him and publishes a magazine in New York City called *The Black Flame*.

In Neo-pagan and Satanic schools like this, we witness a degeneration of sexual magic principles. Everything that was formerly done to make sexuality sacred as part of the ancient mysteries has now been replaced by acts of exhibitionism, ceremonies akin to sideshow spectacles, and pseudo-initiations intended to satisfy neurotic desires. Although they often pay lip service to Crowley, his epigones have not studied the Sanskrit, Egyptian, and Greek texts as thoroughly as he did, nor do they have his sense of asceticism or his artful ability of combining notions from the various religions into a coherent belief system.

It should now be apparent that what I have offered in the present book, which is both demystifying and initiatory, cannot be used to fuel the harebrained ideas and eccentricities of modern false prophets. I have tried to give the reader an orientation in magic while preventing him or her from being led astray in simulacra. In conclusion one may say that the preceding text is defined by three criteria of authenticity. These criteria apply to ceremonial, operative, or speculative forms of magic that can be performed as a group, as a couple, or by one person alone.

The first criterion concerns the esoteric organizations that place sex magic at the highest degree of their initiation cycle. This is perfectly legitimate, presuming the masters are animated by a true religious ideal and that they have explored all the great texts of mystical eroticism from East and West in depth. It would hardly be fair to lump together libertine sects that pursue their vulgar pleasures under cover of a theosophical label with the initiates of a single denomination who use sex as a means of achieving perfection, founded on the teachings passed down by a superior. This was the case with the members of the O.T.O. who, as we have seen, were no ordinary individuals and followed the example of Tantric yoga in which the couple often performs the *maithuna* under the direction of a yogi who guides them every step of the way through its difficult protocol.

The second criterion for authenticating sexual magic is that it is used to increase vital force and not reduce it. The studies of Dr. Hippolyte Baraduc led him to demonstrate the existence of a "condensed *vital force*" through which "man is the center of invisible radiations," dependent upon four "ensouled powers" (cerebral, pneumic, gastric, genital). This vital force forms "our *fluidic body*," which Baraduc was able "to externalize and spill from one subject to another, thereby establishing a vibrational resonance between them." Sex magic heightens the psycho-physical vibration of the fluid body and makes it into "a consummation center of the *Zoether*, that vital cosmic force, the shape of whose line is the curve."[7]

Lastly, the third criterion of this magic is that it does not involve a thoughtless unleashing of sexuality, but instead its subtle regulation. This may variously entail prohibitions of the sex act, intercourse without orgasm or even without penetration, metaphysical masturbations, and meditations visualizing scenes of sacred eroticism. Its purpose is not the satisfaction of the flesh in some Epicurean manner, but to awaken the mind to its transcendent possibilities by overstimulating it by means of sex.

Through sexual magic a man and woman can extract from each other what they are each lacking by way of virility and femininity. Through sex magic the individual brings about a merging of the carnal and the spiritual world. Beyond love and pleasure, it is in humanity's best interest to harness eroticism for the development of magical powers that already lie latent within us.

Notes

[The original French edition of *The Great Work of the Flesh* provided only minimal citations limited to book titles in its footnotes. For the present edition we have endeavored to provide more complete citations, including page numbers, in the case of English-language sources. —*Ed.*]

Preface

1. *Table des 72 anges,* Arsenal Library, Paris, ms. 2495.
2. Levi, *The History of Magic,* 104.
3. Ibid., 104.
4. Ibid., 119–20.

Chapter One: The Love Spell Traditions

1. Agrippa, *Three Books of Occult Philosophy*, bk. 1, pt. 3, chap. xlviii. Translation modernized.
2. Le Loyer, *Discours des spectres.*
3. Del Rio, *Investigations into Magic,* 118.
4. Albertus Magnus, *Le solide trésor des merveilleux* (Geneval, 1748). Translation of the *Libellus de Mirebulus Luci Naturae Arcanis* attributed to Albertus Magnus.

5. *Secrets pour se faire aimer,* Arsenal Library, Paris, ms. 2797.
6. Schwaeblé, *Les Recettes magiques pour et contre l'amour.*
7. Ibid.
8. Laroque, *Magie et sexualité.*
9. Nostradamus, *Excellent et moult utile opuscule.*
10. Ibid.
11. Laval, *Dessein des professions nobles et publiques.*
12. Le Baillif, *Le Demosterion.*
13. Piobb, *Formulaire de Haute Magie.*
14. Vairo, *De fascinatione.*
15. Ibid.
16. Ibid.
17. Bois, *Le Satanisme et la magie.*
18. Ibid.
19. Ibid.
20. Saint-Andre, *Lettres de M. de Saint-André.*

21. Albertus Magnus, *Le Petit Albert.*

22. Albert (Petit), *Le solide trésor de merveilleux.*

23. Saint-André, *Lettres de M. de Saint-André.*

24. Vairo, *Trois livres de charmes.*

25. Ibid.

26. Ibid.

27. Ibid.

28. Ibid.

29. Saint-André, *Lettres de M. de Saint-André.*

30. Ibid.

31. Liébault, *Trésor des remèdes secrets pour les maladies des femmes.*

32. Ibid.

33. Ibid.

34. Ibid.

35. Ibid.

36. Ibid.

37. Ibid.

38. Ibid.

39. Ibid.

40. Ibid.

41. Ibid.

42. Ibid.

43. Ibid.

44. Huarte, *L'Examen des esprits pour les sciences.*

45. Del Rio, *La Controverses et recherches magiques.*

46. Ibid.

47. *Confession faicte par Messire Louys Gaufridi.*

48. Ibid.

49. Ibid

50. Ibid.

51. Ibid.

52. Cavailhon, *La Fascination magnétique.*

53. Ibid.

54. Bastiani, *Bréviaire de l'amour sorcier.*

55. Deleuze, *Introduction pratique au magnetism animal.*

56. Bois, *Le Satanisme et la magie.*

57. Ibid.

58. Ibid.

59. Piobb, *Formulaire de Haute Magie.*

60. Sabazius, *Envoûtement et contre-envoûtement.*

61. Ibid.

62. Ibid.

63. Ibid.

64. Ibid.

65. Ibid.

66. Ibid.

67. Ibid.

68. Ibid.

69. Ibid.

70. Ibid.

71. Ibid.

72. Ibid.

73. Ibid.

74. Ibid.

75. Ibid.

76. Ibid.

77. Ibid.

78. Ibid.

79. Meslin, *Théorie et pratique de la magie sexuelle.*

80. Ibid.

81. Ibid.

82. Ibid.

83. Ibid.

84. Ibid.
85. Sabazius, *Envoûtement et contre-envoûtement.*
86. Ibid.
87. Ibid.
88. Meslin, *Théorie et pratique de la magie sexuelle.*
89. Ibid.
90. Ibid.
91. Ibid.
92. Ibid.
93. Thiers, *Traité des superstitions.*
94. Pliny, *Natural History,* Book XXX, 1.
95. Del Rio, *La Controverses et recherches magiques.*
96. Wier, *De l'imposture et tromperie des diables, enchantements et sorcelleries.*
97. Cf. Le Blanc, *Moyens secrets de défier la torture.*
98. *Secrets pour se faire aimer.*
99. Jessica, *Petit traité de magie pratique.*
100. Ibid.
101. Bastiani, *Bréviaire de l'amour sorcier.*
102. Ibid.
103. Ibid.
104. Meslin, *Théorie et pratique de la magie sexuelle.*
105. Jessica, *Envoûtement et magie en Afrique du Nord.*
106. Ibid.
107. Ibid.
108. Bastiani, *Bréviaire de l'amour sorcier.*
109. Ibid.

Chapter Two.
The White Magic of Love

1. Deveney, *Paschal Beverly Randolph,* 223.
2. Deveney, *Paschal Beverly Randolph,* 185.
3. Randolph and Naglowska, *Magia Sexualis,* 59.
4. Randolph, *The Anseiratic Mystery,* in Deveney, *Paschal Beverly Randolph,* 316.
5. Randolph and Naglowska, *Magia Sexualis,* 25.
6. Ibid., 29–34.
7. Ibid., 35.
8. Ibid., 27.
9. Ibid., 27.
10. Ibid., 62
11. Ibid., 62
12. Ibid., 62–63.
13. Ibid., 69.
14. Ibid., 63.
15. Ibid., 63.
16. Ibid., 63.
17. Randolph, *After Death; or Disembodied Man.*
18. Randolph quoted in Deveney, *Paschal Beverly Randolph,* 223.
19. Randolph, *The Mysteries of Eulis,* in Deveney, *Paschal Beverly Randolph,* 337.
20. Ibid., 337.
21. Randolph and Naglowska, *Magia Sexualis,* 58.
22. Ibid., 57.
23. Ibid., 67.
24. Ibid., 77–82.
25. Ibid., 94.

26. Quoted in Deveney, *Paschal Beverly Randolph*, 240.

Chapter Three.
The High Science
of Sacred Sexuality

1. Quoted in King, *Sexuality, Magic and Perversion*, 97.
2. Ibid., 98–99.
3. Cf. "Aleister Crowley, le maître incompris de la Gnose modern," [Aleister Crowley, the Misunderstood Master of Modern Gnosis] in *Supérieur Inconnu* 15 (June–September 1999). Here, in my own magazine, I corrected the false interpretations surrounding this phenomenal man, without omitting anything of his orgiastic excesses—the authentically religious meaning of which I drew out.
4. Crowley, *Liber Agape & De Arte Magica.*
5. Crowley, *De Arte Magica.*
6. Crowley, *The Magical Record of the Beast 666*, 3–4. In addition to *Rex de Arte Regia*, this book contains his magical journal from Cefalù and Fountainebleu covering the period from 1919–1920.
7. Ibid., 249.
8. Crowley, *Diary of a Drug Fiend*, 330.
9. Crowley, *Magick*, 172. This book includes *Book 4*, along with other treatises like the *Liber Samekh* and the *Liber O* (on the "Greater Ritual of the Pentagram").
10. Crowley, "Artemis iota," *Magick without Tears*, 79–83.
11. Bouchet, *Aleister Crowley et le mouvement thélémite*. This is the abridged version of Christian Bouchet's doctoral thesis in ethnology that he submitted in 1994 to the University of Paris IV.
12. King, *Sexuality, Magic and Perversion*, 116–17.
13. Ibid., 117–18.
14. Ibid., 118.
15. Ibid., 116.
16. Ibid., 119.
17. King, *Modern Ritual Magic*, 163.
18. Introvigne, *Le Magie: les nouveau mouvements magiques.*
19. Bouchet, *Aleister Crowley et le mouvement thélémite.*
20. Pascal, "Lux Evoliana," in *Julius Evola, le visionnaire foudroyé.*
21. Evola, *The Path of Cinnabar*, 95.
22. Evola, *Eros and the Mysteries of Love*, 31.
23. Ibid., 32.
24. Ibid., 31.
25. Evola, "Liberté du sexe et liberté par rapport au sexe," in *L'Arc et la massue.*
26. Ibid.
27. Ibid.

Chapter 4.
The Great Work of the Flesh

1. Rawson, *The Art of Tantra*, 7.
2. Ibid., 14.
3. Ibid., 88–89.
4. Ibid., 87.
5. Ibid., 87.
6. Schipper, *The Taoist Body*, 154.
7. Ibid., 150.
8. Ibid., 150–51.
9. Ibid., 151.
10. Ibid., 151.
11. Anand, *The Art of Sexual Magic*, 48.
12. Ibid., 49–50.
13. Ibid., 56–57.
14. Ibid., 57.
15. Ibid., 134.
16. Ibid., 138.
17. Ibid., 145.
18. Ibid., 161.
19. Ibid., 162.
20. Ibid., 68
21. Ibid., 233.
22. Ibid., 258.
23. Ibid., 192.
24. Ibid., 194.
25. *Procédés secrets du joyau magiques,* eleventh century treatise of Taoist alchemy, with commentary by Farseen Baldrian Hussein.
26. Rawson, *The Art of Tantra*, 92.
27. Schipper, *The Taoist Body*.
28. Chia, *Taoist Secrets of Love*.
29. Ibid.
30. Ibid.
31. Ibid.
32. Ibid.
33. Ibid.
34. Ibid.
35. Ibid.
36. Chia, *Healing Love through the Tao*, 209.
37. Ibid., 220.
38. Piobb, *Vénus, la déesse magique de la chair*.
39. Ibid.
40. Cheng, *Le Tao de l'amour*.
41. Ibid.
42. Ibid.
43. Douglas and Slinger, *Sexual Secrets*.
44. Varenne, *Le Tantrisme, la sexualité transcendente*.
45. David-Neel, *Magie d'amour et magie noire, scènes du Tibet inconnu*.
46. Piobb, *Formulaire de Haut Magie*.
47. Ibid.
48. Ibid.
49. Fortune, *Sane Occultism*, 73.
50. Ibid., 69.
51. Brosses, *Entretiens avec Raymond Abellio*.
52. Ibid.
53. Ibid.
54. Delorme, *Les Vampire humains*.

Chapter Five. How to Make Love with an Invisible Creature

1. Augustine, *The City of God*.
2. David-Neel, *Magie d'amour et magie noire*.
3. The Reverend Father Sinistari d'Ameno, *De la démonalité et*

des animaux incubes et succubes.

4. Ibid.

5. Brodin, *De la démonomanie des sorciers, revue diligemment et repurgée des plusieurs fautes.*

6. Ibid.

7. Montfaucon de Villars, *Le Comte de Gabalis, ou entretiens sur les sciences secrets.*

8. Cazotte, *The Devil in Love.*

9. Grün, *Les Esprits élementaires.*

10. Schwaeblé, *Les Recettes magiques pour et contre l'amour.*

11. Ibid.

12. Alexandrian, *Histoire de la philosophie occulte.*

13. Saint-Martin, *Correspondance inédites.*

14. Ibid.

15. Lalonne, *Les Apparitions materialists des vivants et des morts.* This book is an extravagant monument of pseudo-science.

16. Randolph, *Dealings with the Dead,* 10.

17. Crookes, *Researches in the Phenomena of Spiritualism.*

18. Ibid.

19. Ibid.

20. Ibid.

21. Ibid.

22. Ibid.

23. Ibid.

24. Alexandre-Bisson, *Les Phénomènes dits de materialization.*

25. Ibid.

26. Ibid.

27. Ibid.

28. Ibid.

29. Ibid.

30. Ibid.

31. Ibid.

32. Kremmerz, *Introduction à la science hermétique.*

33. Ibid.

34. Evola, *The Metaphysics of Sex,* 258.

35. Ibid., 258.

36. Kremmerz, *Introduction à la science hermétique.*

37. Introvigne, "De l'hypertrophie de la filiation: le milieu kremmerzien en Italie," in *Symboles et mythes dans les mouvements initiatiques et ésotériques.*

38. Ibid.

Chapter Six. The Art of Riding the Tiger

1. Levi, *Transcendental Magic,* 98.

2. Frazer, *The Golden Bough,* 217.

3. Ibid., 220.

4. Ibid., 170.

5. Papus, *Traité méthodique de magie pratique.*

6. Ouspensky, *In Search of the Miraculous,* 55.

7. Ibid., 256–58.

8. Saint Cyprian, *De la singularité des clercs.*

9. Ibid.

10. Ibid.

11. Ibid.

12. Ibid.

13. Bayle, "François d'Assise," in *Dictionnaire historique et critique.*

14. Alexandrian, *Histoire de la littérature érotique.*

15. Bayle, "Fontevrault" in *Dictionnaire historique et critique.*

16. Ibid.

17. Ibid.

18. Ibid.

19. Ibid.

20. Billon, *Le Fort inexpugnable de l'honneur du sexe feminine.*

21. Navarre, *Heptaméron,* 2nd day, 18th tale.

22. Montaigne, *Essays.*

23. *Histoire de Magdeleine Bavent, avec sa confession générale et testamentaire.*

24. Schubart, *Éros et religion.*

25. Péladan, *Le Vice Suprême.*

26. Ibid.

27. Ibid.

28. Erikson, *Gandhi's Truth,* 351.

29. Ibid., 460.

30. Ibid., 404.

31. Ibid., 403.

32. Ibid., 404.

33. Quoted in Deveney, *Paschal Beverly Randolph,* 181–82.

34. Gozzoli, *Les Saints de Tilly-sur-Seulle.*

35. Ibid.

36. Ibid.

37. Ibid.

38. Ibid.

39. Ibid.

40. Ibid.

41. Crowley, *The Magical Record,* 15.

42. Grant, *Images and Oracles of Austin Osman Spare,* 11.

43. Hartmann, *Magic White and Black,* 98.

44. Grant, *Images and Oracles,* 24.

45. Ibid., 57.

46. Grant, *Images and Oracles,* 57.

47. The preceding quotes are from the Padgett translation of Apollinaire, *The Moon King,* in *The Poet Assassinated and Other Stories,* 76–78.

48. Alexandrian, *Le Doctrinal des jouissances amoureuses.*

49. Stoller, *Sexual Excitement: Dynamics of Erotic Life,* 68.

50. Quoted in King, *Modern Ritual Magic,* 147.

51. Introvigne, *La Magie.*

52. Zürn, *The Man of Jasmine.*

Chapter Seven.
Magical Sex Aids

1. Introvigne, *La Magie.*

2. Belin, *Traité des talismans ou figures astrales.*

3. Ibid.

4. Muchery, *Magie, moyen pratique d'action occulte.*

5. Quoted in King and Skinner, *Techniques of High Magic,* 78–79.

6. Meslin, *Théorie et pratique de la magie sexuelle.*

7. Ibid.

8. Ibid.

9. Christian, *Histoire de la magie, du monde surnaturel et de la fatalité.*

10. Papus, *Traité méthodique de magie pratique.*

11. Muchery, *Magie, moyen pratique d'action occulte.*

12. Ibid.

13. Levi, *Clefs majeures et clavicules de Salomon.*

14. Ibid.

15. Ibid.

16. Papus, *Traité méthodique de magie pratique.*

17. Christian, *Histoire de la magie.*

18. King and Skinner, *Techniques of High Magic,* 79.

19. Downing, *The Massage Book,* 2.

20. Abrassart, *Le Massage californien.*

21. Ibid.

22. Ibid.

23. Ibid.

24. Ibid.

25. Ibid.

26. Ibid.

27. Ibid.

28. Downing, *The Massage Book,* 83.

29. Ibid., 85.

30. Ibid., 127–28.

31. Ibid., 128.

32. Ibid., 129.

33. Ibid., 128.

34. Ibid., 105.

35. Ibid., 121.

36. Tisserand, *Aromatherapy for Lovers,* 70.

37. Ibid., 60.

38. Ibid., 62.

39. Ibid., 61.

40. Ibid., 63–64.

41. Ibid., 24–25.

42. Ibid., 40.

43. Ibid., 69–70.

44. Ibid.

45. Ibid, 35–36.

46. Ibid., 64.

47. Ohashi, *Le Livre du shiatsu.*

48. Ibid.

49. Rioux, *Shiatsu et sensualité.*

50. Ibid.

51. Ibid.

52. Ibid.

53. Ibid.

54. Ibid.

55. Ibid.

56. Ibid.

57. Wan der Heyoten, *Le Massage taoiste.*

58. Ibid.

59. Suzzarini and Suzzarini, *La Thermopuncture amoreuse.*

60. Ibid.

61. Ibid.

62. Ibid.

63. Ibid.

64. Ibid.

65. Piesse, *Histoire des parfums et hygiene de la toilette.*

66. Ibid.

67. Sabazius, *Envoûtements et contre-envoûtement.*

68. Claye, *Les Talismans de la beauté.*

69. Ibid.

70. Ibid.

71. *El Ktab des lois secrètes de l'amour,* according to Omer Haleby in *Abu Othman.*

72. Ibid.

73. Claye, *Les Talismans de la beauté.*

74. *Le Parfumeur royal ou traité des parfums.*

75. Haleby, *El Ktab des lois secrètes de l'amour.*

76. Ibid.

77. Ibid.

78. Piesse, *Histoire des parfums.*

79. Ibid.

80. Tisserand, *Essence of Love.*

81. Sabazius, *Envoûtements.*

82. Ibid.

83. Ibid.

84. Marquès-Rivière, *Amulettes, talismans et pantacles dans les traditions orientales et extrême-orientales.*

85. Piobb, *Formulaire de Haute Magie.*

86. Voyer d'Argenson collection in the Arsenal Library.

87. Albertus Magnus, *LePetit Albert.*

88. Ibid.

89. Cited by Riols in *Les Veritables Moyens pour forcer l'amour.*

90. Dieulafait, *Diamants et pierres precieuses.*

91. Taille de Bondaroy, *Le Blason des pierres precieuses.*

92. Ibid.

93. Ibid.

94. Anand, *The Art of Sexual Magic,* 59–60.

Coda

1. King, *Modern Ritual Magic,* 181.

2. King, *Sexuality, Magic and Perversion,* 7–8.

3. Ibid., 8.

4. *Théléma,* new series, vol. III, no. 7/8, June–October, 1999.

5. Introvigne, *Études scientifiques dur le satanisme.*

6. Ibid.

7. Baraduc, *La Force vitale.*

Bibliography

Abrassart. *Le Massage californien.* Paris: Guy Trédaniel, 1983.

Agrippa, Henry Cornelius. *La Philosophie occulte ou la magie.* Translated and edited by André Levasseur. Paris: Chacornac, 1911.

———. *Three Books of Occult Philosophy.* London: Moule, 1651.

Albertus Magnus. *Le solide trésor de merveilleux.* [= *LePetit Albert.*] Geneva: Aux Dépess de la Compagne, 1704.

"Aleister Crowley, le maître incompris de la Gnose modern." *Supérieur Inconnu* 15 (June–September 1999).

Alexandre-Bisson, Juliette. *Les Phénomènes dits de materialization.* Paris: Payot, 1995.

Alexandrian, Sarane. *Histoire de la littérature érotique.* Paris: Payot, 1995.

———. *Histoire de la philosophie occulte.* Paris: Éditions Seghers, 1983.

———. *Le Doctrinal des jouissances amoureuses.* Paris: Filipacchi, 1997.

Ameno, Father Sinistari d'. *De la démonalité et des animaux incubes et succubes.* Translated by Isidore Liseux. Paris: Isidore Liseux, 1875.

Anand, Margo. *The Art of Sexual Magic.* New York: Penguin/Tarcher, 1995.

Apollinaire, Guillaume. *The Poet Assassinated and Other Stories.* Translated by Ron Padgett. San Francisco: North Point Press, 1984.

Augustine of Hippo. *The City of God.* Translated by Marcus Dods. Buffalo, N.Y.: Christian Literature Publishing Co., 1887.

Baraduc, Hippolyte. *La Force vitale.* Clermont: Daix Frères, 1897.

Bastiani, Ange. *Bréviaire de l'amour sorcier.* Paris: Solar, 1969.

Bayle, Pierre. *Dictionnaire historique et critique,* third edition. Rotterdam: M. Böhm, 1720.

Belin, Jean Albert. *Traité des talismans ou figures astrales,* Paris: Pierre de Bresche, 1670.

Billon, François de. *Le Fort inexpugnable de l'honneur du sexe feminine.* Paris: Jan d'Allyer, 1555.

Bois, Jules. *Le Satanisme et la magie.* Paris: Léon Chailley, 1885.

Bose, Nirmal K. *My Days with Gandhi.* New Delhi: Orient Longman, 1974.

Bouchet, Christian. *Aleister Crowley et le mouvement thélémite.* Nantes: Editions du Chaos, 1992.

Brodin, Jean. *De la démonomanie des sorciers, revue diligemment et repurgée des plusieurs fautes.* Lyon: A. de Harcy, 1608.

Brosses, Marie-Thérèse des. *Entretiens avec Raymond Abellio.* Paris: Belfond, 1966.

Cavailhon, Edmond. *La Fascination magnétique.* Paris: É. Dentu, 1882.

Cazotte, Jacques. *The Devil in Love.* London: Hookham and Carpenter, 1793.

Cheng, Heng. *Le Tao de l'amour.* Paris: Albin Michel, 1994.

Chia, Mantak. *Healing Love through the Tao: Cultivating Female Sexual Energy.* Rochester, Vt.: Destiny Books, 2005.

———. *Taoist Secrets of Love.* Santa Fe: Aurora Press, 1984.

Christian, Pierre. *Histoire de la magie, du monde surnaturel et de la fatalité.* Paris: Furne et Jouve, 1863.

Claye, Louis. *Les Talismans de la beauté.* Paris: Labigre-Duquesne frères, 1864.

Confession faicte par Messire Louys Gaufridi, prêtre en l'église des Accoules de Marseille. Aix: Jean Tholozan, 1611.

Crookes, William. *Researches in the Phenomena of Spiritualism.* London: Burns, 1874.

Crowley, Aleister. *Diary of a Drug Fiend.* New York: Samuel Weiser, 1978.

———. *Liber Agape & De Arte Magica.* Toronto: Kadath Press, 1986.

———. *The Magical Record of the Beast 666.* London: Duckworth, 1972.

———. *Magick.* London: Routledge & Kegan Paul, 1977.

———. *Magick without Tears.* Hampton, N.J.: Thelema Publishing Co., 1954.

David-Neel, Alexandra. *Magie d'amour et magie noire, scènes du Tibet inconnu.* Paris: Plon, 1938.

Deleuze, Joseph. *Introduction pratique au magnetism animal.* Paris: Germer-Baillière, 1850.

Delorme, Roger. *Les Vampire humains.* Paris: Albin Michel, 1979.

Del Rio, Martín. *Investigations into Magic.* Translated by P. G. Maxwell-Stuart. Manchester University Press, 2000.

———. *La Controverses et recherches magiques.* Translated by André Chesne. Paris: Régnaud Chaudière, 1611.

Deveney, John Patrick. *Paschal Beverly Randolph.* New York: SUNY Press, 1997.

Dieulafait, Louis. *Diamants et pierres precieuses.* Paris: Hachette, 1874.

Douglas, Nik, and Penny Slinger. *Sexual Secrets.* New York: Destiny Books, 1979.

Downing, George. *The Massage Book.* New York: Random House, 1972.

Erikson, Erik H. *Gandhi's Truth: On the Origins of Militant Nonviolence.* New York: W. W. Norton, 1960.

Evola, Julius. *The Path of Cinnabar: An Intellectual Autobiography.* Translated by Sergio Knipe. N.p.: Traditio, 2009.

———. *The Metaphysics of Sex.* New York: Inner Traditions, 1983.

———. *Eros and the Mysteries of Love.* Rochester, Vt.: Inner Traditions, 1991.

———. "Le troisième sexe." In *L'Arc et la massue.* Translated by Philippe Baillet. Paris: Pardès–Guy Trédaniel, 1983.

———. "Liberté du sexe et liberté par rapport au sexe." In *L'Arc et la massue.* Translated by Philippe Baillet. Paris: Pardès-Guy Trédaniel, 1983.

Fortune, Dion. *Sane Occultism.* N.p.: Aziloth Books, 2013.

Frazer, James. *The Golden Bough: A Study in Magic and Religion.* Abridged Edition. New York: Macmillan, 1922.

Gozzoli, Adrien. *Les Saints de Tilly-sur-Seulle.* Caen: 1846.

Grant, Kenneth. *Images and Oracles of Austin Osman Spare.* London: Fulgur, 2003.

Grün, Karl. *Les Esprits élementaires.* Paris: Guy Trédaniel, 1996.

Haleby, Omer. *El Ktab des lois secrètes de l'amour.* Translation and commentary by Paul de Régla. Paris: Georges Carré, 1903.

Hartmann, Franz. *Magic White and Black.* New York: Theosophical Publishing Company, 1911.

Histoire de Magdeleine Bavent, avec sa confession générale et testamentaire. Paris: J. Le Gentil, 1602.

Huarte, Juan. *L'Examen des esprits pour les sciences.* Translated by Vion d'Alibray. Paris: J. Le Bouc, 1645.

Introvigne, Massimo. "De l'hypertrophie de la filiation: le milieu kremmerzien en Italie." In *Symboles et mythes dans les mouvements initiatiques et ésotériques.* Paris: Éditions Arébe/Table d'émeraude, 1999.

———. *Études scientifiques dur le satanisme.* Paris: Dervy, 1995.

———. *Le Magie: les nouveau mouvements magiques.* Paris: Droguet & Ardant, 1993.

Jessica. *Envoûtement et magie en Afrique du Nord.* Paris: Omnium littéraire, 1964.

———. *Petit traité de magie pratique.* Paris: Self-published, 1966.

King, Francis. *Modern Ritual Magic.* Dorset, U.K.: Prism Press, 1989. [Revised edition of *Ritual Magic in England: 1887 to the Present Day.* London: Neville Spearman, 1970.]

———. *Sexuality, Magic and Perversion.* Los Angeles: Feral House, 2002.

King, Francis, and Stephen Skinner. *Techniques of High Magic.* Rochester, Vt.: Destiny Books, 2000.

Kremmerz, Giuliano. *Introduction à la science hermétique.* Paris: Axis Mundi, 1986.

Lalonne, Gabriel. *Les Apparitions materialists des vivants et des morts,* vol. II. Paris: Leymarie, 1911.

Laroque, René. *Magie et sexualité.* Paris: Éditions René Laroque, 1962.

Laval, Antoine de. *Dessein des professions nobles et publiques.* 1605.

Le Baillif de La Riviere, Roch. *Le Demosterion.* Rennes: Pierre le Bret, 1578.

Le Blanc, Edmond. *Moyens secrets de défier la torture.* Paris: N.p., 1867.

Le Loyer, Pierre. *Discours des spectres,* 2nd edition, revised and expanded. Paris: Nicolas Buon, 1608.

Le Parfumeur royal ou traité des parfums. Paris: Sangrain l'aîné, 1761.

Levi, Eliphas. *Clefs majeures et clavicules de Salomon.* Paris: Niclaus, 1975.

———. *The History of Magic.* Translated by A. E. Waite. Boston: Red Wheel/Weiser, 2001.

———. *Transcendental Magic: Its Doctrine and Ritual.* Translated by A. E. Waite. London: George Redway, 1896.

Liébault, Jean. *Trésor des remèdes secrets pour les maladies des femmes.* Paris: Jacques Du Puys, 1535.

Marquès-Rivière, Jean. *Amulettes, talismans et pantacles dans les traditions orientales et extrême-orientales.* Paris: Payot, 1938.

Meslin, Henri. *Théorie et pratique de la magie sexuelle.* Paris: Librairie Astra, 1938.

Montaigne. *Essays.* London: Reeves & Turner, 1877.

Montfaucon de Villars. *Le Comte de Gabalis, ou entretiens sur les sciences secrets.* Paris: Claude Barbin, 1670.

Muchery, Georges. *Magie, moyen pratique d'action occulte.* Paris: Éditions du Chariot, 1931.

Navarre, Marguerite de. *Heptaméron, Deuxième jour, dix-huitième nouvelle.* Paris: Bordas, Classiques Garnier, 1991.

Nostradamus. *Excellent et moult utile opuscule.* Lyon: A. Volant, 1555.

Ohashi, Wataru. *Le Livre du shiatsu.* Montreal: L'Étincelle, 1986.

Ouspensky, P. D. *In Search of the Miraculous.* New York: Harcourt, 1949.

Papus. *Traité méthodique de magie pratique.* Paris: Dangles, 1973.

Pascal, Pierre. "Lux Evoliana." In *Julius Evola, le visionnaire foudroyé.* Paris: Copernic, 1977.

Péladan. *Le Vice Suprême.* Paris: Chamuel, 1884.

Piesse, Septimus. *Histoire des parfums et hygiene de la toilette*. Paris: J.G. Baillière, 1905.

Piobb, Pierre V. *Formulaire de Haute Magie,* revised, and expanded edition. Paris: Dangles, 1938.

———. *Vénus, la déesse magique de la chair*. Plan-de-la-Tour: Editions d'Aujourd'hui, 1979.

Pliny, *Natural History*. Vol. VIII. Translated by W. H. S. Jones. Cambridge, MA: Harvard University Press, 1963.

Procédés secrets du joyau magiques. Commentary by Farseen Baldrian Hussein. Paris: Les Deux Océans, 1984.

Randolph, Pascal B. *After Death; or Disembodied Man*. Boston: Self-published, 1868. A fourth, revised, and corrected edition was published in 1873 by Colby & Rich in Boston.

———. *The Anseiratic Mystery*. Toledo, Ohio: Sun, Liberal Printing House. 1873.

———. *Dealings with the Dead; The Human Soul, Its Migrations and Transmigrations*. Utica, N.Y.: M. J. Randolph, 1861.

———. *The Mysteries of Eulis*. Toledo, Ohio: Randolph Publishing, 1874.

Randolph Pascal B., and Maria de Naglowska. *Magia Sexualis*. Translated by Donald Traxler. Rochester, Vt.: Inner Traditions, 2012.

Rawson, Philip. *The Art of Tantra*. London: Thames & Hudson, 1985.

Reuss, Theodor. *Oriflamme*. 1912.

Riols, Santini de. *Les Veritables Moyens pour forcer l'amour*. Paris: Chez les libraires, 1922.

Rioux, Yuki. *Shiatsu et sensualité*. Montreal: Éditions de l'Homme, 1983.

Sabazius, R. P. *Envoûtement et contre-envoûtement, method pratique d'action et de protection selon les traditions kabbalistiques des sciences magiques*. Paris: Leymarie, 1991.

Saint-André, François. *Lettres de M. de Saint-André, conseilleur-médcin du Roy, au sujet de la magie, des malefices et des sorciers*. Paris: Jean-Baptiste Maudrouyt, 1725.

Saint Cyprian. *De la singularité des clercs*. Paris: Gabriel Valleyre, 1718.

Saint-Martin, Louis-Claude de. *Correspondance inédites*. Paris: E. Dentu, 1862. English translation from Mircea Eliade, *Journal III, 1970–1978*. Translated by Teresa Lavender Fagan. Chicago: University of Chicago Press, 1989.

Schipper, Kristofer. *The Taoist Body*. Berkeley: University of California Press, 1994.

Schubart, Walter. *Éros et religion*. Translated by Joseph Feisthauer. Paris: Fayard, 1966.

Schwaeblé, René. *Les Recettes magiques pour et contre l'amour.* Paris: Payot, 1926.

Secrets pour se faire aimer. Bibliothèque de l'Arsenal, ms. 2797.

Spare, Austin Osman. *Zoëtic Grimoire of Zos.* In Kenneth Grant and Steffi Grant, *Zos Speaks!*

Stoller, Robert J. *Sexual Excitement: Dynamics of Erotic Life.* New York: Pantheon, 1979.

Suzzarini, François, and Michel Suzzarini. *La Thermopuncture amoreuse.* Paris: Guy Trédaniel, 1988.

Table des 72 anges. Arsenal Library, Paris, ms. 2495.

Taille de Bondaroy, Jean de la. *Le Blason des pierres precieuses.* Paris: Lucas Breyes, 1574.

Théléma, vol. III, no. 7/8, June–October, 1999.

Thiers, Jean-Baptiste. *Traité des superstitions.* Paris: Antoine Dezallier, 1679.

Tisserand, Maggie. *Aromatherapy for Lovers.* London: Thorsons, 1993.

———. *Essence of Love.* New York: Harper, 1995.

Vairo, Leonardo. *De fascinatione.* In *Trois livres de charmes, sorceleges ou enchantements, faicts en latin par Léonard Vair, espagnol.* Paris: Nicolas Chesneau, 1583.

Varenne, Jean. *Le Tantrisme, la sexualité transcendente.* Paris: Colt, 1977.

Wan der Heyoten, Louis. *Le Massage taoiste.* Paris: Guy Trédaniel, 1990.

Weyer, Johann. *De Praestigiis Daemonum et Incantationibus ac Venificiis.* 1563. French edition: Wier, Johann. *De l'imposture et tromperie des diables, enchantements et sorcelleries.* Translated by Jacques Grévin. Paris: J. Dy Ouy, 1567.

Zürn, Unica. *The Man of Jasmine.* Translated by Malcolm Green. London: Atlas Press, 1994.

Index